ENDING SPAM

ENDING SPAM

Bayesian Content Filtering and the Art of Statistical Language Classification

by Jonathan A. Zdziarski

NO STARCH
PRESS

San Francisco

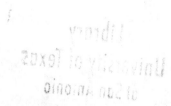

Publisher: William Pollock
Managing Editor: Karol Jurado
Production Manager: Susan Berge
Cover and Interior Design: Octopod Studios
Developmental Editors: William Pollock, Elizabeth Zinkann
Copyeditor: Rebecca Pepper
Compositor: Riley Hoffman
Proofreader: Stephanie Provines
Indexer: Ted Laux

For information on book distributors or translations, please contact No Starch Press, Inc. directly:

No Starch Press, Inc.
555 De Haro Street, Suite 250, San Francisco, CA 94107
phone: 415.863.9900; fax: 415.863.9950; info@nostarch.com; http://www.nostarch.com

Library of Congress Cataloging-in-Publication Data

Zdziarski, Jonathan A.
  Ending spam : Bayesian content filtering and the art of statistical language classification /
Jonathan A. Zdziarski.-- 1st ed.
       p. cm.
  Includes index.
  ISBN 1-59327-052-6
1. Electronic mail systems--Security measures. 2. Unsolicited electronic mail messages. 3. Filters
(Mathematics) I. Title.
  TK5105.73.Z35 2005
  005.7'13--dc22
                                                    2005008221

To Christ, who gives me new ideas every day and occasionally
lets me think they're my own

ACKNOWLEDGMENTS

This book was not written in a vacuum. Many of the world's brightest minds in the spam-filtering arena have helped to provide the information I present here. The spam-filtering community exists today only because of the collaborative efforts of many individuals and their selfless contributions to computer science. Many special thanks to Bill Yerazunis, Brian Burton, John Graham-Cumming, Paul Graham, Gary Robinson, Marty Lamb, Terry Sullivan, Matthew Prince, and the many others who contributed their thoughts, insight, and experience to this book. If you experience any success in filtering spam, it is most definitely because of the efforts of one or more of these individuals.

BRIEF CONTENTS

CONTENTS IN DETAIL

3
LANGUAGE CLASSIFICATION CONCEPTS   45

PART II
FUNDAMENTALS OF STATISTICAL FILTERING

6
TOKENIZATION: THE BUILDING BLOCKS OF SPAM   97

7
THE LOW-DOWN DIRTY TRICKS OF SPAMMERS   111

8
DATA STORAGE FOR A ZILLION RECORDS   141

9
SCALING IN LARGE ENVIRONMENTS
157

PART III
ADVANCED CONCEPTS OF STATISTICAL FILTERING

10
TESTING THEORY
177

11
CONCEPT IDENTIFICATION: ADVANCED TOKENIZATION

197

12
FIFTH-ORDER MARKOVIAN DISCRIMINATION

215

13
INTELLIGENT FEATURE SET REDUCTION   227

14
COLLABORATIVE ALGORITHMS   241

APPENDIX
SHINING EXAMPLES OF FILTERING   257

INTRODUCTION

The battle cry of a true die-hard spam fighter consists of colorful metaphors usually shouted when a single unsolicited message evades their filter. Whatever the spam is about, you can be sure the nerd at the keyboard is going to spend the next 20 minutes analyzing every possible scenario of why their filter failed to catch the stupid thing, shout a few more expletives, and then move on with their everyday routine. This book is designed for those individuals who feel passionately about spam, and it is written to illustrate the different techniques involved in the artful science of spam filtering. Whether you're a seasoned hacker or completely new to spam filtering, this book should provide some great inspiration and instruction.

This book will spark your interest if you are one of the following types of people:

- You are passionate about spam, would like to design and implement your own spam filter, and need the information contained in this book to help you understand present-day "best practices."

- You would like to or have already implemented an existing spam-filtering solution on your network and want to understand not only the different approaches to implementing such a solution, but also what it is the thing actually does.

- You are a geek and, while not directly hung up on spam filtering, would like to acquire a general understanding of how spam filters work and the tactics spammers are using to evade them.

- You are a spammer and have been racking your brain for the past few years trying to figure out how to push your trash to those of us who sit behind a neat and tidy inbox, free from you.

If you are a spammer, I'm afraid I have bad news: Statistical, adaptive spam filtering is very effective and capable of learning far quicker than spam is capable of evolving, as we illustrate in this book.

If you are *not* a spammer, I have very good news: Statistical, adaptive spam filtering is very effective and capable of learning far quicker than spam is capable of evolving, as we illustrate in this book.

In short, this is a book about the low-down dirty details of spam filtering, how real-world filters are working to protect you, and how spammers are squirming in their eBay-bought shoes trying to find new ways to push their poison into your inbox.

This book is predominantly about statistical filtering or, rather, intelligent machine learning. Intelligent machine learning has become very popular in the spam filtering arena over the past few years, as it is capable of dynamically adapting to a particular user's behavior and learning what that user believes is and isn't spam. While there are a number of myths to dispel (which I hope this book will help do), statistical filtering has proved to be extremely effective against the diverse permutations of spam out there, and it requires very little effort at the systems administrator level. Statistical filtering is one of the last remaining efforts in fighting spam before larger entities attempt to usher in solutions such as Bonded Sender (Slashdot for email, only getting modded down costs you money) or to rewrite core networking and messaging components entirely. Should statistical filtering fail, it will signal the beginning of a significant shift in the design of the Internet and the privacy rights of the individuals using it. That, among other reasons, is why an entire book has been devoted to this type of filtering. Our future is looking bright, however, and as the world slowly begins to catch up to attacking the issue of spam, technology has started to side with us.

This book covers both the fundamentals of statistical learning—the efficacy and efficiency of which have been proven over the past few years—and many algorithms that are fresh, new approaches I believe will be around for many years to come. Topics such as Markovian discrimination, Bayesian noise reduction, and neural mesh networking have never been covered in depth because they are all new technologies applied to spam filtering. Although new, they have been found to be quite adaptive and have brought language classification to new levels of accuracy that will not likely be outdated. This book provides a good balance between best practices and exciting, fresh ideas, with the goal of providing only information that is going to be pertinent and useful over the long haul. All the information has been laid out in an easy-to-understand format, forgoing many of the formalities usually found in technical books. This book isn't designed to make the author look smart and the reader look dumb; instead, it's designed to bring the reader into an understanding of important filtering concepts and to make it easy for the reader to absorb every bit of information.

As with most of the Internet's technologies, a majority of the concepts used by large corporations today to fight spam have their roots in the work of the hacker community. As you'll see in the first few chapters, many of the innovative ideas for dealing with spam were originated by grassroots hackers, only to be glitzed over with marketing glamour by large companies. This book traces many popular innovations directly to their hacker sources. Some hackers are well-developed masters of their trade; others are mildly eccentric or completely nuts. However, they all have one thing in common: They founded the art of spam filtering and continue to design new concepts. They're usually more than happy to discuss spam, the Internet, and philosophy over a carton of Chinese food. (No hackers harmed me in the writing of this book.)

The world needs more people to run spam filters—more people to help make spamming even less lucrative and eventually put spammers out of business. The social problem with spam is that people who would normally click a link in response to spam aren't going to run a filter for themselves. They must be educated and coaxed along by administrators who can provide the right tools for them so they never have to be confused by a spam.

History tells us that a monoculture by any name is bad. That's why the world needs more spam filters. Every filter is prone to some minor weakness, but diversity in spam-filtering technology prevents spammers from cashing in on these occasional weaknesses. When you hear about spam filters being a "dime a dozen," it shouldn't be seen as a negative but as something to get jiggy about! Holes are bound to be found in any software, no matter how well written, and in a world of malicious spammers, a single flaw could be devastating if everyone used the same filter. A diverse selection, with many "best of breed" filters, will help ensure that spammers are never able to invade a significant number of mailboxes.

Spam filtering can become addictive, so as you learn more about the different techniques you'll undoubtedly want to jump in and get your hands dirty. Filtering spam is surprisingly satisfying, and this book should give you plenty of inspiration to geek out and start hacking. Paul Graham, who is considered the father of Bayesian content filtering, put it perfectly when he described the fascination many of us share in this area:

> For me, the most significant change was when I started having a
> filter that worked, because spam suddenly became entertaining—
> as a rainstorm can be, once you're inside.

The reason many of us fight spam in the first place is probably the satisfaction of it. It is certainly much easier to press the Delete button a few hundred times per day than it is to put time into writing and implementing a spam filter. As trivial as spam filtering sounds, it's quite amazing to see some of its results and how they can affect even quality of life. Saving companies millions of dollars is nice, but receiving thanks from your users, some of whom have weaknesses such as online gambling or pornography, can give you an even better feeling of satisfaction. On top of that are the people who will probably never be tempted with some of the trash that's out there because of what you're doing.

Not only can spam filtering be remarkably satisfying, but there is simply a wonderful community to work with in this area. Filter authors are always working together, sharing ideas over a bag of steak teriyaki (note that I brought up food again—food is a major component in this community, so be prepared to eat a lot of it). The annual MIT Spam Conference draws a certain energy every year, as more individuals become zealous about the art. Email lists are frequently noisy with chatter about new techniques, mixed with a dose of the hacker subculture to make it more entertaining. The spam-filtering community truly is reminiscent of the home-brew hacker groups of olde.

It's my hope that this book will inspire you to become a part of this growing community of hackers and contribute to the art of spam filtering— as either a developer or a user. Both hats are equally important, and equally satisfying. So step up, refuse to obfuscate your email address, and let the spammers bring it on . . . this book will give you the ammunition you need.

PART I

AN INTRODUCTION TO SPAM FILTERING

1

THE HISTORY OF SPAM

I receive between 500 and 600 spams per day. So does anyone who's had an email account for a while. Like other victims, I take particular interest in the history surrounding the violation of my mailbox. The spam isn't even that useful—I'm trapped in a world of Viagra ads and Nigerian diplomats. I don't need any Viagra (yet), and I've never been to Nigeria. If you're going to send me something, at least send me something I can use. Getting spam is like watching a bad television commercial. I'm quite certain the first marketing advertisement for the wheel was far more interesting than some of the spam I receive today. So what's the history behind this nuisance? Did spam just "appear" one day in mass quantities?

While the bulk of this book deals specifically with fighting spam from the low-level inner workings of spam filters, this chapter takes a look at the evolution of spam. It's fascinating but mildly depressing to look at how spam has developed and where all of this garbage came from.

The Definition of Spam

There are a few conflicting schools of thought as to the actual definition of spam, but just like something hanging out of your nose, everyone knows it when they see it. To many, spam is simply unwanted email. If that's true, then every email I get from my boss asking me to work for a living is spam. To others, spam is "unsolicited commercial email," which covers advertisements for products and other types of solicitations. That too is incomplete. Others just refer to spam as "junk email," which raises the recursive question, "And what is that?" Lately the community at large is leaning toward a definition of spam as "unsolicited bulk email," which seems a bit more sane but still lacks a bit of effervescence. Until the gurus figure out how to describe spam, we'll just have to continue using the expletives we're using today.

We really are terribly ignorant in terms of knowing the roots of spam. It's almost as if we've been on a 30-year-long high and suddenly woke up with the munchies. In fact, we don't even know definitively where the term "spam" came from. Many believe that it originated from MUDs in the 1980s. A MUD (multiuser dungeon) is a virtual gaming environment using text-based chat as a medium of play. MUDs are borderline obsolete. They've been all but replaced by the more graphical environments offered by newer commercial games where, rather than appreciate the literary beauty of hacking someone to pieces with a blunt instrument, you can experience it as if you were actually there. MUDs used the term "spamming" to describe flooding a computer with information.

Others believe the word "spam" was borrowed from Monty Python's "Viking Spam" skit, in which the characters could not communicate with one another over the loud chanting of "spam, spam, spam," and that it was introduced later into either MUDs or relay chats (the predecessor to Internet Relay Chat) to describe flooding behavior. This parallels today's spam problem in most people's inboxes.

Finally, one of the more amusing explanations is that spam was named after the concept of throwing a handful of processed meat at a fan and watching it splatter into pieces; when the Spam hits the fan, it makes a mess, covers everything, and smells quite ill. This is certainly an accurate illustration of what most people feel like when they get spam in their inboxes. It makes us feel dirty, as though we just took a shower in meat juice.

Ultimately, the true origin of the term is just as mysterious as what's really in that mystery meat of the same name. Regardless of where it came from, however, "spam" has got to be the best possible name we could have chosen.

The Very First Spam

No matter how you actually define spam, or where the term came from, most would agree that the very first "spam" distributed on a wide area network can be traced all the way back to 1978 as an advertisement from Digital Equipment Corporation. The original advertisement was sent over what was known as the Arpanet, for which a printed directory of addresses was at one time available (imagine that). Email clients weren't nearly as advanced as they are today, and so the spammer had to manually type in the addresses of all the recipients (what a quiet world it would be if spammers still had to do this; perhaps that should be a feature request). Fortunately, due to buffer space issues in the SNDMSG program the spammer used, only 320 of the email's intended recipients actually received the spam on the first broadcast. The original spam, minus the more than nine pages of To: lines, is as follows.

```
Mail-from: DEC-MARLBORO rcvd at 3-May-78 0955-PDT
Date:   1 May 1978 1233-EDT
From: THUERK at DEC-MARLBORO
Subject: ADRIAN@SRI-KL

DIGITAL WILL BE GIVING A PRODUCT PRESENTATION OF THE NEWEST MEMBERS OF THE
DECSYSTEM-20 FAMILY; THE DECSYSTEM-2020, 2020T, 2060, AND 2060T. THE
DECSYSTEM-20 FAMILY OF COMPUTERS HAS EVOLVED FROM THE TENEX OPERATING SYSTEM
AND THE DECSYSTEM-10 <PDP-10> COMPUTER ARCHITECTURE. BOTH THE DECSYSTEM-2060T
AND 2020T OFFER FULL ARPANET SUPPORT UNDER THE TOPS-20 OPERATING SYSTEM. THE
DECSYSTEM-2060 IS AN UPWARD EXTENSION OF THE CURRENT DECSYSTEM 2040
AND 2050 FAMILY. THE DECSYSTEM-2020 IS A NEW LOW END MEMBER OF THE DECSYSTEM-
20 FAMILY AND FULLY SOFTWARE COMPATIBLE WITH ALL OF THE OTHER DECSYSTEM-20
MODELS.

WE INVITE YOU TO COME SEE THE 2020 AND HEAR ABOUT THE DECSYSTEM-20 FAMILY AT
THE TWO PRODUCT PRESENTATIONS WE WILL BE GIVING IN CALIFORNIA THIS MONTH. THE
LOCATIONS WILL BE:

                TUESDAY, MAY 9, 1978 - 2 PM
                    HYATT HOUSE (NEAR THE L.A. AIRPORT)
                    LOS ANGELES, CA

                THURSDAY, MAY 11, 1978 - 2 PM
                    DUNFEY'S ROYAL COACH
                    SAN MATEO, CA
                    (4 MILES SOUTH OF S.F. AIRPORT AT BAYSHORE, RT 101 AND RT
92)

A 2020 WILL BE THERE FOR YOU TO VIEW. ALSO TERMINALS ON-LINE TO OTHER
DECSYSTEM-20 SYSTEMS THROUGH THE ARPANET. IF YOU ARE UNABLE TO ATTEND, PLEASE
FEEL FREE TO CONTACT THE NEAREST DEC OFFICE FOR MORE INFORMATION ABOUT THE
EXCITING DECSYSTEM-20 FAMILY
```

The sender of this message was an individual by the name of Gary Thuerk, who worked in DEC's marketing department. Thuerk thought the recipients would respond to an invitation to learn about DEC's Arpanet support. They did. A series of controversial discussions and flames started regarding the message, and as a result the message was propagated even further so that everyone could read it and contribute to the discussion. The need for everyone to rant about this first spam was apparently what made it so popular. The spam created a significant amount of load on what are now considered low-bandwidth lines, usually 56 Kbps in capacity (the speed of dialup today). With limited disk and bandwidth resources, the distribution was a borderline "denial of service attack" for some.

The reactions to the first spam were quite mixed. Surprisingly, there was a bit of a debate about the correctness of the message, which wasn't at that point known as spam. Richard Stallman, the founder of the Gnu project and president of what is now the Free Software Foundation, was working as a staff hacker at the MIT Artificial Intelligence Lab at the time. Stallman initially sent this message in response to the spam:

```
0-MAY-78 23:20:30-PDT,2250;000000000001
Mail-from: MIT-AI rcvd at 7-MAY-78 2316-PDT
Date: 8 MAY 1978 0213-EDT
From: RMS at MIT-AI (Richard M. Stallman)
Subject: MSGGROUP# 697  Some Thoughts about advertising
To: stefferud at USC-ISI
Redistributed-To: [ISI]<MsgGroup>Mailing.List;154:
Redistributed-By: STEFFERUD (connected to MSGGROUP)
Redistributed-Date:  8 MAY 1978

1) I didn't receive the DEC message, but I can't imagine I would have been
bothered if I have. I get tons of uninteresting mail, and system announcements
about babies born, etc. At least a demo MIGHT have been interesting.
2) The amount of harm done by any of the cited "unfair" things the net has
been used for is clearly very small. And if they have found any people any
jobs, clearly they have done good. If I had a job to offer, I would offer it
to my friends first. Is this "evil"? Must I advertise in a paper in every city
in the US with population over 50,000 and then go to all of them to interview,
all in the name of fairness? Some people, I am afraid, would think so. Such a
great insistence on fairness would destort everyone's lives and do much more
harm than good. So I state unashamedly that I am in favor of seeing jobs
offered via whatever.
3) It has just been suggested that we impose someone's standards on us because
otherwise he MIGHT do so. Well, if you feel that those standards are right and
necessary, go right ahead and support them. But if you disagree with them, as
I do, why hand your opponents the victory on a silver platter? By the
suggested reasoning, we should always follow the political views that we don't
believe in, and especially those of terrorists, in anticipation of their
attempts to impose them on us. If those who think that the job offers are bad
are going to try to prevent them, then those of us who think they are
unrepugnant should uphold our views. Besides, I doubt that anyone can
successfully force a site from outside to impose censorship, if the people
there don't fundamentally agree with the desirability of it.
4) Would a dating service for people on the net be "frowned upon" by DCA? I
hope not. But even if it is, don't let that stop you from notifying me via net
mail if you start one.
```

You've got to wonder how lonely some engineers had to be back then—just think what would have happened (and what the Free Software Foundation would be) had RMS started that dating service. The position Stallman took on what is now known as spam is similar to that of many new Internet users—

namely the ones who don't mind clicking ads or are easily tricked into thinking they've got a prize waiting for them. Stallman's rebellious point of view made for a bit of an embarrassment once he actually saw the spam with all of its nine pages of recipients, at which point he must have gotten a real vision of what was happening. His opinion quickly changed, and he ended up eating his own words by sending this follow-up.

```
10-MAY-78 23:20:30-PDT,685;000000000001
Mail-from: MIT-AI rcvd at 9-MAY-78 1528-PDT
Date: 9 MAY 1978 1827-EDT
From: RMS at MIT-AI (Richard M. Stallman)
Subject: MSGGROUP# 698  DEC message [VERY TASTY!]
To: Stefferud at USC-ISI
CC: Geoff at SRI-KL
Redistributed-To: [ISI]<MsgGroup>Mailing.List;154:
Redistributed-By: STEFFERUD (connected to MSGGROUP)
Redistributed-Date:  9 MAY 1978


Well, Geoff forwarded me a copy of the DEC message, and I eat my words. I sure
would have minded it! Nobody should be allowed to send a message with a header
that long, no matter what it is about.
Forward this if you feel like it.
```

After the controversy, DEC finally decided to pull the plug on the campaign and never sent another one. DEC ended up running the DECWRL Service Center, which was considered a major Arpanet repository, for the next 20 years or so. Bill Yerazunis of Mitsubishi Electric Research Laboratories recalled that this was considered an act of contrition by many.

Spam: The Early Years

Over the next several years, annoyances popped up occasionally but with increasing frequency. Charity and money-making scams appeared, but in controlled quantity. They usually came in the form of a single message to a group or a handful of groups and quickly resulted in a series of due flames. At this point, all message posting was still performed by hand, which therefore required resources on the sender's part.

Jay-Jay's College Fund

In 1988, a struggling student sent the following message to several newsgroups, asking for financial assistance.

```
From: JJ@cup.portal.com (JJ@cup.portal.com)
Subject: HELP ME!
Date: 1998-05-23 17:00:08 PST


Poor College Student needs Your Help!!  :-(
```

Hi. I just finished my junior year in college, and now I'm faced with a major
problem. I can't afford to pay for my senior year. I've tried everything. I
can't get any more student loans, I don't qualify for any more scholarships,
and my parents are as broke as am I. So as you can see, I've got a major
problem. But as far as I can see, there is only one solution, to go forward.
I've come along way, and there is no chance in hell that I'm going to drop out
now! I'm not a quiter, and I'm not going to give up.

But here is why I'm telling you all this. I want to ask a favor of every one
out here on the net. If each of you would just send me a one dollar bill, I
will be able to finish college and go on with my life. I'm sure a dollar is
not much to any of you, but just think how it could change a person's life.
I'd really like to encourage all of you to help me out, I've no other place to
go, no other doors to knock on. I'm counting on all of you to help me!
(PLEASE!)
If you would like to help a poor boy out, please send $1 (you can of course
send more if you want!! :-)

Jay-Jay's College Fund
PO BOX 5631
Lincoln, NE 68505

PS. Please don't flame me for posting this to so many newsgroups, I really am
in dire need of help, and if any of you were as desparate as I am, you just
might resort to the same thing I am. Also, please don't tell me to get a job!
I already have one and work over 25 hrs a week, plus get in all my classes,
plus find time to study! So hey, please consider it! It would really mean a
lot to me. Thank you!

NOTE: Any extra money I receive will go to a scholarship fund to help others
in the same situation. :-)

This message, along with the many other network mailings that occurred
during this period, sparked much concern over the commercialization of the
Internet. The network of the time, much as it is today, was based primarily on
etiquette. Many predicted an abrupt end to the once-peaceful network now
that "commoners" were able to log on more and more often.

In the 1980s, many email chain letters began to come into existence and
were quickly stamped out. The very first email chain letter was recorded in
February 1982. It, along with another in August 1985, were quickly flamed
and canceled.

Date: 15 Feb 1982 17:21:57-EST
From: Mark.Boggs

Trust in the LORD with all your heart and HE will acknowledge and HE will
light the way.

This prayer has been sent to you for good luck. The original copy is from the
Netherlands. It has been around the world nine times. The luck has now been
brought to you. You will receive good luck within four days of receiving this

letter, provided in turn, you send it back out. DO NOT SEND MONEY, FOR FAITH
HAS NO PRICE. Do not keep this letter. It must leave your hands within 96
hours after you receive it. An RAF officer received $70,000. Joe Ellito
received $450,000 and lost it because he broke the chain. While in the
Phillipines, General Welch lost his wife four days after he received this
letter. He failed to circulate the prayer. However, before his death, he
received $775,000. Please send 20 copies and see what happens to you on the
fourth day. This chain comes from Venezuela, and
was written by Saul Anthony deOziof, a missionary from South America. I,
myself, forward it to you. Since the chain must make the tour of the world,
you must make 20 identical copies to this one. Send it to your friends,
parents, or associates. After a few days you will get a suprise. This is true
even if you are not superstitious. Take note of the following. Constantine
Dino received the chain in 1953. He asked his secretary to make 20 copies and
send them. A few days later, he won a lottery for $2,000,000 in his country.
Carlo Caditt, an office employee, received the chain. He forgot it and a few
days later he lost his job. He found the chain letter and sent it to 20
people. Five days later he got an even better job. Dolon Fairchild received
the chain and not believing it, threw it away. Nine days later he died. For no
reason whatsoever should this chain be broken. Remember, SEND NO MONEY.

Please do not ignore this. IT WORKS!

The Jesus Spam

In the early 1990s, the commercialization of the Internet finally happened
in full force, and with that came lots of spam. Around 1994, the more
notable spams began materializing. This type of spam was given particular
attention because it was the first to be overtly abusive of mail and news
systems, using automated software to mail to the lists. The first widespread
spam comparable to today's spams has been referred to as the "Jesus" spam.
The Jesus spam was posted in January 1994 to every single group on Usenet.

From: Clarence L. Thomas IV (clarence@orion.cc.andrews.edu)
Subject: Global Alert For All: Jesus is Coming Soon
Date: 1994-01-17 21:38:43 PST

The earthquake in Los Angeles, California, the flood in Europe, the seemingly
unstoppable war in the former Yugoslavia, the devastating fires in Australia,
the flood in the Midwest of the United States of America, the devastating
fires near Los Angeles, California, the rapid and appalling increase in
violence in cities, towns, villages all over the world, the famines, the
diseases, the rapid decline of the family unit, and the destructive earthquake
in India (in 1993) are signs that this world's history is coming to a climax.
The human race has trampled on God's Constitution, as given in Exodus 20:1-17
(King James Version Bible), and Jesus is coming to set things right. These
rapidly accelerating signs are an indication that Jesus is coming soon
(Matthew 24).

God's Holy Spirit is gradually withdrawing its protection from the earth and
the devastating events you see are demonstrations of Satan's power. All those
who are not guarded by God are in danger of forever losing eternal life.

If you want to know what's about to happen, please study the books of Daniel and Revelation which are located in God's Word, the Bible. They are not sealed or closed books. They can and must be understood by all. Every word in the Bible from Genesis to Revelation is true. The Bible and the Bible only must be your guide.

When God's Law (the Constitution for the Universe) is consistently ignored, disregarded, changed, and questioned, He permits certain events to occur to wake us up. I would urge all, wherever you are and regardless of the circumstances, to directly call on Jesus and ask Him to intervene in your life. Jesus who created this planet and every living creature in it and on it, died on the cross, was raised from the dead by God the Father, and is now in Heaven interceding for you. Jesus is the only One who can rescue us from the slavery, misery, and death Satan is causing us.

The message was posted by a systems administrator at Andrews University, and therefore it sparked a bit of controversy about whether it should in fact be considered spam. Until this point, a systems administrator position was one of honor—or at least was considered a position with much responsibility, unless you were fortunate enough to have a job allowing you to be the operator from hell. Since the commercialization of the Internet, however, systems administrator positions have, unfortunately, lost much of the respect they deserve, and the role has degenerated into a mere baby-sitting job. A systems administrator used to be able to freely call up another Internet service provider or the InterNIC and receive priority assistance, possibly even cooperation in an exchange of information to track down problem users. Today's systems administrators don't even get better coffee in the coffee machine, and the best support they can hope for is from cocky little neophytes on the other end of the line who think they know something about the Internet while getting paid based on the number of calls they can "handle" in a day. Too, privacy rights and lawsuits have completely eliminated any chances of sharing information to actually solve problems, even if you have a subpoena. But I digress. . . .

Canter & Siegel

Probably the most notable spam in history, or at least the most talked about, was the Canter & Siegel spam. A husband and wife team, attorneys Laurence Canter and Martha Siegel, decided to hire a programmer who could write software to post an advertisement to every single newsgroup in existence. This gave birth to the first known bulk mailer software. Several different permutations of the spam were sent over a short period of time. Many were short, while others were several pages long and included an attached application that one could fill out and send in.

From: Laurence Canter (nike@indirect.com)
Subject: Green Card Lottery- Final One?
Date: 1994-04-12 00:40:42 PST

```
Green Card Lottery 1994 May Be The Last One!
THE DEADLINE HAS BEEN ANNOUNCED.

The Green Card Lottery is a completely legal program giving away a certain
annual allotment of Green Cards to persons born in certain countries. The
lottery program was scheduled to continue on a permanent basis. However,
recently, Senator Alan J Simpson introduced a bill into the U. S. Congress
which could end any future lotteries. THE 1994 LOTTERY IS SCHEDULED TO TAKE
PLACE SOON, BUT IT MAY BE THE VERY LAST ONE.

PERSONS BORN IN MOST COUNTRIES QUALIFY, MANY FOR FIRST TIME.

The only countries NOT qualifying are: Mexico; India; P.R. China; Taiwan,
Philippines, North Korea, Canada, United Kingdom (except Northern Ireland),
Jamaica, Domican Republic, El Salvador and Vietnam.

Lottery registration will take place soon. 55,000 Green Cards will be given to
those who register correctly. NO JOB IS REQUIRED.

THERE IS A STRICT JUNE DEADLINE. THE TIME TO START IS NOW!!

For FREE information via Email, send request to cslaw@indirect.com


--
****************************************************************
Canter & Siegel, Immigration Attorneys
3333 E Camelback Road, Ste 250, Phoenix AZ  85018   USA
cslaw@indirect.com    telephone (602)661-3911  Fax (602) 451-7617
```

This software bulk mailing infuriated people. But what really ticked people off about this particular team of spammers was that the more people complained about them, the more famous Canter & Siegel actually became. The spam made it into the newspapers, the duo gave interviews, and soon everyone knew who Canter & Siegel were. Amid all of the public outcry, they then had the audacity to announce plans to provide this mass-mailing service to others as a commercial service. This made them two of the most revolutionary—and hated—marketers of their time.

Things got very intense for a brief time. Such strong hatred for Canter & Siegel grew throughout the general Internet community that newspapers writing articles in support of the two attorneys were threatened by anonymous callers and found their email bombarded with letters of protest.

Canter & Siegel became so well known that they somehow convinced a publisher to publish a book titled *How to Make a Fortune on the Information Superhighway*. The book was a flop, and eventually Canter & Siegel faded out, but not before revolutionizing the advertising and marketing industries by introducing software bulk mailing—a disease that continues to infect inboxes today—thanks guys!

In 1997, Laurence Canter was disbarred by the state of Tennessee, in part for spamming.

News Release
Contact: William W. Hunt, III
[Tennessee] Board of Professional Responsibility
615-361-7500

June 16, 1997

Arizona Attorney Disbarred

On June 5, 1997, The Supreme Court of Tennessee entered an order disbarring Laurence A. Canter with law offices in Scottsdale, Arizona; Cupertino and San Rafael, California, but licensed to practice law in Tennessee. Mr. Canter also received a one year suspension to be served concurrently with a disbarment. This order was based on a recommendation of a hearing panel after a hearing in this case.

Mr. Canter was fould guilty of numerous offenses of the Attorneys' Code of Professional Responsibility (Rule 8, Rules of the Supreme Court of Tennessee). In 1994 in an incident reported in the national media he placed an advertisement that appeared on more than 5,000 of the Internet's news groups as well as 10,000 of E-Mail lists. The posting appeared on computer screens unsolicited and each reader was required to read at least a portion of the message. The hearing panel found that the posting violated Tennessee's advertising rules DR 2-101 and was an improper intrusion into the recipient's privacy violating Disciplinary Rule 1-102(A)(1)(5)(6).

Mr. Canter also represented Mr. Shafgul Islam in an immigration matter. Mr. Canter failed to adequately communicate with Mr. Islam, charged Mr. Islam an improper non-refundable retainer, failed to return Mr. Islam his file and improperly demanded Mr. Islam provide him a "full release."

Mr. Canter was also hired by Mr. A. M. Jaffee relative to an incorporation of a business and two immigration matters. Mr. Canter Failed to adequately communicate with his client, neglected his client's matters and misappropriated $350 he held in trust for his client.

In a fourth matter, Mr. Canter withheld funds from the paycheck of an employee Sandra Colvis to pay taxes and health insurance premiums, misappropriated funds to his own use and failed to pay them to the proper authorities. The paychecks made out to Ms. Colvis were also returned for insufficient funds.

Bill Yerazunis is the author of the CRM114 Discriminator, which is considered one of the "best-of-breed" language classifiers and spam filters available today. He's also a very bright guy who holds several patents and had the entire geek world rooting for him as "Doctor Crash" on Junkyard Wars not too long ago. Yerazunis recalls the Canter & Siegel spam as giving birth to one of the most important events in spam history:

> The initial Arpanet realization that the Net is designed to deal with censorship in the same way it deals with any other kind of damage—to simply route around the problem.
>
> In my opinion, the issue is that the people running the Arpanet were honest, reasonable, and intelligent folks; they didn't have the necessary "hungry Doberman smelling steak" attitude to dealing with Canter & Siegel. Nor did anyone simply drive over to their house with ten buddies and baseball bats and . . . well, fix the situation. That would have worked too, not as well, but it would have worked for a while. Rather, the Internet community treated C&S rationally but not sufficiently radically. If C&S's ISP had been blacklisted FOREVER, that would have fixed the problem within two ISPs' worth of iteration.
>
> So instead we'll spend some billions of dollars this year and _not_ fix the problem. And we'll spend billions next year, and billions the year after that . . . Do you see my problem with this scenario? :) If, even back then, it was realized that routers needed the ability to detect flooding attacks from single IP addresses or small groups of IP addresses sending millions of message packets, not only would we _not_ have spam, but as a side effect we'd have an effective Internet-wide antivirus system.

If Yerazunis is right, had we taken more radical action against Canter & Siegel and their service provider, it's possible we may have set the right precedents in motion to prevent the spread of spam. The Internet community's inability to police itself would soon present an opportunity for some radical individuals to get the community cheering for them.

Cancelmoose

Canter & Siegel weren't the only ones sending out spam during that time period. Michael Wolff & Company Inc. (Random House) decided to start spamming to promote some of Wolff's books, starting with one called *Net Chat*. Wolff sent out about 150 different ads for the book in December 1994. These were followed by advertisements for other books in the series.

```
From: editors@ypn.com (Michael Wolff)
Date: 20 Oct 1994 18:43:57 -0400
Organization: Michael Wolff & Company, Inc.
Nntp-Posting-Host: bill.ypn.com


We've just finished our new book Net Games--a guide to the world of online
games. It's stuffed with addresses and hints for playing games over the Net
from chess to Doom to FurryMUCK. We've put up a sampling of pages from the
book as GIF's that can be downloaded from ftp://www.ypn.com/pub/pages.
```

This incident popularized an anonymous individual who went by the hacker alias Cancelmoose, the first spam-fighting superhero. Cancelmoose started operation in November 1994 and used a cancelbot to perform mass cancellations of Usenet postings that he or she believed were spam.

NOTE *To this day, only a few people know the true identity of Cancelmoose. Unfortunately, a very small group of free speech activists were able to publicly push Cancelmoose into exile. During this time period, however, supporting Cancelmoose was one of the ways many felt they could fight back against spammers.*

Cancelmoose's run sparked many heated discussions concerning Wolff's spamming. Cancelmoose responded to Wolff's claims of victimization personally, stating, "They were deemed spam because it was the same thing posted 150 times. I don't care if your message was newsgroup opinions or religious sermons or the recipe for chocolate chip cookies. The nature of the opinions expressed are irrelevant to spam determination." Wolff's credibility was reduced even further when people noticed that he didn't appear to know how to correctly cross-post to three different newsgroups, but rather posted individual messages to each newsgroup in response. Eventually both Wolff and his books faded away.

NOTE *Cancelmoose helped coin one of the original attempts to define spam in December 1994 as "mass sending of mail to legitimate mailing lists."*

It was at this same time that the very first spam filters came on the scene in very primitive form, such as Nancy McGough's 1994 Procmail Tutorial. These filters used a very basic rule set to determine whether a message was spam. They will be discussed in more depth in Chapter 2.

Jeff Slaton, the "Spam King"

In 1994, spam began to grown exponentially. Come April 1995, Jeff Slaton, who called himself the Spam King, started taking over the industry by flooding mailing lists with ads for everything from small businesses to political ads.

Indirect.com, the company Slaton was using to send his spams, allegedly terminated his accounts, but they appeared to keep creeping back into active status. Slaton is one of the early individuals who made spamming appear lucrative, claiming to make $425 per distribution and between 15 and 30 distributions every week, which, if accurate, would have raked in from $300,000 to $600,000 annually. Slaton had the audacity to charge disgruntled recipients a $5 fee to be removed from all of his lists.

If you would like to be removed from any future E-Mailings ... Please send $5.00 for a computer search and I will remove you from the mailing list.

This infuriated many, and rightly so. In fact, emotions ran so high that some individuals started calling for public punishment for Slaton (some using the legal system, others using a baseball bat). Many threats were made, but in November 1995—just seven months after he started his spam campaign—Slaton claimed that he no longer believed in his marketing approach (that it was "self-defeating") and that he was "done spamming."

Slaton introduced the idea of "plausible deniability" for his customers, who claimed to be completely ignorant of any network abuse. This type of deniability is still used today by many well-known commercial organizations that quietly contract with individuals like Mr. Slaton to push spam.

"Krazy" Kevin Lipsitz

1995 was truly the year of the entrepreneur spammer. "Krazy" Kevin Lipsitz began a notorious newsgroup-spamming campaign. Specializing in many types of scam promotions, he began the now-popular practice of using AOL.com's domain name as a reply-to address and was responsible for getting all of AOL moderated on many mailing lists. Ray Everett-Church, an assistant postmaster for AOL at the time, helped defuse the situation by responding to the idea of moderation and making it clear that AOL would pursue legal action against Lipsitz.

In 1997, Lipsitz was convicted of fraud and ordered to pay up to $500 per violation of general business law. Unfortunately, he returned to spamming in October 1999.

Stanford Wallace, Cyber Promotions

Stanford Wallace (also known as "the uber-spammer" and "Spamford" Wallace) was another individual going into business during 1995. In November of that year, Wallace began a one-man spam campaign and later founded Cyber Promotions (CyberPromo). Wallace made several attempts to make junk email legitimate, and his company ended up suing AOL after it decided to block all mail from the advertising company. Cyber Promotions claimed that some of AOL's users were opt-in customers or even clients of the company, and therefore AOL was violating its right to free speech. The judge shot down this argument, stating that AOL's systems were considered private property, but eventually a settlement was made between AOL and Wallace, allowing him to continue his campaign using a different set of AOL domains.

Wallace swore off spamming for good in March 1998 and has since helped track a few other spammers down; however, Wallace himself pops up in the news every so often with suspicion. All of this hasn't come without a price, though, as Wallace was sued by many network providers, including CompuServe and AOL. A judge declared CompuServe's network private property and unsolicited mail to be trespassing.

Cyber Promotions has continued to fan the flame of "First Amendment rights for spammers," an issue that is still raised today by many spammers whenever they find themselves on the losing side of the battle.

Floodgate—The First Spamware

The first commercially streamlined spamware to hit the streets was called Floodgate. Naturally, Floodgate was marketed using the same techniques it touted.

```
                MAIL THOUSANDS OF EMAIL MESSAGES
                   PER HOUR - NO KIDDING !!
                SEND YOUR EMAIL MESSAGES OUT, AT
                1,000's MESSAGES / HOUR (28.8K modem)
                 YES, 1,000's Of Messages An Hour
********************************************************
          MILLIONS OF EMAIL ADDRESSES
          ******** $100.00 *******
********************************************************
   YOU'LL RECEIVE 2 HIGH-SPEED EMAIL SOFTWARE PROGRAMS
Introducing...."FLOODGATE BULK EMAIL LOADER"
          AND...."GOLDRUSH STEALTH MASS MAILER"
This is the same software that all bulk emailing services use!
----------------------------------------------------
Floodgate Bulk Email Loader Version 5.2 AND
Goldrush Stealth Mass Mailer Version 3.215
for Windows 95 and Windows 3.1 now Supports 17
(really more with the free form filter) File Formats
```

Floodgate ushered in a new generation of do-it-yourself spammers and helped bring several independent entrepreneurs into the scene. Today, a majority of spam is still sent by only a few large entities, but at a time when there were only a couple of "professional" spammers, Floodgate provided the tools for just about anybody to jump on board. Compared to the $400 to $500 spammers were charging to send a single distribution, $100 was a great deal.

Other Significant Events in 1995

In August 1995, the very first known list of public email addresses was offered for sale: 2 million total addresses.

In September 1995, "abuse@" email addresses were finally becoming popular. This provided a way for end users and systems administrators to report network abuse to a company's network operations center. At first, this was a great idea, as it allowed service providers a standard way to manage spam complaints. As time went on, however, abuse boxes continued to fill up, and the resources required to manage an abuse box resulted in a very slow response time.

In November 1995, the first "remove lists" were created, allegedly to remove individuals from lists they did not want to be subscribed to. There was much debate about this issue, with most believing that using the unsubscribe mechanism only served to confirm to the spammer that the email address was valid. The "remove list" seemed to be merely a front to claim a legitimate "opt-in" business.

War Waged on Spam

During 1996, the largest growth occurred in the spam arms race, in terms of arsenal. A few anti-spam concepts were birthed, including Spamblock, Internet Death Penalty, and a network abuse newsgroup, but unfortunately the spam industry landed some major blows with the development of many tools to aid spamming. While network administrators were still tinkering with possible solutions, spamware had become huge. Some of the tools that came into existence in 1996 were Lightning Bolt, Ready-Aim-Fire, and E-Mail Blaster. Several new spammers also popped up, including Yuri Rutman, Walt Rines, and Dave Mustachi.

Spamhaus

Spamhaus was formed in July 1996 to provide a way of tracking spammers; it provided the first semblance of a blacklist. Today, Spamhaus provides many valuable resources to Internet service providers fighting spam. Two popular blackhole lists are hosted at Spamhaus, including the SBL (Spamhaus Blackhole List) and XBL (Exploits Blackhole List). It provides many different articles and other resources as well. Spamhaus originally provided a searchable database of domains, whois information, names, addresses, and phone numbers. During Spamhaus's first few years, it received threats from many spammers. Spammers would also attempt various types of legal attacks to intimidate Spamhaus, which made light of them by posting their messages on its website.

```
Return-Path: ds98@submit1.com
Received: from [209.24.168.19] (HELO DesktopServer98) by
hercules.ultradesign.net (Stalker SMTP Server 1.8b3) with SMTP id S.0000041853
for <abuse@combat.uxn.com>; Sat, 17 Apr 1999 16:49:11 +0100
From: Anthony <ds98@submit1.com>
To: <abuse@combat.uxn.com>
Message-Id: <419.436267.36408287ds98@submit1.com>
Subject: REMOVE FROM SITE
Mime-Version: 1.0
```

```
Content-Type: text/plain; charset="us-ascii"
Content-Transfer-Encoding: 7bit
Date: Sat, 17 Apr 1999 16:49:12 +0100

Discontinue the illegal use of our trademarked domain on your site!!!

www.bulkemailstore.com
```

WARNING

The threat below is particularly amusing, as the spammer couldn't even spell "defamation" correctly; they were threatening to sue Spamhaus for "deformation"!

```
Return-Path: ds98@bulkemailstore.com
Received: from mail.netmagic.net ([206.14.125.10] verified) by
hercules.ultradesign.net (Stalker SMTP Server 1.8b3) with ESMTP id
S.0000041787 for <abuse@combat.uxn.com>; Sat, 17 Apr 1999 16:25:40 +0100
Received: from anthonym (ppp4-19.sj.netmagic.net [209.24.168.19]) by
mail.netmagic.net (8.8.7/NetMagic) with SMTP id IAA15681 for
<abuse@combat.uxn.com>; Sat, 17 Apr 1999 08:23:00 -0700
Reply-To: <ds98@bulkemailstore.com>
From: "DS98" <ds98@bulkemailstore.com>
To: "UXN Spam Combat" <abuse@combat.uxn.com>
Subject: Warning
Date: Sat, 17 Apr 1999 08:20:45 -0700
Message-ID: <000901be88e5$dd6318a0$13a818d1@anthonym.netmagic.net>
MIME-Version: 1.0
Content-Type: text/plain
Content-Transfer-Encoding: 7bit
X-Priority: 1 (Highest)
X-MSMail-Priority: High
X-Mailer: Microsoft Outlook 8.5, Build 4.71.2173.0
X-MimeOLE: Produced By Microsoft MimeOLE V4.72.3110.3
In-Reply-To: <v03110701b33deec2c2d3@engineering.uxn.com>
Importance: High

Okay, that was the polite request.

Any further illegal use of our Trademarks on your site will be prosecuted to
fullest extent of the law. Our fee is $1000 per day for the use of our
Trademark, you will be invoiced accordingly. Although we appreciate the Free
advertising it is "unauthorized".

If that is your position, we will now make you very sorry for your position.
Legal proceedings have begun and we will seek an injunction against you and
your site and email addresses will be targeted, you sent me this email so we
have the right to reply as many times deemed necessary.

You will also be sued for deformation and slander.
```

And finally, this threat, in which CyberCreek, manufacturer of spamware, threatens criminal charges against Spamhaus, is particularly humorous. Ironically, CyberCreek was shut down less than a week after sending this message.

```
From: "Andrew Brunner" <abrunner@cybercreek.com>
To: "UXN Spam Combat" <abuse@combat.uxn.com>
Date: Mon, 23 Aug 1999 23:36:35 -0500
Subject: Re: REQUEST.NET listed on Spam Support Services Tracking Site
X-Mailer: CyberCreek Mail Professional with MSIE Support; CyberCreek RSR Build
= 1580


Keep dreaming spam nazi.

We will see how far you get when we haul your ass in front of
a magistrate ;-)

Andrew Brunner
CyberCreek LLC
```

Unsolicited Commercial Email

In April 1996, the term "unsolicited commercial email" (UCE) was coined. The Usenet abuse FAQ does a good job of defining UCE.

```
UCE: Unsolicitied Commercial Email

Email containing commercial information that has been sent to a recipient
who did not ask to receive it.

This is widely used, and confused with UBE, (see above). UCE must be
commercial in nature but does not imply massive numbers. Several ISPs specify
a threshold for unsolicited commercial email:

    ----- sending one UCE is a violation -----

In a specific case, individuals took offense at having been sent commercial
messages regarding their web sites. Their addresses were posted for the
purpose of comments and suggestions about the site; the messages received were
commercial offerings to buy ad space on the site or sell something to the site
maintainer.
```

Spam Out of Control

As if spam wasn't already out of control by the end of 1996, the volume grew exponentially by the end of 1997. Many statistics show that spam volume grew by as much as a factor of 10 during the second half of the year. Many new spammers also joined the pack, and newer spam tools such as Extractor Pro, Stealth, and Goldrush were designed to evade the primitive spam filters that were available at the time. During the first part of 1997, the term "open relay" was coined, which referred to a mail server that would relay mail to a different Internet provider by an unauthorized sender (namely one who was not a customer). A significant amount of open relay work was done during the year to close down servers at the Internet service providers. Even today, open relays still exist, although more SMTP software is now configured out of the box to prevent this. Many databases like *ORBS (Open Relay Behavior-modification System)* popped up to track systems with open relays.

During 1997, more than 200 million email addresses were sold on a handful of email list CDs. This was due in part to the appearance of email harvesters, which scoured newsgroups and websites for email addresses. Thus started the chain reaction of address obfuscation, reversing the direction of technological advances such as the at sign (@).

The first spam hearings with the Federal Trade Commission took place in 1997. They were technically about "consumer online privacy" but were relevant enough to spam for big-name spammers, such as Stanford Wallace from CyberPromo, to show up and lie through their teeth to the commission. The hearings lasted four days and basically ended by acknowledging the problem but being unclear about exactly how to solve it. A few bills were presented, and although it was known exactly what needed to be done, as usual the politicians stood in the way of any real progress.

Toward the end of 1997, the last well-known spammer haven—AGIS—kicked off the major spam players, including CyberPromo and Nancynet. This sparked a major effort to close spammer accounts across the United States. Paul Vixie's RBL (real-time blackhole list) was announced, which provided a blackhole interface directly to an Internet service provider's routers, enabling them to stop blacklisted networks from even communicating with theirs. The war on spam had finally started to strengthen, with people like Vixie providing the ammunition.

1998, 1999, and 2000: Three Years of War on Spam

During the next three years, spam was fought in full force and was kept at bay, at least in terms of volume. Between 1998 and 1999, spam would be fought back down from a factor of 10 to a factor of about 3 or 4, but by the end of 2000, it would start creeping back up again. This would eventually lead to a massive spike in volume that has only grown since 2001.

Some notable happenings during this three-year period included a massive growth in spamware, several new websites and networks touching on the spam scene, and a massive spike in lists of email addresses for sale.

Several organizations were touted to provide a "universal remove service," such as the IEMMC (a spammer's organization), remove-list.com, and SAFEeps. These services didn't appear to do much other than cause people to willingly supply their email addresses. Some believe the lists were a front to harvest addresses; others think it was just a way to keep the lawyers at bay.

Around the beginning of 2000, the most famous and widely circulated spam to date was forged: the world's first Nigerian spam. This scam has since outlived four years of spam fighting, with several permutations of it showing up today in inboxes around the world. These spams were quickly dubbed 419 spams, after the article of the Criminal Code of Nigeria enacted by Nigerian president Olusegun Obasanjo to ban this type of fraud. Obasanjo stated that the scam was causing "incalculable damage to Nigerian businesses" and "[placed] the entire country under suspicion." The typical 419 spam begins with something to this effect:

Attention:Sir

It is my pleasure to contact you for an assistance and business co-operation. I know the content of this letter might be surprising to you but I assure you that every word of it is true. Even though we hardly know each other I believe you can help me ...

The 419 Coalition has posted an excellent description of the typical 419 scam on its website at http://home.rica.net/alphae/419coal:

> The Scam operates as follows: the target receives an unsolicited fax, email, or letter often concerning Nigeria or another African nation containing either a money laundering or other illegal proposal OR you may receive a legal and legitimate business proposal by normal means. Common variations on the Scam include "over invoiced" or "double invoiced" oil or other supply and service contracts where your Bad Guys want to get the overage out of Nigeria; crude oil and other commodity deals; a "bequest" left you in a will; "money cleaning" where your Bad Guy has a lot of currency that needs to be "chemically cleaned" before it can be used and he needs the cost of the chemicals; "spoof banks" where there is supposedly money in your name already on deposit; "paying" for a purchase with a check larger than the amount required and asking for change to be advanced; fake lottery 419; and ordering items and commodities off "trading" sites on the web and then cheating the seller. The variations of Advance Fee Fraud (419) are very creative and virtually endless.

> At some point, the victim is asked to pay up front an Advance Fee of some sort, be it an "Advance Fee," "Transfer Tax," "Performance Bond," or to extend credit, grant COD privileges, send back "change" on an overage cashier's check or money order, whatever. If the victim pays the Fee, there are often many "complications" which require still more advance payments until the victim either quits, runs out of money, or both. If the victim extends credit on a given transaction, etc., he may also pay such fees ("nerfund" etc.), and also be stiffed for the goods or service with NO effective recourse.

The 419 spam is particularly famous, or rather infamous, because it actually dates back to the 1980s, when the scam was faxed or mailed to its victims. Unfortunately, today a number of new users still fall victim to the 419 scam.

Network Solutions

Network Solutions Inc. was founded in 1979 under government contract to provide, among other things, domain name resolution to the world. It marked its 20th anniversary in 1999, and a significant wind of change moved the company's now-commercial focus into the spotlight. Network Solutions had been selling information that is normally collected when a company or individual registers a domain name. By 2001, these sales efforts were in full force, and many "domain name directory" CDs began popping up for sale by individuals trying to make a buck. Although the information sold was technically public, one would have had to query Network Solutions' machines a few million times to collect the data. Network Solutions openly admitted this, and while they claimed their market was primarily Internet service providers and other telecommunications companies, the selling of an individual's phone number, email address, and even physical address infuriated many. The company provided an opt-out mechanism, but by the time its customers had even heard of this feature, their names had in many cases already been sold many times. It is no surprise that these events paralleled the distribution of some of the biggest third-party CDs, with more than 240 million addresses per set.

2001 to the Present: Exponential Spam Growth

Since 2001, spam has grown exponentially. By the end of 2002, spam had grown in volume by a factor of nearly 60 compared to its volume just six years prior. Spam is now utterly and completely out of control. Websites such as SPEWS (Spam Prevention Early Warning System) have cropped up in an attempt to provide many different blacklisting services to service providers. Over the past several years, more complex spam filters have been designed and implemented, using everything from basic heuristic rule sets to modern-day statistical filters. Statistical filtering now yields accuracy rates higher than a human would be capable of achieving, yet there is still a margin of error that annoys some.

The spam problem is only growing. Users are finding more and more spam in their inboxes every day. Many researchers now believe that spam is responsible for anywhere from 35 percent to 65 percent of all email traffic on the Internet today, with a whopping annual growth rate of 15 percent to 20 percent. Many are concerned that spam could be the end of email.

Final Thoughts

Computer users' philosophy toward spam has shifted dramatically. What used to be passionate feelings against the commercialization of the Internet have now been dulled into a mild frustration. Spammers still make arguments for free speech, but these have been so overused that even the courts have found no merit in them. It is considered commonplace to receive spam, and many novice Internet users have learned the bad habit of spamming miscellaneous information to smaller lists of acquaintances.

The few people who remain passionate about fighting spam today have made considerable headway in last couple of years. The CAN-SPAM Act was signed into law in the United States, and while this legislation hasn't been shown to have any true effect on spam, it is helping to bring spam-fighting efforts to the federal level of attention. If anything, it's given firepower to prosecutors by defining criminals. Still, until enforcement of this type of network abuse is made effective on a large scale, the general public will have to depend on spam filters to keep their inboxes free from spam.

2

HISTORICAL APPROACHES TO FIGHTING SPAM

In 1994, automated approaches to sending spam began to emerge, triggering an inter-network nerd battle between spammers and anti-spammers in the Internet community. An arms race quickly developed, and several new technologies emerged to counter the growing rate of spam, with the goal of saving companies huge amounts of bandwidth, server resources, and time spent on abuse management. The very first technologies to emerge were quite primitive, but as people learned what to look for through trial and error, many useful approaches would emerge. In this chapter, we'll examine some of the popular ways individuals have fought and are fighting spam, the weaknesses of various approaches, and some concoctions that hackers have thrown together that work remarkably well.

Primitive Language Analysis

Primitive language analysis is the process of matching specific phrases of text to an email. The very first spam filters were quite primitive and were not really filters at all. Before real spam filters emerged, these primitive tools used a very simple approach to language analysis by simply scanning email for known senders in the message headers, multiple Usenet cross-postings (messages sent to a large number of different forums), or for phrases that were indicative of spam such as "Call Now!" and "Free Trial!" Between 1994 and 1997, there wasn't much else the world could do about spam. The technology to fight it was too limited.

In the early days of spam, before spammers learned many of the nasty tricks they use today (as we'll discuss in Chapter 7), filters that cross-checked against lists of junk mail sender lists were somewhat effective only because it was possible to filter based on a known list of words and phrases which most of the world believed only existed in spam. Filtering based on a single word alone had a potential success rate of around 80 percent, with very little chance of catching legitimate messages.

Most of these early spam-catching tools were home-brewed solutions. Some tools, such as procmail (a utility for mail processing), were used to create recipes to filter for certain basic words and phrases in incoming email. As new spams were being distributed on a daily basis, the word and phrase lists required continued maintenance. Many individuals found themselves with better things to do with their time, and so a few commercial solutions became popular during this period. These commercial solutions were sold in conjunction with a subscription nightly-update service to automatically download and apply new filtering phrases.

This primitive approach to spam filtering became mainstream for a while. Early versions of some email clients such as Microsoft Outlook implemented simple junk mail sender lists that would check for known sender addresses in message headers. Although this approach had some weaknesses, it worked well enough up until it didn't.

One major weakness of primitive language filtering is that a single guilty phrase, such as the words "toll free," could condemn an entire legitimate message to a user's junk mailbox. The simplicity of these spam filters eventually led to a high false-positive rate. Although some of these guilty phrases applied to a majority of spam, they also began to apply to a small collection of legitimate mail. As a result, a user had to check their bit-bucket frequently to make sure that no legitimate messages were caught. It also became clear that there were some gray areas to spam filtering: As the phrase "one man's spam is another man's ham" (which grew out of this period) suggests, some messages (like a bulk invitation to a conference) might be considered wanted mail by some users and spam by others.

One of the advantages of primitive filtering was that it was so simple to implement that users generally custom-tailored these filters to match their own email behavior. But this was also one of the biggest problems; it required a lot of maintenance in order to work properly. As spam began to grow, the lists of guilty words and phrases became longer and less manageable. The complexity of filtering spiked around 1997, when struggling spammers began to look for new ways to trick users into reading their emails. The new ways they found to change and obfuscate messages left most filters ineffective. Updating them took too much work, and primitive filters were effectively extinguished.

Pros	Only solution available at the time, easy to customize.
Cons	Required heavy maintenance, low accuracy, high error rates.
Ideal For	Obsolete.

Blacklisting

In 1997, Paul Vixie deployed the first free, subscription-based *RBL*, or *real-time blackhole list*, thus marking the first significant public effort to control spam at the Internet service provider (ISP) level. The blackhole list was a system for "creating intentional network outages *(black holes)* for the purpose of limiting the transport of known-to-be-unwanted mass email." Specifically, a blackhole list maintains a list of known spammer networks (its blacklist) and provides its participants with the ability to ignore traffic from them. The philosophy of blacklisting is simple enough and is reminiscent of the *Meidung* used by the Amish—also known as the *shunning*. Basically, once a blacklist maintainer receives enough complaints about a particular network, that network is added to the blacklist, at which point all list subscribers automatically ignore inbound traffic from the blacklisted network until the spammer repents (or dies of old age).

A blacklisted network may appeal its blacklisting after taking care of the problem (namely tossing the spammer off their network), at which point it may be removed from the list at the maintainer's discretion (and sometimes the maintainer's mood). Blacklists allowed people to filter spam based on its origin rather than its contents. Subscribers no longer needed to maintain their own content-based filtering lists (although many did) and could instead rely on the blackhole to tell them what mail to filter.

Vixie called his list the *MAPS (Mail-Abuse Prevention System)* RBL. Subscribers accessed the MAPS RBL by establishing an intercommunication between their network equipment and the blacklist. Their routers, the machines responsible for directing traffic across the Internet, were configured to accept blacklisted routes from the blacklist. The routers then blackholed these routes used by spammers, causing all traffic from the spammer to be ignored and giving rise to the phrase "intentional network outages." The advantage of performing blacklisting at the network level is that it conserves resources and has the muscle to make an entire network "disappear" until the problem is dealt with. Smaller businesses that "rented" their network from a local ISP could configure their mail servers to perform lookups on the blacklist server to determine whether a sender's Internet address belonged to a known spammer.

The concept of blackholing became immediately famous, as it not only helped to filter spam but also conserved a provider's bandwidth and server resources. Between 1997 and 1999, the MAPS RBL was the tool of choice for preventing spam from entering a network. Then, in 2001, an anti-spam organization named SPEWS caught onto the idea and launched its own blacklist, followed by many other organizations and individuals.

The availability of many different types of blackhole lists helped bring some level of filtering diversity to the networking community, giving the ISP the freedom to choose just how strict a spam-filtering policy it wanted to implement. Each blackhole list had a different set of terms and conditions for identifying spam—some more strict than others. Some lists were so strict and so broad that participants risked rejecting mail from legitimate senders. Others were a bit more laid back and reserved the blackhole listings for the most serious offenders.

Propagation and Maintenance Problems

Blackhole lists have two significant weaknesses. The first is propagation time. Unfortunately, blackhole lists don't list networks until they've already begun sending spam. While this worked great in the earliest versions of these lists, because spammers were fairly immobile, in today's world of stolen dialup accounts, sacrificial shell boxes (machines a spammer will voluntarily sacrifice by placing them in an ISP's colocation facility to send spam), and open relays (mail servers that are misconfigured to send mail for anyone outside of their network), new spam hosts can pop up instantly and be gone by the time they are added to a blackhole list. This leads to the second problem with many blackholes: quality of maintenance.

In an attempt to be proactive with new spam hosts, many lists began blacklisting the address space of dialup and ISDN users. The big problem with this was that address spaces frequently changed. Companies renumbered their addresses and sometimes would go out of business (especially between 2000 and 2002), leaving the blacklisted address space a headache for the next tenants to deal with.

Many of today's blackhole lists today are also poorly maintained or are managed by vigilantes who don't adhere to any form of proper procedure before blacklisting networks. As a result, some networks that have been added to a blacklist are never removed, are removed slowly, or are blacklisted for political reasons. All of these issues make some blacklists very unreliable and result in the blocking of legitimate emails.

The Osirusoft List

One particular incident occurred with a now-defunct blacklist called the *Osirusoft list*. This blacklist, run by an individual named Joe Jarad, was a distributor for the SPEWS network and was designed primarily as an *open relay blacklist*, a blacklist specifically for the purpose of blackholing individuals who were running mail servers vulnerable to abuse by spammers.

Once Osirusoft blacklisted you as an open relay, you were told to submit an email to the list's automated system for retesting, and you would allegedly be removed from the blacklist if your mail server tested clean. The problem was that the Osirusoft server was designed to keep people blackholed indefinitely: It was configured to reject email from blacklisted hosts, and since you had to send your retest message from the blacklisted host, it was impossible to get off the list.

The Osirusoft list was picked up by SpamAssassin (a popular spam-filtering tool) and sendmail (a popular email server package), and so even if you didn't intentionally subscribe to the list, you were automatically subscribed if you used either of these two tools with RBL support enabled. To make matters worse, Osirusoft was a member of a community of blacklists that was quite popular, and therefore many ISPs inadvertently used Osirusoft without even knowing it.

In the end, Osirusoft was a shining example of stupidity. The system got DDoSed (knocked out of commission by many distributed denial of service attacks), many lawsuits were threatened, and at one point power was even mysteriously lost to the facility, bringing the list down for days (and causing many network interruptions in the process). Eventually the maintainer decided to blacklist the entire world, which caused all participants tied to the blacklist to reject mail from everywhere. This caused a lot of people to believe that the maintainer was an idiot, at which point Osirusoft was immediately decommissioned.

Heuristic Filtering

Heuristic filtering was developed in the late 1990s. This type of filtering uses a set of commonsense rules intended to identify specific characteristics of spam. These characteristics can include content or specific observations about particular constructions typical of spam. Unlike primitive filters, heuristic filters have rules to detect both spam and legitimate mail. Messages having somewhat spammy characteristics can quite possibly be delivered as legitimate mail if they also set off a number of alarms that the message isn't spam.

Brightmail

In 1999, the Brightmail Corporation released what most believe was the first commercial anti-spam solution. Brightmail offered both free and commercial versions of its solutions, including a POP3 proxy service for end users that allowed a user to filter spam without having to install any new software. Instead, users configured their email client to connect to Brightmail's server (instead of their ISP's). Brightmail's server would then establish a connection to the user's ISP and filter mail as the user was downloading it (see Figure 2-1).

Brightmail was a cross between primitive and heuristic filtering. It used a "database" for spam that was initially maintained by people called "spam experts" or "spam masters," who would pick out special characteristics from a large collection of spam and add these characteristics to the database.

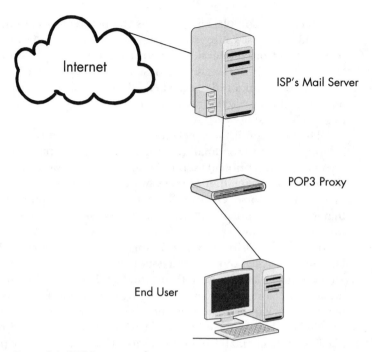

Figure 2-1: POP3 proxy architecture

The initial version of Brightmail required a lot of manual maintenance. Users were instructed to forward any errors (both spam misses and false positives, which included people's private correspondence) to a human at Brightmail, with full headers intact, where it would be added to the database for future filtering.

We will forward the caught message to our Spam Masters, who will analyze it and update our filters accordingly. That way, we can make sure our filters don't make the same mistake again.

SpamAssassin

When it was introduced, Brightmail was one of the only widely available filtering solutions, but that was about to change. In 2001, the first true heuristic filter, SpamAssassin, made its appearance on Sourceforge. SpamAssassin was one of the first open-source, freely available spam filters, and it had a noticeable positive effect on people's sanity.

SpamAssassin used many different "rule sets" to measure whether a message was spam or not, and no single characteristic condemned a message. Instead, a score was calculated based on the matching characteristics, and if the score exceeded a certain threshold, the message was considered spam. As summarized on its website, SpamAssassin's basic functionality initially included three features. First, it analyzed the message headers to detect a number of tricks spammers had begun using to mask their identities or to fool users into thinking the message was valid. Next, SpamAssassin performed a textual analysis of the message, looking for specific words and phrases that match spam. Lastly, SpamAssassin performed lookups on many existing blacklists.

In addition to basic pattern matching, SpamAssassin used many true "heuristic" type commonsense rules, including one that detects malformed (or simply bad) headers and another that detects From: addresses that don't resolve correctly (meaning they're faked).

Drawbacks to Heuristic Filtering

Heuristic filtering has a couple of significant weaknesses that make it increasingly ineffective. Their primary weakness stems from the fact that the rule sets were designed for everybody to use. Therefore, the rules have to be somewhat watered down to avoid a significant number of false positives (legitimate mail that was incorrectly marked as spam). As a result, the first version of SpamAssassin had an error rate (rate of missed spam or false positives) of about 1 in 10 messages, though later versions improved this rate to 1 in about 20 messages, providing about 95 percent accuracy.

But the more significant problem with heuristic filtering seems to be that, because everyone uses the same set of rules, spammers can use the filter to learn how to evade it. Since the rule sets and scoring mechanisms are mostly static, spammers are able to download the latest heuristic tool and run their spam through it. As they begin to identify the parts of their spam that set the software off, they can change their message to evade the rules, even setting off a few rules to identify legitimate mail. Spammers did just that. They then sent their modified messages, knowing that they would pass through every default installation of the software that used the same set of rules. As a result, accuracy became very volatile and dropped significantly, with some systems administrators noticing decreases to as low as 40 percent on some occasions. Accuracy would increase as the filter authors added new rules but would drop again once the spammers tried something new.

Maintenance Headaches

The maintenance headaches associated with heuristic filters have never gone away. Although many heuristic filters are very effective at reducing spam by 85 percent or more, the rule sets still require constant updating due to the evolution of spam.[1]

As of this writing, SpamAssassin uses anywhere from 900 to 950 different heuristic rules, and that rule set appears to need significant maintenance approximately every six months to maintain accuracy. That's a lot of maintenance. Systems administrators haven't got the time to audit 900 rules, and so the responsibility for maintaining them has been deferred to the maintainers of the software, resulting in the need for an upgrade every time new rules are added.

---

[1] At the MIT Spam Conference in 2004, Terry Sullivan illustrated the evolution cycle of spam with his paper entitled "The Myth of Spam Volatility." Sullivan argued that the feature set of spams generally has a life span on the order of months (and not minutes, as was previously thought by some).

Scoring

Another downfall of the heuristic approach is that each rule has its own *score*, which determines the significance of the rule in analyzing a message. However, since the significance of each rule is very different for each user, the scores provide only a blanket scenario defining the "normal" behavior of the majority of individuals. As spam has evolved, these different scores have become a bit out of tune, requiring the systems administrator to constantly tweak their sensitivity. But perhaps more problematic is that the scores don't really represent anything specific; they're just numbers, and they're not based on any mathematical equation or statistic. The arbitrariness of the scoring system has caused systems administrators to leave the scores alone, which has resulted in a further drop in accuracy. Many users today complain that they get only 70 percent to 80 percent accuracy rates using some heuristic filters, with some delivering as low as 30 percent.

NOTE *SpamAssassin has recently adopted a Bayesian filter as part of its decision matrix, in an effort to boost accuracy. As the code begins to mature, this will likely bring the filter's accuracy levels up to more acceptable levels. Bayesian filters are described in the next chapter.*

Pros	Much more accurate than primitive filtering, easy to distribute rule sets.
Cons	Rule sets still require maintenance, accuracy not as good as newer statistical filters, rule sets can be used by spammers to evade the filter.
Ideal For	Systems administrators who need out-of-the-box filtering and can tolerate a 5 percent or greater error rate, with fluctuating levels of accuracy.

Whitelisting

Whitelisting is the opposite of blacklisting and uses an inclusionary list. Everybody is blacklisted by default unless they are specifically named on the whitelist. If you've ever tried to make it into a ritzy club, you'll probably have a good understanding of what it's like not to be whitelisted (especially if you're reading technical books like this one for a living).

The biggest difference between whitelisting and traditional content filtering is that content filtering requires that we identify spam, while whitelisting requires us to identify senders. Most whitelisting implementations are managed individually by each user, for the obvious reason that there are on the order of a few hundred million legitimate email addresses to keep track of.

A Little Too Effective

Whitelisting is touted as having 100 percent accuracy, primarily because nothing that is not explicitly allowed can get through. This is claimed as a big advantage, but that is a bit of an embellishment. Since all mail from unknown senders is rejected, messages from members of newsgroups you belong to or from people who simply want to contact you for legitimate reasons will be rejected. You might not know that they've even attempted to contact you.

There are several ways to compensate for the overzealousness of whitelists. One way is to create whitelist email addresses, a special email address that can be given to senders who are not yet whitelisted. Other workarounds involve throttling the sender (limiting the speed and number of messages an unknown sender can send) and sending a challenge/response (discussed later in this chapter). The important thing to remember when considering whitelists as a solution is that the stricter safeguards require more work on the user's part, which can be considerable, especially when compared to just deleting spam.

Still, in spite of the manual labor involved in maintaining whitelists, many savvy users find this to be the best method to prevent spam, especially those who don't have very diverse email behavior or who use email only to talk to a select group of individuals.

Forgeries

Enter the forgery problem. Many whitelisting systems whitelist only based on the email address rather than on the entire From: header. This is done to make whitelisting easy for unsavvy users, enabling them to simply plug in their friends' email addresses. The From: field is considered a trusted field, when in reality it's quite easily forged. For example, a spam advertising antivirus software might forge an address of support@mcafee.com, an email address many antivirus software users are likely to have in their whitelist. Since no authentication is performed by the recipient, spammers can forge whatever address they like; if they can find an address common enough to a large group of people, they can send you as much spam as they want, and there's nothing you can do about it.

Whitelisting is a black-and-white approach, with very little room for a gray area. A user is either trusted or not trusted. Most people don't "trust" everyone who sends them mail not to also send them spam, as a lot of people get added to many personal mailing lists or have been subjected to spammers masquerading as legitimate users—on mailing lists, for example.

To add insult to injury, if a spammer does manage to forge an address in the user's whitelist, the recipient can't simply remove that address from the whitelist, or they'll block all mail from the legitimate sender. But if they keep the address whitelisted, they allow all spam from the forged sender using the address. There is no middle ground; whitelisting either works or it doesn't.

Many content-based filters use whitelisting on top of the existing content filtering to boost accuracy. A lot of people believe this is a mistake, though, as it exposes the software to the types of vulnerabilities just discussed. It has the potential to also pull attention away from improving the accuracy of content filtering. Whether you like whitelisting or not, it's here to stay and is a viable option for those who prefer to close their windows to outsiders.

Pros	Very accurate, not based on learning message content.
Cons	Can be forged, all users are trusted, requires manual work.
Ideal For	Users who want high accuracy rates don't mind doing the work and can risk losing occasional emails.

Challenge/Response

Challenge/response (C/R) takes an approach similar to whitelisting and is much more despised by many users. C/R pushes the burden of maintaining a user's whitelist onto the message sender—something a lot of people see as a slap in the face because it forces senders to do the work of a spam filter, requiring them to click on a link in order to send their first message to the recipient.

Subject: Re: Hi There!

Greetings,

You just sent an email to my spam-free email service. Because this is the first time you have sent to this email account, please confirm yourself so you'll be recognized when you send to me in the future. It's easy. To prove your message comes from a human and not a computer, click on the link below:

http://[Some Web Link]

Attached is your original message that is in my pending folder, waiting for your quick authentication.

Many people find this annoying and will simply refuse to communicate with individuals who require a response to an email challenge.

Problems with Challenge/Response

Most of the basic flaws found in whitelisting also apply to challenge/response. Forgeries are still fairly easy to perform, and to make matters worse, C/R users themselves can add their address as a trusted sender to the recipient's whitelist.

Another complaint specific to C/R is the amount of email traffic it generates. Instead of helping to conserve resources, C/R uses additional resources by sending verification emails to every unknown sender. As a result, large quantities of mass email go out daily to the forged addresses spammers use, or whenever there's a new virus. This can total millions of emails per day for a small ISP.

People also complain that challenge/response delays their email. For example, if a sender fails to reply to the challenge to an urgent email, that email would be delayed until the next time the sender checks his or her own email—which could be minutes, hours, or even the next day.

Many advocates of challenge/response note that it has one of the lowest false-positive rates and one of the highest accuracy rates. This is true until you consider the number of people who simply won't bother responding to a challenge. Still, C/R does provide a high level of accuracy for those who are willing to live with the caveats. And if you're antisocial, it's probably one of the greatest solutions on the planet.

Pros	Very accurate, not based on learning message content.
Cons	May cause people not to want to email you. Slows down email. Generates high email traffic loads. Can be forged. Requires manual work on the sender's part.
Ideal For	Users who want senders to verify themselves prior to conversation and are willing to miss an occasional email or limit the number of people who want to talk to them.

Throttling

Throttling is probably one of the most sensible ways to fight spam for small- to medium-sized service providers, as it doesn't stop any legitimate mail from entering the network. Instead, it simply slows down the rate at which a single network or host can send traffic. This prevents any significant resources from being used by the spammer and can even result in fewer spams entering a network (if the connection is throttled down enough to outlive the spammer's distribution).

Think of throttling as a slow grocery store cashier: If you have only a few items to buy, a slow cashier is no big deal—you can sit and yak about the weather and his new perm for a few minutes and then be on your way. But if you're trying to buy the whole farm, you'll be there for a while. Throttling is used for both inbound traffic and outbound bulk detection/prevention at many ISPs. What's nice about throttling is that it conserves resources without having much effect on legitimate mail, and it also uses more of the spammers' most expensive resources: time and processing.

The philosophy behind throttling is that a legitimate mail distribution would never need to send more than a certain threshold of traffic to any particular network. For example, a legitimate mailing list may send out huge quantities of mail, but each message is going to different recipients on different networks. At most, only a handful of the messages going out would be directed to any one network. A spammer, on the other hand, may have scripts designed to bombard a network with spam by using a dictionary attack, in which every possible username is generated. A good throttling tool will accurately determine whether the sender is abusing the network and limit the amount of bandwidth the sender is capable of pushing. Messages will eventually get where they're going if they are legitimate, but because throttling also uses more of the sender's resources, spammers are more likely to hang up when they realize they're talking over a slow network connection. Next time a telemarketer calls you, try repeating, "What?" in a real slow southern drawl. You'll either get them to hang up or at the very least gain an extremely satisfying feeling by frustrating them within an inch of their sanity.

TarProxy

TarProxy is a "recipient-satisfaction" program written by Marty Lamb of Martian Software (http://www.martiansoftware.com) and is the embodiment of true throttling. TarProxy talks directly to a spam filter and will perform throttling as well as many other more satisfying tasks, such as rejecting mail outright from known spammers, in which the mail server sends a status code informing them that their message is not accepted.

```
554 I don't need any Viagra. Go Away.
```

TarProxy can use a feature of SMTP called *tempfail* to convince the spammer's mail server that it is out of resources and to try again later (most spammers won't).

```
451 I'm tired of this. Spam me later.
```

Probably the most popular feature in TarProxy is its ability to *tarpit* a spammer, which basically means using up all of the spammer's resources by putting them on "hold" indefinitely, telling their mail server to wait . . . and wait . . . and wait some more. It's like saying "Whaaaaaaaaaaaaaaaat?" to that telemarketer. Like sticking the spammer in a pit of tar, TarProxy sends a status code asking the sender's mail server to wait until it is ready to receive the message.

```
451-Your spam is important to us. Please stay on the line...
451-Your spam is important to us. Please stay on the line...
451-Your spam is important to us. Please stay on the line...
451-Your spam is important to us. Please stay on the line...
```

According to the TarProxy documentation, tarpitting uses up resources at the service provider, but with a firewall and a little smoke-and-mirrors trick, it's easy to convince the spammer you're still there when you're not.

NOTE   *Since TarProxy depends on a spam filter to tell it what to throttle, the accuracy of the tarpit is only as good as the filter. The negative side to this type of throttling is that it may delay legitimate mail whenever the spam filter experiences a false positive. The solution to this is to use a spam filter that has a very high level of accuracy and to combine the tools with a type of network-based whitelist.*

Other Throttling Tools

Many other throttling tools exist that are designed to throttle everyone based on total throughput, number of messages, and other types of conditions. These tools have an advantage over other throttling solutions in that they don't rely on a spam filter, but they become a disadvantage if the tool is too aggressive. For example, many legitimate mailings could be throttled if the threshold is crossed. If the CEO of a hosted company emailed all of his employees, who are located behind an ISP's servers, emails could get delayed.

Overall, throttling is a great feature and helps to cut back on the amount of spam traffic that overtakes your network. Since it's not really a solution to spam, it should always be used in conjunction with other tools that prevent spam delivery.

Pros	Helps conserve resources, very satisfying to use.
Cons	Not a solution to spam, could upset legitimate users.
Ideal For	Service providers and large companies that need to conserve resources.

Collaborative Filtering

Collaborative filtering is a generic approach used to describe any type of filtering in which a network of intelligence is used to identify spam. A collaborative intelligence network can take many forms, such as a collection of lexical data in which characteristics of spam are described. In most cases, collaborative networks take advantage of the misfortune of others receiving spam to build better intelligence for future filtering efforts. Bill Yerazunis, who coauthored an Internet draft on message inoculation (one of many collaborative approaches to filtering spam), described collaborative filtering in an email to a community of other filter authors, eventually leading to the development of a proposed message inoculation standard:

> Part of the problem is that spam isn't stationary, it evolves. That pesky .1% error rate is in some part due to the base mutation rate of spam itself. Maybe the answer is "vaccination." Vaccination is letting one person's misery be used to generate some protective agent that protects the rest of the population; only the first person to get the spam actually has to read it.
>
> My expectation is this: say you have ten friends, and you all agree to share your training errors. Each of you will (statistically) expect to be the first to see a new mutation of spam about 9% of the time; the other ten friends in this group will have their Bayesian filter trained preemptively to prevent this. Net result: you get a tenfold decrease in error rate—down to 99.99% accuracy. With a hundred such (trusted) friends, you may be down to 99.999% accuracy.

Spam filters have started to implement support for a proposed message inoculation standard[2] that will allow individuals in trusted groups to share message inoculations with one another in order to pre-seed each other against a particular type of spam. Other tools, such as Vipul's Razor, are designed to provide a distributed, collaborative network whereby large masses of users can share this type of fingerprinting. In either case, information about spam (such as content, construction, and other characteristics) is gathered and shared among a group of individuals or filters. The many different types of collaborative filtering will be discussed in Chapter 14.

---

[2] Some trial tests were performed with small groups in a study using live users for testing. A group of ten users was placed in what is referred to an *inoculation group*, which is a group where forwarded spams result in an inoculation being propagated to all other members of the group. Each mailbox was mirrored, so that there was an uninoculated mailbox and an inoculated mailbox for each user. At the end of a 30-day trial cycle, each inoculated mailbox had approximately ten fewer spams than the uninoculated mirrors. Ten spams per user alone doesn't sound significant, but statistically it is very significant—ten errors could easily represent the difference between 99.95 percent accuracy and 99.5 percent accuracy, or, put more numerically, 1 error in 2,000 versus 1 in 200. On a large scale, this could mean millions of emails per month.

Collaborative filtering gives a boost to some existing spam filtering mechanisms by giving them the time (and/or resources) to adapt to new types of spams being sent. It also helps a majority of users avoid having to go through the misery of receiving the spam that others are getting.

The weakness of collaborative filtering is the participating community itself. In large communities, there is either a high maintenance loop or, if automated, a high risk of false positives. Larger networks with high maintenance loops generally experience latency in updating their databases, in the same way that blacklisting has a propagation delay. Automated networks run the risk of false information being propagated or possibly injected by a malicious party. Smaller networks are generally more accurate and more real-time but lack the ability to cover a wide pool of fresh inbound spam. There are different types of collaborative networks, depending on the goal of the implementer. A good balance between the two approaches is usually best, and collaborative filtering can provide a good increase in filtering accuracy if done properly.

Pros	Proactive protection from new types of spam.
Cons	Reliability must be carefully watched. Propagation delay.
Ideal For	An additional layer of protection from within spam filters.

Address Obfuscation

```
j0nathan| /* who's yo daddy */ |at or near| domain (dawt) [X]COM [ ]NET [ ]ORG
```

One approach to fighting spam that seems to have become the norm lately is to obfuscate one's email address to hide it from spammers. This is done in an attempt to make harvest bots obsolete (*harvest bots* are automated pieces of software that scour millions of web pages and newsgroups in search of new email addresses to add to spammers' lists).

The concept of address obfuscation is fairly simple. Instead of displaying your email address as bob.smith@myisp.com, you may see "bob dot smith |at| myisp dot com." However, this approach really doesn't work quite as well as people think it does, and spammers are finding ways to work around it. Harvest bots are getting smarter at reassembling email addresses, so unless users feel like obfuscating their addresses into piles of mush (like the example above), it is unlikely they'll outsmart the newer bots. Spammers also receive information about a user's email address from places other than the Web. For example, many ISPs and credit card companies sell lists of addresses to spammers or enter into in third-party advertising agreements with spammers.

Anyway, if you've ever used your email address in its natural form—anywhere—you can be sure the harvest bots have already gotten to it. Even if you haven't, there's a good chance your address has made it to a list somewhere.

The bottom line is that while address obfuscation might keep someone's name off a few lists, it's ultimately not a real solution to fighting spam. The myth that obfuscating one's email address alone can prevent spam has been disproved on many occasions. It also sends a message to the spammers that they're winning.

NOTE *One possible solution to fighting harvest bots, rather than obfuscating your address, is to employ collaborative filtering and set up several honey pots on the Internet.* Honey pots *are mailboxes that are set up specifically to catch spam before real users get it. These spams can then be injected into a collaborative filter to inoculate the community, turning harvest bots against the spammers that use them. Setting up an address and hiding it in white-on-white text is a sure way to get it harvested by bots, to protect your real addresses by means of inoculation. Project Honey Pot is an attempt to exploit and track harvesters. Visit the project at http://www.projecthoneypot.org.*

Pros	May keep you off a few mailing lists.
Cons	Gives a concession to spammers, doesn't solve spam.
Ideal For	Overzealous spam fighters with lots of time on their hands.

New Standards

Over the past few years, many have proposed new standards or bolt-ons to the SMTP protocol. *SMTP* stands for *Simple Mail Transfer Protocol* and is the way mail servers communicate with each other. SMTP was designed to function anonymously to guarantee the privacy of Internet users. Spammers have taken advantage of this aspect of email servers to send spam anonymously. Many fixes have been proposed, ranging from simple add-ons to complete rewrites of the protocol.

Authenticated SMTP

Authenticated SMTP was originally thought to be an answer to spam, but it turned out to be useful only for identifying legitimate senders of mail on a system. Authenticated SMTP requires users to provide their password before they are allowed to send mail. It is still used by some ISPs to allow mobile users to relay and for abuse and tracking purposes, though many of today's mail clients today still lack an implementation for authenticated SMTP and a majority of ISPs don't use it. Authenticated SMTP has recently started increasing in popularity again with the birth of SPF (Sender Policy Framework), discussed next.

The big reason that authenticated SMTP isn't used to fight spam is that it wasn't really designed to fight spam—marketing somehow managed to get ahold of the concept and confuse themselves. It prevents individuals from sending spam through a server by requiring a legitimate logon, but it doesn't prevent spammers from sending the messages themselves or from establishing their own mail server to spam from. Many spammers today build their own mail servers and host them on unsuspecting networks in order to belt out the mail, thereby bypassing any security added to the ISP's mail server. These boxes are considered sacrificial because they are usually confiscated by the ISP on which they are hosted once the ISP becomes aware of them. By this time, the sacrificial mail server has already paid for itself many times over. Who's to prevent spammers from setting up their own authenticated

SMTP machine? A central authority would be one of the only ways to enforce this type of authentication, and that concept is far too Orwellian for most people to accept.

Many users also take issue with the breakdown of anonymity that authenticated SMTP helped usher in. Most individuals in the community are strong proponents of anonymity on the Internet, and being able to trace every message back to an authenticated sender would be much like having a rental car with an onboard computer that calls home whenever you speed. Even simple, noninvasive methods of accountability are shunned on the Internet.

Sender Policy Framework

One of the more recent proposals for fighting spam is called *Sender Policy Framework (SPF)*, proposed by an organization called the *Anti-Spam Research Group (ASRG)*. SPF is one of those brain-dead simple ideas that make people wonder why no one thought of it before. It defines which machines on a network are allowed to send mail.

SPF functions as a bolt-on to the SMTP protocol that takes advantage of text records in DNS (records that exist for adding comments and extra information to Internet name records) and allows ISPs to identify "reverse MX records," which are mail servers on their network that are permitted to send mail. Any host that is sending mail but is not in the permitted-from list can then be identified and either discarded, quarantined, or evaluated with additional scrutiny by a spam filter. SPF is presently in use at AOL, and many other large providers are beginning to follow suit. An SPF record is one line in DNS and looks like this:

```
vanitydomain.com  IN TXT  "v=spf1    mx  -all"
    hotmail.com  IN TXT  "v=spf1   ptr  -all"
     pobox.com  IN TXT  "v=spf1 a mx  ?all"
```

The goal of SPF is not to prevent spam but to prevent forgery. In coming years, as SPF grows more popular, sending forged mail "from" a domain that is using SPF will become more difficult. Many believe that pushing the means of identifying spammers out to the domain level instead of the host level will make it easier to find and prosecute spammers (making it more difficult for spammers to operate), as they will have to register and use real domains. With new products like prepaid credit cards, it is relatively easy to register a domain while maintaining your anonymity, however. Still, it is much more difficult to move an entire domain every day than it is to just jump on a newly stolen dialup account.

SPF is best explained by the FAQ available on the SPF website (http:// spf.pobox.com):

Suppose a spammer forges a hotmail.com address and tries to spam you. He connects from an IP address somewhere. When he declares MAIL FROM: <forged_address@hotmail.com>, you don't have to believe him. You can ask Hotmail if the IP address comes from their network. (In this example) Hotmail publishes an SPF record. That record tells you how to find out if the client IP address belongs to them.

```
        hotmail.com  IN TXT  "v=spf1  ptr  -all"
```

You execute the "ptr" mechanism, which means: find out the hostname of the client; if it ends in hotmail.com, it's legit.
If the message fails SPF tests, it's a forgery. That's how you can tell it's probably a spammer.

One caveat to SPF is that implementing it requires SMTP etiquette to change a bit. This isn't necessarily a bad thing. It used to be customary to send mail using whatever SMTP server was available on the network you were using—so if you were staying at a hotel with high-speed Internet access, you would send your mail from the hotel's server. SPF prevents this from happening and requires that the sender send mail only from the authorized mail hosts for the domain in their email address. This, of course, requires a bit of reworking for companies that are set up using the "old-school" method. The shift in mail server etiquette may ultimately help popularize authenticated SMTP by providing a genuine need to authenticate users who are outside an ISP's network.

Litigation

Several attempts are being made to fight spam with litigation. Unspam (http://www.unspam.com) is a consulting company formed to provide creative solutions to the spam problem.[3] Regardless of whether they win or lose the lawsuits they file, the idea is to cost spammers so much in litigation that it puts them out of business.

There are many different ways to sue spammers, but the key to doing so is first to identify them and then to give the lawyers legal ground for a lawsuit. One idea is to bind harvest bots and other automated tools to a specific set of terms and conditions that govern the use of content on your website, and then track these harvest bots. This is exactly what Project Honey Pot (http://www.projecthoneypot.org) is attempting to do, and with great success. The terms and conditions for use of email addresses can be embedded in the comments of the HTML page, restricting nonhuman visitors (namely, harvest bots) from using the email addresses displayed on the site or other resources to send bulk mail. The following sample was provided by the good folks at Unspam.

TERMS & CONDITIONS

[COMPANY] provides this website, all the content under this domain, and its services to you subject to the following conditions. Whether you or your agents visit any site provided by [COMPANY], by visiting this website you accept these conditions. Please read them carefully.

COPYRIGHTS

---

[3] Matthew Prince of Unspam presented his organization's latest attempts to decrease spam through litigation at the 2004 MIT Spam Conference.

All content included on this site or under this domain, such as text, graphics, logos, button icons, images, audio clips, digital downloads, data compilations, and software, as well as the compilation of that content into one, conherent website, is the property of [COMPANY] and protected by United States and international copyright laws. You or your agents may only access or make copies of this site or any of its content pursuant to the terms of this license. You are allowed under this license to use a browser to access this site for your personal use. Your browser may make a copy of the contents of the site in order to display its contents. Reproduction beyond the copying necessary to access and display the website is prohibited without written consent.

SPECIAL LICENSE RESTRICTIONS FOR NON-HUMAN VISITORS

Special restrictions on a visitor's license to access this site apply to non-human visitors. "Non-human visitors" include, but are not limited to, web spiders, bots, indexers, robots, crawlers, harvesters, or other computer programs designed to automatically access and read content from this website. Such non-human visitors are restricted from taxing the resources of this website or any service it provides beyond what would be typical of a human visitor.

Because of their potential for abuse, in consideration for access to the site, non-human visitors are required to read and observe the industry-standard restrictions as set forth in the robots.txt file included at the root level of every domain governed by this agreement. The restrictions provided for in this file shall be considered an addendum to this agreement when applicable to non-human visitors. The robots.txt file specifies restrictions to the directories non-human visitors may access. Non-human visitors accessing directories beyond what is allowed by the robots.txt file is recognized by the parties to this agreement as trespass and expressly prohibited. Any non-human visitors to this site shall be considered agents of the individual(s) who control or author them. These individuals shall ultimately be responsible for the behavior of their non-human agents and are liable for violations of this license.

Furthermore, as specified by the "no-email-collection" flag in the header of every web page and the robots.txt file, email addresses on this site are considered proprietary intellectual property of the author of this website. It is recognized that these email addresses are provided for human visitors alone, and have value in part because they are only accessible to said human visitors. You further acknowledge and agree by accessing this site that each email addresses the site contains has a value not less than $1,000 derived from their relative secrecy. The compilation, storage, and potential distribution of these addresses by non-human visitors substantially diminishes the value of these addresses. Intentional collection, harvesting, gathering, or otherwise storing email addresses by non-human visitors is recognized under this agreement as theft or diminution of value of [COMPANY'S] intellectual property and expressly prohibited.

APPLICABLE LAW

By visiting any site under this agreement, you agree that the laws of the [YOUR COUNTRY] and, specifically, those of the state of [YOUR STATE], without regard to principles of conflict of laws, will govern these Terms and Conditions and any dispute of any sort that might arise between you and [COMPANY].

Matthew Prince of Unspam sees many new attempts at legislation on the horizon, with a focus on child protection:

> A bunch of states are considering Children's Protection Registries. The bills allow parents to register their children's electronic contact points (email addresses, IM ids, mobile phone numbers, etc.) as being off-limits to certain inappropriate messages including those advertising pornography, gambling, prescription drugs, alcohol, tobacco, etc. Utah already passed it. Illinois, Michigan, and Georgia are currently considering it.

The recently passed Utah legislation can be found at http://www.le.state.ut.us/~2004/bills/hbillenr/hb0165.htm.

These new approaches to legislation would not only provide additional legal muscle to attorneys, but also help file criminal charges against pornographic spammers once finding them becomes easier. The idea is that a stranger on the street would be arrested for showing your child pornography, so why is sending it to them via email any different? Excuses like, "Dude I swear I thought she was 18," won't work against laws like this.

And that's the catch—it's easy to file lawsuits and even criminal charges if you know who it is you're after. Unfortunately, most legislation fails due to the inability to identify the spammers. Many new identification registries are being built to help track both the behavior and the identity of spammers. Project Honey Pot does this by creating a series of one-time-use email addresses and releasing them to harvest bots. They're then able to track which spams came from which harvest bots, and therefore correlate most spams to their respective spammers.

Spammer Fingerprinting

Terry Sullivan has been working on a spammer fingerprinting method called SpammerPrinting to fingerprint individual spams in an attempt to identify their author. SpammerPrinting, according to Sullivan, is "an unsupervised machine learning technology designed to assist in identifying likely sources of unsolicited bulk email." The construction, choice of words, and lexical patterns in an email are all characteristics used to identify messages of similar origin. SpammerPrinting analyzes a collection of messages originating from an arbitrary collection of sources and develops a series of analytical profiles that allow similar messages to be grouped together. Using these profiles, SpammerPrinting is then able to categorize the different messages into groups based not on content but on sender.

Other tools, such as SPF and new legislation, are helping to force the identities of spammers out into the open. Once they are pushed into the open, spammer fingerprinting provides a way to sufficiently prove who sent what spams.

Intellectual Property

Intellectual property is usually established and then licensed for legitimate purposes, giving legal ground for suing spammers when they abuse email addresses or other claimed intellectual property (as they are expected to). There are both simple and complex ways to use intellectual property for this purpose. Simple ways including covering all information on a website with a license, as discussed in the previous section. A more advanced approach to using intellectual property can be illustrated by the Habeas Haiku.

The Habeas Haiku was one of the more well-known failed attempts to give lawyers a platform to sue spammers, this time for copyright infringement. The Habeas Haiku was a piece of copyrighted intellectual property owned by a company named Habeas and licensed for legitimate (nonspam) use only—a set of nine lines of text that a legitimate sender could paste into legitimate email. It was marketed by Habeas as a way to help get messages through spam filters. In order for this to work for end users, spammers would have to avoid using the Habeas Haiku in their emails. In order for this to have worked for Habeas, spammers would have had to use the copyrighted haiku in their own spams, which they did, so that Habeas could sue them for it.

As a result of this paradox, the presence of the Habeas Haiku is now a great way to detect spam and has provided a means for Habeas to sue spammers (assuming they can find them). The unfortunate outcome is that the Habeas Haiku has really done nothing to help fight spam other than provide another revenue stream. It could have worked had Habeas been successful in suing spammers and putting them out of business, but so far it hasn't had any effect on spam. If the Habeas Haiku had been directed at the law-abiding Internet community, we all would have had a fit. Since it was directed at spammers, nobody seemed to mind twisting this type of legislation to suit our needs, but all too often, we see this kind of legal twisting applied to innocent parties.

Final Thoughts

In this chapter, we've taken a look at some historical approaches to fighting spam, many of which are still used today. From primitive word matching to advanced heuristic analysis, the technologies employed to detect and fight spam have evolved significantly over the past ten years. Many hybrid solutions exist today, and as long as spam detection remains a challenge, the best solutions will likely incorporate several of these methods.

In the chapters to come, we'll illustrate the heuristic principles of yesterday's technology and describe why they're fading out as the volume of spam continues to increase. We'll discuss why heuristic filtering, as a dying animal, has been easily beaten by spammers as we demonstrate the need for a newer, more dynamic solution.

3

LANGUAGE CLASSIFICATION CONCEPTS

Chapters 1 and 2 described nearly ten years' worth of attempts to put an end to spam. At this point, you are probably wondering whether fighting spam is more of a lesson in futility than in computer science.

Until sometime in 2002, heuristic filtering was the closest programmers could come to solving the spam problem. Sadly, heuristic filtering (writing new rules to detect the latest variants) has proven to be not much better than putting a Band-Aid on the problem of spam. Spammer sends spam. Author writes rules. Spammer changes spam. Author changes rules. This is how spam filtering progressed throughout the 1990s and into the new century.

In this chapter, we'll discuss the concepts behind the next-generation technology being used to combat spam: language classification. *Language classification* is the process of identifying the disposition of a presented text, such as classifying an email or a text document into a particular category. Classifying text can involve determining the genre of a book, categorizing a document, or in our case deciding whether an email is spam. The idea behind language classification is to teach the computer to be a filing clerk.

Spam filters that employ language classification read and filter your email by *learning* your personal email behavior (what you think is and isn't spam). In contrast to the old-school approach of having humans write rules to identify spam, language classifiers analyze email and write their own "rules" or, rather, develop a set of characteristics they look for. This returns the work of fighting spam back to computers, giving them the innate ability to make their own decisions rather than being told how to respond. Language classification has some distinct AI (artificial intelligence) properties, such as learning and decision making, and tackles the next challenge in artificial intelligence: teaching a computer not just to recognize shapes or play chess, but to read—and understand what it's reading (well, sort of).

Understanding Accuracy

To understand the benefits of language classification, it's important to understand the meaning of accuracy and why there is a push for a new generation of spam filters. It's all too common to see percentages thrown around when discussing accuracy in the world of spam filtering. What do they mean? Accuracy refers to the performance and reliability of the filter. Many heuristic filters advertise a 95 percent level of accuracy, which sounds impressive enough. However, the very lowest level of accuracy that should be expected from any language classifier is around 99.5 percent.

You might be thinking that there's not much difference between 95 percent and 99.5 percent. But you would be wrong. A filter with a 99.5 percent accuracy rate is not merely 4.5 percent more effective than one that is 95 percent accurate, but 900 percent more effective! As you might recall from your high school statistics class, every decimal place represents a factor of 10, and so even though 95 percent looks a lot like 99.5 percent, the two are very different.

Let's illustrate. A 95 percent error rate is equivalent to five errors for every 100 messages (or one error for every 20 messages). A 99.5 percent error rate, however, is equal to only one error in every 200 messages. That's a tenfold improvement in accuracy, which can ultimately lead to a similar financial savings for a company. Achieving 99.5 percent accuracy is trivial with today's technology; even a very basic language classifier is able to reach this level of accuracy. Most best-of-breed filters today exceed 99.9 percent, which is one error in 1,000 messages. A few open source filters have been able to produce levels of one error in 7,000 or even 8,000 (99.987 percent) and are only getting better with time.

It's important to keep these levels of accuracy in mind when examining the next generation of spam-filtering technology discussed in this book. Differences that may appear to be trivial are actually quite significant.

Machine Learning

We've introduced language classification, which involves teaching the computer to be a filing clerk. We've also mentioned that this involves learning different types of email. How does that work? At the core of language classification is machine learning. *Machine learning* is the ability of a machine to improve its performance based on previous results and is a significant part of the next two chapters. It's by way of machine learning that spam filters move into a new science where they can learn for themselves.

Machine learning technology predates spam, but until recent advances were made in the technology, it was thought to be too expensive in terms of resources to possibly be used for anything but the most important applications. It was a technology believed to have its place on powerful servers at large corporations or universities, not something we'd want to waste on spam. Once ways to get the technology working on average desktop hardware were discovered, it was quickly applied to common, everyday problems, just as the first Jedi probably used their lightsabers to slice bagels.

This chapter deals specifically with the conceptual aspects of machine learning in the setting of language classification. Special care has been taken to abstract these concepts from the mathematical topics surrounding how these wonderful filters work. In the next chapter, we'll dive into the more statistical components and explore many of the mathematical algorithms behind the concepts discussed here. Some of the concepts will then begin to make sense numerically, and by the end of the next chapter, we will have covered all of the ingredients of a basic statistical spam filter.

Concept Learning

When classifying email, machine learning uses what is referred to as the *concept-learning* approach. Imagine sitting a child down at a table and showing them pictures of different types of cars. After teaching the child what different types of cars look like (sports cars, sedans, and SUVs), you then show them some new pictures (which they haven't yet seen) and ask them to tell you what kind of car they're looking at. In spam filtering, this approach is all about showing the filter what both spam and legitimate mail *(nonspam)* look like as two concepts so that we can teach the computer to tell us which concept new messages look the most like. Spam is surprisingly obvious to spot, and by showing our filter "pictures" of spam, it will eventually be able to identify them on its own, based on the characteristics it previously learned.

Spam and nonspam are the two concepts most commonly used in spam filtering, but other concepts may also be included in a language classifier. Some spam filters use a third *virus* concept, and some are even designed to recognize user-defined categories such as *work mail* and *personal mail* (Bill Yerazunis's CRM114 and John Graham-Cumming's POPFile, to name a few).

Using Language Classification to Fight Spam

When used for fighting spam, language classifiers analyze email (usually incoming mail). Most filters perform the same basic functions. They analyze the message and learn to identify the words, headers, and other text (characteristics) that stick out the most. As the filter analyzes more message text, it's also able to identify particular characteristics belonging to spam, nonspam, or other categories.

The more we teach the filter, the more it learns and the better the decisions it makes. Eventually the filter becomes capable of making accurate decisions about whether a message is spam based on the characteristics it has learned to identify. The filter's final output is the believed *disposition* of the message.

Training

Because spam filters use a concept-learning approach, it's necessary to present the filter with examples of all of the different types of text we want to learn. This is referred to as *training*. If the goal is to have the filter classify spam, it needs to be trained with several examples of spam (and nonspam). This type of training can be performed in two ways:

- The software can be presented with a corpus (a collection of mail) consisting of spam and nonspam.
- Some filters are also designed to learn from scratch by reading email as it arrives.

In both cases, the filter can quickly learn the difference between the different types of mail, based on their content and (initially) with the help of a human to tell it what goes where.

Computers are very proficient at this, in fact. When it comes to identifying spam, modern filters are roughly five to ten times more accurate than a human![1] And because they are much more methodical than we are, they frequently identify patterns we would not have noticed. For example, text like "#FF0000" (the hexadecimal color for red text) and "multipart/alternative" (a type of content formatting that spammers like to use) are things that humans are likely to overlook.

Concept learning also allows the computer to learn from its mistakes. Just like a child will re-evaluate a wrong answer, you can teach a filter to learn the same. In yesterday's world of spam filters, a mistake meant that a rule had to be changed by a human. But if a language classifier makes a mistake, we can simply show it what category the email belongs in, and it will adjust its internal clockwork on its own. It can even learn our own specific email behavior, rather than implementing some generic rule set written by someone else. This takes a significant amount of burden off of the programmer and lessens our dependence on the maintainers of a particular project to keep it up to date.

Whatever I want to train my filter to classify, I can make it classify, and it's just between me and my filter. No programmer has to sit there tweaking the program to get it to mimic my behavior, and that's good news for those who can't afford a personal programmer.

---

[1] According to a study by Bill Yerazunis, the author of CRM114, the average human is approximately 99.84 percent accurate. Yerazunis arrived at this number after manually classifying more than 3,000 of his own personal emails repeatedly. John Graham-Cumming repeated this test on a larger scale in 2004 and achieved similar results, which he presented at the MIT Spam Conference in January 2005.

Statistical Filtering and Bayesian Analysis

Statistical filtering is an approach many spam filters use to perform language classification. It uses statistics and probability to determine the likelihood of a message being spam, along with the machine learning concepts just discussed, as we'll see in the different types of statistical filtering described in this book.

Bayesian content filtering (BCF), also known as *Bayesian analysis*, is a popular implementation of statistical filtering. It incorporates concepts developed in the mid-1700s by British mathematician and Presbyterian minister Thomas Bayes and was introduced in his book *The Doctrine of Chances*. Bayesian analysis is based on a mathematical theorem called *Bayes' Theorem*, and is a popular approach to statistical language classification. We'll discuss Bayesian content filtering in depth in Chapter 4.

Bayes' Theorem is an approach to quantifying uncertainty. It introduced a rule that can be used to factor together many different variables to determine the degree to which a given probability is true. Paul Graham released the first of several research papers, "A Plan for Spam," in 2002, applying Bayes' Theorem directly to spam filtering. Graham's approach uses Bayes' Theorem to combine independent characteristics of an email to achieve a single result, which in turn led to the development of today's Bayesian filters.

Much of the framework comprising what are considered Bayesian content filters today originated from Graham's research. However, the Bayesian functions of these spam filters are only one piece of how the filters function. Because of this, most statistical filters today are said to have Bayesian qualities. Some statistical filters, such as Bogofilter, do not use Bayes' Theorem at all but are sometimes thrown into the same bucket as Bayesian filters because of their similarities to Graham's original research. We'll discuss these other approaches in Chapter 4 as well. For now, we'll focus on Bayes.

Components of a Language Classifier

There are three central components to a language classifier:

Historical dataset
> The filter's memory. It contains a rather large catalog of characteristics that the filter has learned to be identifying characteristics of spam (and nonspam). The dataset is also known as the *wordlist*, *database*, *lexicon*, or *dictionary*.

Tokenizer
> The filter's eyes. It is responsible for reading and interpreting an email, which it does by breaking it down into smaller components (called *tokens*). The tokenizer works with the historical dataset to determine the significance of each token, based on memory.

Analysis engine
> The filter's reasoning. It chooses key characteristics in an email and weighs them to determine whether or not a message is spam.

Figure 3-1 outlines the basic operation of a language classifier. An incoming email is first analyzed by the tokenizer. It is examined and broken down into smaller components. The tokenizer queries the dataset to identify the importance of each component and passes this information to the analysis engine. The analysis engine then calculates the disposition of the message (spam or nonspam). Depending on the determination of the analysis engine, additional actions may be taken, such as delivering a message, training, or other action.

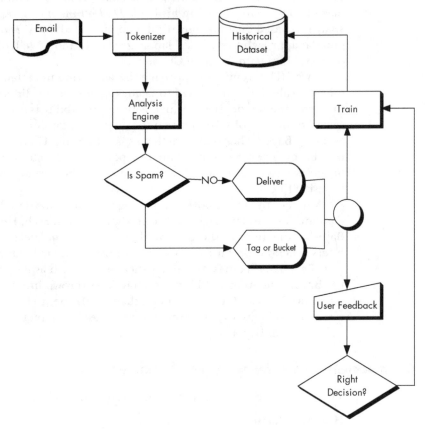

Figure 3-1: Process flow of a language classifier

The Historical Dataset

A *historical dataset* is a catalog of characteristics learned over a period of time. It provides memory to the other components of the filter and the information necessary to identify the most important characteristics of a user's email. This could include the word "Viagra," a piece of text from the message headers, or any other identifying characteristic.

Since every user's email is different, most language classifiers can maintain a separate catalog of data for each user. For example, the types of email I receive are vastly different from, say, those received by Oprah, and such a filter can tell the difference between my mail and her mail. Other systems maintain a global catalog for all users (to conserve disk space) or combine a global catalog with a smaller user catalog. Higher levels of accuracy can be expected from data that is more specific to individual users.

One of the most common ways in which humans determine whether a message is spam or not is by reading it. No matter what a spammer sends us, or what type of writing style they use, the one damning characteristic of the message is the content itself. As Paul Graham puts it,

> The Achilles heel of the spammers is their message. They can circumvent any other barrier you set up. They have so far, at least. But they have to deliver their message, whatever it is. If we can write software that recognizes their messages, there is no way they can get around that.

Language classifiers learn from the message content itself, rather than using preprogrammed rules. The message content is analyzed and individual words and phrases are used to construct characteristics that are recorded in the dataset. The historical dataset of a statistical filter contains counters to record the number of times each identifying mark was found in each class of text, the number of messages analyzed, and other information necessary to determine the nature of each characteristic.

When a language classifier encounters a new type of spam, it identifies new words and phrases. These are immediately added to the dataset as new criteria for distinguishing spam. For example, as words and phrases such as "Viagra" and "Call Now!" are discovered in spam, they are recorded. Over time, the recurrence of these words makes them excellent identifiers of spam. Innocent words are identified too. Specific topics that the user might chat about, such as "calculus" or "Africa," will be stored in the dataset, and their presence in legitimate email will make them stand out as good characteristics.

A single message may include a few hundred words and phrases, and so over time a dataset may grow to include several thousand entries—possibly even a hundred thousand or more.

NOTE   *If you are implementing a statistical filter, there are usually a few different options for the historical dataset, depending on your needs. If your disk space is limited, some filters allow a single historical dataset to be used for all users, rather than one for each user on the system. This always reduces the accuracy of the filter but uses only megabytes of disk space instead of gigabytes. Additional features, such as merged groups, will be discussed later in this book. There is always a trade-off between specificity and accuracy to keep in mind when considering a dataset strategy.*

The Tokenizer

The *tokenizer* is responsible for breaking a message into its colloquial pieces, using a process called *tokenization*. The tokenizer is instantiated every time a new message is processed. It identifies the different components of the message so that they can later be analyzed by the analysis engine and eventually stored in the dataset. These components are frequently referred to as *tokens.* A token can be a word, phrase, header, web address, or any other small piece of text in an email. When a message is tokenized, the process usually results in many tokens (sometimes hundreds or thousands), depending on the type of approach used and the length of the message.

The first, and simplest, approach to tokenizing originated from Graham's original essay on spam, "A Plan for Spam." He described his approach this way:

> I scan the entire text, including headers and embedded html and javascript, of each message in each corpus. I currently consider alphanumeric characters, dashes, apostrophes, and dollar signs to be part of tokens, and everything else to be a token separator. (There is probably room for improvement here.) I ignore tokens that are all digits, and I also ignore html comments, not even considering them as token separators.

Graham later revised his basic tokenization approach to include more advanced features, such as identifying specific header information and URLs. Other developers have enhanced his original approach and added their own spin. We'll discuss the tokenizer in detail in Chapter 6.

NOTE   *Some filters allow you to use different tokenizers or tokenizer approaches by choosing a lightweight option. Some "diet" versions of a tokenizer can result in an improvement in execution time and CPU resources, but the trade-off is accuracy. The fewer (and less complex) the tokens generated, the fewer important characteristics will stick out in an email. Disabling features such as "chained tokens" or "multiword tokens" can result in faster operation but lower accuracy. Unless you're strapped for CPU resources, it's generally a good idea to use the recommended configuration for your filter, rather than choosing a lightweight option.*

Assigning Token Values

In statistical filtering, each token is assigned a numerical value based on its historical appearance. This value represents the statistical probability that the message fits into a particular category (for example, spam). The tokenizer works in tandem with the historical dataset to determine each token's value based on how often it has appeared in spam and legitimate mail. A numeric value representing the token's disposition is assigned to each token and is later used to determine the overall spamminess of the message. If most of a message's tokens are spammy in nature, the message itself will be classified as spam.

The value assigned to a token is referred to as the token's *probability* because it reflects the likelihood that the message containing the token belongs to a particular class of mail (such as spam). The actual value is calculated differently by different statistical filters, based on the specific mathematical approaches implemented. (We'll discuss the formulas used to assign probabilities to tokens in Chapter 4.)

Probabilities in most forms of filtering can range from 0 percent to 100 percent and are assigned to a token based on the token's historical appearances in email. For example, if every message that the word "click" appeared in had historically been classified as spam, the word "click" would be assigned a very strong probability of being spam. Bayesian filters would assign this word a probability close to 100 percent. In contrast, if the word "Africa" appeared only in legitimate mail, it would be assigned a value indicating a very weak probability of being spam (close to 0 percent in a Bayesian filter). A message occurring just as often in both spam and legitimate email would resolve to some value in the middle (50 percent in a Bayesian filter). This is called a *neutral* value because it doesn't support any particular decision. Neutral tokens generally don't affect the outcome of a classification in any way.

In real-world use, it is common to see tokens with a wide range of values. For example, a token may be assigned a probability of 93 percent, telling us that it has appeared in a significant amount of spam but in a few legitimate messages also. A token with a probability of 23 percent is likely to have appeared in many legitimate messages but also in some spam. The most useful tokens are those that appear primarily in one particular class of message, with values closer to either 0 percent or 100 percent.

The Analysis Engine

The *analysis engine* analyzes the individual tokens (and their values) extracted from an email message to make a reasonable judgment about the disposition of the email. The analysis engines used in statistical spam filters identify the more important characteristics of a message and use them to make a decision about spamminess.

These characteristics are used to build a decision matrix. A *decision matrix* is a table used to evaluate problems or possible solutions. In most cases, a decision matrix is a list of the most telltale characteristics of a message that can be used to reach a decision—a collection of the most meaningful tokens and their values in the dataset. For example, some of the identifying marks of a Viagra spam may include "Viagra," "buy online," and "$ave." The identifying marks of legitimate mail may include the user's name or topics the person discusses frequently.

The analysis engine builds a new decision matrix for each message analyzed. It populates the decision matrix with the strongest characteristics of a message and then combines them to create a single result (the believed disposition of the message).

Building a Decision Matrix

The decision matrix is formed by taking the most useful tokens from an email and adding them to the matrix. Most modern-day Bayesian filters limit the number of tokens in a decision matrix, usually to 15 or 27 of the most interesting tokens. This number is referred to as the *peak window value*. The number of elements in a decision matrix is referred to as the matrix's *window size*. Since most decision matrices have a very limited window size, only the most meaningful data is used to populate them. This allows the analysis engine to focus on the most useful parts of an email without being confused by less important text, such as those long, multilevel marketing spams that tend to tell you the person's entire life story.

Meaningful data is chosen based on how strongly the data is associated with a particular disposition. The statistical formulas used to determine the strength of a particular token are based on the algorithms being used (as we'll discuss in Chapter 4).

Evaluating a Decision Matrix

Once a decision matrix has been created, we need to figure out how to interpret it and how to weigh each characteristic. For example, in my dataset the presence of the word "save" in a message suggests an 80 percent likelihood that the message is spam. The presence of the word "book" suggests an 80 percent likelihood that the message is legitimate mail. If we used only one of these characteristics to determine the nature of a message, we'd be wrong about 20 percent of the time—either a spam would make it past the filter or a *false positive* would lead to a loss of good mail. Add that up and you have several errors over a short period of time.

What if an email contained both words? There is a 50 percent chance of being completely wrong in either case. We'd be accurate about half the time, but the rest of the time we'd be canning legitimate mail. Clearly the best single token just isn't enough to go by in making a decision.

The solution is to combine the decision matrix's elements, using a statistical combination algorithm such as Bayes' Theorem, Fisher-Robinson's inverted chi-square, and others (which we'll discuss in the next chapter). These *combination algorithms* allow us to merge all of the information in the decision matrix to arrive at a single result.

Providing Feedback

Once the filter has reached an educated guess about a message, it needs to know if it has made a mistake. In order to improve the quality of the filter's results, it must be provided with feedback. The feedback we generally provide to a spam filter is that of error. When the filter erroneously classifies a message, we tell it and it corrects itself accordingly. If particular characteristics in a message were incorrectly learned as spam in the dataset, they would be relearned as nonspam once we informed the filter of its error. To avoid high end-user maintenance, most language classifiers assume that their decisions are correct unless they are told otherwise.

Feedback loops vary depending on the type of software being deployed. For example, correcting a spam filter written inside an email client (such as Thunderbird or Mail.app) may simply involve clicking a button labeled "This is Spam." Server-side filters, on the other hand, generally use a slightly more complicated feedback loop, such as having the user forward the spam to a virtual email address or making a correction from a web page. The feedback process doesn't necessarily need to be visible to the end user, as there are many ways to customize a filter for ease of use.

NOTE   *If you are implementing a statistical filter on your network, finding an easy way for your users to correct errors is essential. If you are running POP3 email, you'll want to use a filter that allows the user to forward (or bounce) a spam into the system. If you are* *running IMAP or web-based mail, you have many other options. Since the original message is stored on the IMAP server, many spam filters provide an easy way to build a custom interface for training. Many how-tos are available for setting up a system using X-TMDA headers and/or drag-and-drop functionality. Find the easiest, most effortless way for your users to report spams to the system.*

Training

Training a filter to identify spam is tricky and error-prone compared to training it to identify other types of email. Spammers use all kinds of nasty little tricks designed to trip up spam filters, but the filters we'll discuss in this book are all quite resilient to these types of attacks. Still, statistical filters must be trained, and any training philosophy should assume that there will be errors, in order to improve accuracy over time.

Four primary training philosophies are used in spam filtering: TEFT (train-everything), TOE (train-on-error), TUM (train-until-mature), and TUNE (train-until-no-errors).

Train-Everything (TEFT)

Training everything, also known as *unsupervised learning,* trains the filter with every single email that comes in. TEFT can be implemented by adding all the tokens from a message to the dataset whenever a message is processed. The advantage to training everything is that the user's dataset builds in tandem with the email they receive. If the user changes their email behavior (such as subscribing to a new mailing list), TEFT will quickly propogate the new form of behavior into the dataset, helping the filter learn them before any classification errors are made.

Most statistical filters (including Bogofilter, DSPAM, and CRM114) support TEFT, but it is not always the recommended approach. TEFT's weakness is that the dataset can become too volatile if the user deals with lots of email, in which case token values in the dataset may fluctuate, leading to errors.

For example, if the user receives an unusually large amount of spam but not much legitimate mail, the filter will begin to learn spammy tokens in abundance, without enough innocent mail to offset the learning. While most mathematical functions are fairly tolerant of large skews in the message balance, the absence of legitimate mail can cause a token to look spammy simply because the dataset will never have ever seen it in a legitimate message.

Still, in spite of its weaknesses, TEFT-mode training works remarkably well for most users who receive a fair amount of spam. Users with up to 70 percent spam or with constantly changing email should experience good performance using TEFT-mode training. Users who have very static behavior or who receive an excessive amount of email daily should consider the next mode of training, TOE.

Train-on-Error (TOE)

The TOE approach is designed to allow the user's dataset to be trained only when an error has occurred. TOE is supported by many spam filters, including CRM114, DSPAM, and POPFile. Many users prefer the TOE approach to training because large volumes of email may change the values of data too frequently, leading to errors. For example, if a user receives 10,000 emails per day, using TEFT there will be 10,000 sets of changes to the user's dataset. TOE, on the other hand, would require only one change for every error made by the classifier.

Systems administrators love TOE because it involves exponentially fewer writes to disk. Instead of writing every time a message is processed, TOE filters write to disk only when they need to correct an error. TOE also stores fewer tokens in a user's dataset (due to the way the algorithm functions), which results in much lower disk-space utilization.

NOTE   *TEFT-mode training generally yields about 70 percent uninteresting data in a user's dataset, which is purged out of the system incrementally. TOE-mode training, however, yields a much lower rate of useless data, as only data present from an error is used. This could save hundreds of gigabytes of disk space on large implementations.*

TOE's strength is also its weakness. Because it learns only when the filter has made a mistake, it will not learn a user's new email behavior until it has already caused some false positives, which can get annoying. Users who change their email behavior frequently may find that TOE provides very poor accuracy.

TOE is also slower at detecting new types of spam. Spam evolves very slowly. As a result, it is not necessary to constantly "tweak" the filter to maintain its accuracy, which is why TOE works well. However, spam does evolve, with very subtle permutations over a period of months. A filter whose training mode permits proactive learning (such as TEFT) is able to identify and learn the new permutations in these spams as they evolve, with the dataset adapting to match the new permutations. The downside of TOE is that it is too static and too slow to evolve. While TEFT is too volatile, TOE is too static.

TEFT and TOE both work well in spite of their caveats, though one or the other may be slightly more accurate depending on the current evolution rate of received spam (and that of the user's own email). TOE-mode training is generally good for users who have very high spam ratios (90 percent or more) or who receive a significant amount of email (5,000 or more messages per day). TOE is not good for users who have a very dynamic pattern of email behavior, such as those who correspond over newsgroups and in public forums, where they're likely to receive email from strangers.

Train-Until-Mature (TUM)

TUM is a mode of training that attempts to find a middle ground between TEFT and TOE. It is supported by spam filters such as SpamProbe and DSPAM, and comes in various forms. TUM is stubborn. Once it has decided how to classify individual tokens, it won't change its mind unless a mistake has been made. Like TEFT, it learns new types of data, but it will stop learning specific tokens once they have matured (that is, once sufficient data has been collected to make an accurate decision). Like TOE, TUM trains *everything* whenever an error is being corrected.

TUM's advantage is with new data. It learns new data immediately, and mature data can more quickly be retrained when an error has been made, because less data exists to reverse. Many implementations of TUM also include a fail-safe to train whenever the filter is uncertain about the message.

Train-Until-No-Errors (TUNE)

Unlike TOE or TEFT, TUNE is more of a training-loop-specific function. It runs only when instructed to perform a training cycle and may take several hours to complete. It involves training and retraining a user's entire mail corpus until few or no errors are made in a test loop. TUNE is presently supported only by the CRM114 Discriminator, and many users have found that it delivers higher levels of accuracy than TOE. It isn't particularly popular as a spam filter, because it requires a significant amount of both user effort and time to perform the training. On top of this, it doesn't learn at all until told to retrain. To correct an error using TUNE, the user must add the message to their mail corpus and run a training cycle on the entire corpus, until few or no errors occur. TUNE also requires the user to retain their entire mail corpus for occasional retraining, which can be impractical with high-volume users or users who simply aren't savvy enough.

Like TOE, TUNE learns only when errors occur, and only when the user takes the time to retrain the whole dataset. In most cases, TUNE requires too much work and maintenance to be widely adopted, but in spite of its warts, many experienced users still use TUNE to achieve the higher levels of accuracy it delivers.

When to Train

There are three different times that a filter might train. Some filters train only when you turn them on, processing a user's mail corpus during an initial training phase, while others train as incoming messages are classified (to adapt to a user's email behavior in real time). Finally, some filters train only when an error has occurred (and not when a message is processed). Many filters refer to this as the "if it's not broken, don't fix it" philosophy.

NOTE *Most filters are configurable to the systems administrator's preferences. Finding the best time(s) to allow training depends on the organization's needs, its computing resources, and the behavior of its users. On very high-volume systems, it makes sense to train only on error to avoid a significant amount of processor load and disk-space consumption. Medium-sized systems with reasonable levels of email traffic may also benefit from TUM, while low-volume systems should probably use TEFT to help speed up training.*

An Example of a Filter Instance

To close our discussion of statistical filtering concepts, let's look at how a typical statistical filter will process a message. For this, we will examine the process used by a mock-up filter representing the plain vanilla Graham approach to filtering, and apply some real data. Here is the sample message we feed to our mock-up filter.

```
From: "Julie Ellison" <gcgbswamlgqy@sbcglobal.net>
Reply-To: "Julie Ellison" <gcgbswamlgqy@sbcglobal.net>
Subject: Don't Pay For Name Brand Drugs
Date: Sun, 11 Apr 2045 10:21:05 +0600
Content-Type: text/plain

CANADIAN GENERICS NOW HAS VALIUM!

Know where to find discounted Prescriptions? Buy your personal prescr.iption
drugs on the internet and $ave! Allergies, Weight Loss, Muscle and Pain Relief
Men and Womens Health, heartburn, migraines, Impotence Get meds from Canada
here:

http://$scribbleheterozygous.zzstrore2.com/gp/default.asp?id=gm03
Order Some HERE
```

Step 1: Tokenize the Message

The first step is to tokenize this message. The words and phrases that follow represent the colloquial components of the message as identified by Graham's approach to tokenizing. Many alternative approches to tokenization have been devised, as we'll discuss in Step 2, but we'll use Graham's approach here because it is has already been discussed and is the simplest to understand.

Tokens prefixed with "Url*" were found in a URL contained in the message. Tokens prefixed with a header such as "From*," "Reply-To*," or "Subject*" were found in specific message headers. As you can see, the entire message has tokenized into just over 70 individual tokens. If we look at the tokens, we can already begin to identify the ones that stick out.

From*Julie	From*Ellison	From*gcgbswamlgqy	From*sbcglobal
From*net	Reply-To*Julie	Reply-To*Ellison	Reply-To*net
Subject*Don't	Subject*Pay	Subject*For	Subject*Name
Subject*Brand	Subject*Drugs	Date*Sun	Date*Apr
Content-Type*text	Content-Type*plain	Url*http	Reply-To*sbcglobal
Url*$scribblehetero	zygous	Url*zzstrore2	Url*com
Url*gp	Url*default	Url*asp	Url*id
Url*gm03	Reply-To*gcgbswamlgqy		

CANADIAN	GENERICS	NOWHAS	VALIUM	Know	where
Weight	find	discounted	Prescriptions	Buy	your
prescr	iption	drugs	on	the	internet
and	$ave	Allergies	to	Loss	HERE
Muscle	Pain	Relief	Men	Womens	Health
heartburn	migraines	Impotence	Get	meds	from
Canada	here	Order	Some	personal	

Step 2: Build a Decision Matrix

Once we have our set of tokens, our spam filter finds the most relevant ones to include in its decision matrix, as shown here. Tokens are ranked based on their level of spamminess (and nonspamminess). Tokens close to 0 percent spamminess or 100 percent spamminess are the ones the filter will be most interested in. We are left with a set of tokens with the strongest disposition (spam or nonspam). The numbers next to the tokens below represent some example token values our filter has assigned, based on each token's historical appearance in spam and nonspam (we'll discuss how this happens in Chapter 4). Numbers close to 1.0 represent a stronger disposition toward spam, and numbers close to 0.0 represent a stronger disposition toward legitimate mail.

SPAM	[0.999900]	NOW
SPAM	[0.999900]	drugs
SPAM	[0.999900]	meds
SPAM	[0.999900]	Loss
SPAM	[0.999900]	Date*Apr
SPAM	[0.999900]	here
SPAM	[0.999900]	Relief
SPAM	[0.999900]	Weight
SPAM	[0.938004]	Url*http
SPAM	[0.932180]	Content-Type*text
SPAM	[0.885617]	and
INNOCENT	[0.127251]	personal
SPAM	[0.856461]	HERE
SPAM	[0.851932]	Url*gp
SPAM	[0.830545]	Pain

Step 3: Evaluate the Decision Matrix

There's not much evaluation to be done in this example, because we can determine just by looking at it that this message is spam. As with most spams, an abundance of spammy data is present in the decision matrix for this message. Our analysis engine identifies the strongest characteristics of this email and easily determines that the message is spam. The filter then quarantines, tags, or drops the message, depending on how the filter was designed.

Step 4: Train the Message

Depending on which training mode we're using, the filter will train the message differently. If we are training whenever a message is classified (and not only on error), tokens from this message are then added to the user's historical dataset. This new information will adjust the values returned the next time the filter is run.

Step 5: Correct Errors

If the filter's decision was incorrect, the user notifies the filter by marking the message as "not spam," at which point the correction adjusts the historical data, reversing and relearning the original data. Unless the user marks the message as "not spam," the filter assumes that the classification was correct and moves on.

Efficacy of Statistical Filtering

The principles of statistical filtering involve learning new types of messages as they evolve. Spammers are using a number of different tricks to try to evade statistical filters—so many that we've devoted an entire chapter to them. Statistical filtering is designed to be adaptive, and so its biggest strength against spammers is that they can no longer just mutate the email they're sending out. Older-generation filters, whether based on heuristic rules, primitive pattern matching, or any other technology, all had one thing in common, in that the *author* told them what spam looked like, and the *author* told them what characteristics to watch for. Statistical filters, on the other hand, rely on the user to initially tell them what messages are spam, and then they learn to identify future spam as well as new characteristics on their own. Graham describes the efficacy of previous-generation filters in this same light:

> Indeed, most antispam techniques so far have been like pesticides that do nothing more than create a new, resistant strain of bugs.

Not only have new strains of spam emerged as a result of spam filtering, but until now we've had to recode for them all. Research performed by Terry Sullivan, who presented at the MIT Spam Conference in 2004, has shown us that the sea changes at least once or twice a year, which caused us in the past to reanalyze spams (reading thousands of them in the process) and come up with a new set of ways to identify them. Thanks to statistical filtering, we can let the computer do the work, and all we have to do is submit an occasional error for retraining. Filter authors certainly have better things to do than read spam all day, and becoming desensitized to raunchy porn and pyramid schemes isn't healthy for anyone (unless you're running a pyramid porn scheme). Statistical filtering saves time not only for the user but also for the developer.

The Future of Language Classification

Although language classification has proven quite effective at fighting spam, it is not yet as popular as other approaches have been in the past. Migrating filters to use this next-generation technology is not a step that will happen overnight. Many are concerned about the long-term efficacy of language classifiers, and there is even some resistance to this new approach on the part of a few developers and manufacturers, who insist that their older tools are better designed (even if they experience poor levels of accuracy).

For example, SpamAssassin still incorporates more than 900 heuristic rules, although it has recently implemented a Bayesian filter "rule" to quiet the masses. Many people still believe that it hasn't been implemented well enough to compete with next-generation filters, as the effectiveness of the software is still dropping. In the words of one SpamAssassin user, "SpamAssassin doesn't learn, it just tolerates you to make you feel like you're actually accomplishing something." The Bayesian learning mechanism *does* improve accuracy, but holding on to the heuristic portions of the program keeps it from becoming a filter that will outperform statistical products.

Some commercial appliances still refuse to adopt language classification technology altogether. As a result, many systems on the market today promise a "Bayesian element" but aren't really dedicated to statistical analysis; this Bayesian element is given a slice in the filtering chain (usually at the bottom), front-ended by heuristic rules, blackhole lookups, whitelists, and a hodge-podge of other solutions that have been worked into the product—and they end up starving the Bayesian filter of data or causing it to degenerate to the point that it reflects the same results as the higher-level components. Many commercial anti-spam companies simply misunderstand Bayesian filtering or make incorrect statements about it (such as its level of accuracy) to push their own products.

The Sovereignty of Statistical Filtering

The primary concern that commercial appliance manufacturers have with language classification is that to be most effective it should be implemented as a first-line defense against spam. Statistical filtering is its own sovereign state and functions best with its own militia. Since it is more accurate than any other spam-fighting technology to date, placing any of these less accurate tools in front of it only hurts the accuracy of the filter. Most manufacturers are a bit concerned with the idea of deploying a box that learns on its own. Their customers will no longer need annual contracts for nightly updates (of rule sets) or as many software upgrades, which certainly puts them in a precarious financial position. By dumbing down the filtering appliance with heuristic tools (relying on annual subscriptions), manufacturers are able to continue generating residual revenue while implementing a lesser technology. Most people think in terms of arsenal, and so this makes sense.

Eventually, a new business model will be sorted out, but until then, some corporations have marketed Bayesian content filtering as an incomplete solution, for financial reasons. They have sought to convince the public that statistical filtering is ineffective. However, Bayesian content filtering hasn't turned out to be *ineffective*, but rather *too effective*. Due to the financial risk of deploying technology that improves itself, many open source language classifiers have been left outperforming commercial solutions.[2]

Many other types of appliances tout five 9s accuracy. Brightmail makes this claim, but some who have implemented its solution have reported accuracy as low as 83 percent, unless they use their glorified whitelists. Other solutions require the use of challenge/response or other annoying technologies in order to achieve these inflated levels of accuracy. In nonstatistical filters, the price of accuracy is human effort. Paradoxially, saving human effort is one of the primary reasons most companies choose to filter spam.

Final Thoughts

This chapter has introduced you to language classification, with a focus on the conceptual pieces of a language classifier. These components are generally very similar, providing a common framework for both filter developers and systems administrators to understand and tune them.

It's important for systems administrators to find the right filter for their network. Filters come with many different sets of features and are aimed at different implementations. If you operate a very large network with hundreds of thousands of users, find a filter that can scale to support your storage and processing constraints. We'll cover many different ways to tune statistical filters as we explain their technical details throughout the book.

Over the past few years, language classification has become quite popular. It is widely used for filtering spam, but several different companies are also using it to categorize documents and route incoming emails. Companies with high volumes of customer support requests that have previously had to dedicate an entire department of people just to the task of forwarding customer requests have now found a way to save time, space, and money by automating these tasks with language classification.

In the next chapter, we'll explore the mathematics behind these components as they apply to statistical filtering. Statistical filtering is a mathematical harmony—an artful masterpiece. If you're a developer, understanding the mathematical components should prove rather refreshing. If you are a systems administrator, the next chapter will explain the science behind statistical filtering and describe many of the different tuning knobs related to these components.

---

[2] With the exception of one purely statistical commercial solution, Death2Spam. Death2Spam achieves accuracy levels of up to 99.9 percent, higher than most other commercial solutions on the market that implement a hybrid solution.

4

STATISTICAL FILTERING
FUNDAMENTALS

This chapter builds a mathematical world around the foundational concepts we covered in the last chapter and illustrates the clockwork inside statistical filters. If you're a developer, this chapter will provide you with answers to most of the questions you may have from Chapter 3 and give you the procedural information necessary to develop a typical Bayesian filter. If you're a systems administrator, this chapter will explain, specifically, how the statistical filter you are using functions and what some of its configuration options may do, so that you can better understand what's going on behind the scenes.

Statistical filtering involves measuring probability. One of the great benefits of statistical language classification is that you're actually measuring something, as opposed to guessing scores. Heuristic-based filters, on the other hand, assign a "score" to each feature, which is really just an arbitrary number without mathematical significance. As Paul Graham puts it, "The user doesn't know what it means, but worse still, neither does the developer of the filter." It's very difficult for a systems administrator to interpret the meaning of a score, since it doesn't relate to any real measurement. It's even more difficult for a developer, who's supposed to be coding new rules, to do their job without being able to understand the effects of their changes (which cannot be measured).

Statistical classifiers, on the other hand, measure something very specific—mathematical probability. The idea that "there is an X percent chance that this message is spam" is a lot easier to comprehend than "this message scored a 3.52." It also gives filter authors and systems administrators a look into the thought process of the filter, so they can better ensure its correct operation. By mathematically weighing even the simplest characteristics of an email—such as the probability of the word "Viagra" meaning spam, we end up with more reliable information—and more reliable spam filters.

Statistical language classification has become very popular for many different types of solutions, in addition to spam filtering. While it is used in fighting spam, it has also become a mainstream approach to solving problems once considered to be solvable only by a human—and in fact many employees have been hired in the past to spend hours doing what statistical language classifiers do today in fractions of a second—making decisions about documents.

Thanks to bright mathematicians like Thomas Bayes, computers are now making our more trivial decisions for us.

An Imperfect Solution

Language classification is imperfect—a small margin of error will always remain. Since language classifiers learn based on historical decisions, they are always going to make decisions based only on what they already know. In other words, it is impossible to design a perfect algorithm to solve the problem of language classification, because decisions are based only on historical information (namely, what the classifier knows so far about the recipient). Because email evolves, language classifiers must act to some degree as a crystal ball to predict how the user will classify new messages.

From a philosophical perspective, language classification is more of an art form than a science. Instead of approaching it with the idea that it can be made perfect, you will save a considerable amount of time when you realize that the process is *im*perfect; the goal should be to design and implement a system that is "good enough," with practical resources in mind.

This is the same philosophy used to find square roots. The term "good enough" as we use it here denotes the ideal balance between accuracy and system resources, making use of software that is practical in a wide range of scalable environments.

Building a Historical Dataset

The historical dataset (discussed in Chapter 3) includes the memories of previous messages and meaningful words, phrases, and combinations to watch for in future emails. In order to reach a decision about a particular message, the historical dataset must first be built.

The characteristics used in statistical filtering are generated based on the content of the message; therefore, no matter how much spam changes over time, it will always have some unique content we can use to identify it. As new words begin to appear in spam, they're automatically added to the filter's memory.

Building a historical dataset can be the responsibility of the systems administrator or the end user. The systems administrator is responsible for building and maintaining any dataset used globally and for providing a way for end users to train their own dataset (if they will have one). It is the developer's responsibility to provide the tools necessary for building and maintaining the dataset, either by feeding the filter a collection of saved messages (a corpus) or from scratch.

Corpus Feeding

Corpus feeding involves building a historical dataset by analyzing a collection *(corpus)* of saved mail. We start off with a small collection of both spam and legitimate mail that has been presorted and classified (by a human). The filter will process each message and build a table containing the occurrence of every token (how many times it has appeared in both spam and legitimate mail). When we're finished, we end up with a very large collection of tokens and their corresponding counters, representing their appearance in the corpus.

The following example shows a small slice of preliminary data from such an exercise.

Feature	Appearances/Spam	Appearances/Ham
fun	19	9
girlfriend	4	0
mariners	0	7
tell	8	30
the	96	48
vehicle	11	3
viagra	20	1

NOTE *The occurrence of a token counts only once for each message analyzed.*

As you can see, the word "the" has appeared in 96 messages that were considered spam and in 48 legitimate messages. In a perfectly balanced email corpus, this would suggest that the word is more likely to be present in spam, but most corpora are unbalanced. In order to determine the true disposition of each token, we'll also need to know how much spam and nonspam is in the corpus.

Two additional counters are created in the dataset for this purpose. For simplicity's sake, our sample corpus will comprise twice as much spam as nonspam (which is usually about right in the real world):

Total Spam	224
Total Legitimate Mail	112

Anywhere from several hundred to a few thousand messages are processed in this fashion, building one large table at the end of the process. Once complete, the table is stored as our dataset, on disk, so that it can be accessed every time an email arrives.

NOTE   *Analyzing a corpus of mail collected over three to six months will allow the filter to see more of the user's personal behavior than one collected over a few days. It will also seed the filter with more information useful for identifying spam, since the characteristics of spam change occasionally. For this reason, 10,000 messages collected over a period of a week are not as useful as 1,000 messages collected over a month's time. If you are building a historical dataset for use globally, it's also important to use mail from several diverse users on the system. The more diverse the data, the less likely it will be to generate erroneous classifications.*

Starting from Scratch

It's not entirely necessary to build the dataset from a historical corpus of mail. In fact, many spam filters prefer to start from scratch and build the dataset as email is received. The filters CRM114, POPFile, and DSPAM, for example, all function best when building a dataset from scratch. The philosophy is that building from an empty corpus prevents the filter from getting hung up on stale data, which can hurt long-term accuracy.

Starting from scratch means that the filter knows nothing until a message is trained. Once a message is trained, either the tokens are added to the dataset or their counters are incremented if they already exist. For example, if the word "calculus" is already present in the dataset, either its innocent counter or its spam counter will be incremented whenever a message is trained containing that word. If the word is not present in an email, it's left alone in the dataset.

Depending on the training mode used (as we discussed in Chapter 3), the filter will add information to the dataset at different times. The training mode can also dictate which specific tokens are incremented. Since we also keep track of message totals, the total number of messages is also updated whenever a message is trained, so that we know the size of the dataset at any point in time.

Building from an empty dataset generally takes time and messages. Even with many messages over a short period of time, certain areas of a user's email behavior may not be well represented, and infrequent emails such as monthly newsletters may end up in the bit bucket unintentionally. However, accuracy rises over time using this approach, eventually reaching a plateau once enough training has taken place.

Correcting Errors

As the historical dataset is built, training errors are likely to occur while the filter learns. When this happens, it's important to reverse whatever information has been previously recorded about the message.

If the message has been previously learned, it must first be unlearned. This is done by decrementing the counters under which the message was originally classified. It can then be learned by incrementing the correct counters. This is referred to as *retraining* the message.

For example, if the spam filter originally thought a message containing the word "free" was legitimate, the data may initially look like the following.

Token	Nonspam Hits	Spam Hits
free	10	32

Total Spam:	65
Total Nonspam:	20

Once the message is submitted for retraining, the data will be reversed.

Token	Nonspam Hits	Spam Hits
free	9	33

Total Spam:	66
Total Nonspam:	19

NOTE *In some environments (such as train-on-error, or TOE), the original message was never learned, so the message needs only to be learned (and not unlearned).*

When relearning a message, it's important to relearn all of the original tokens used in the original (erroneous) classification. This includes the original full headers of the message, message body, and all content.

This can be done in several ways. Some spam filters allow the user to bounce the message back to the server, where it is processed. Bouncing is a feature supported by many email clients and involves sending the original message (with all headers intact) back into the filter. Another way to ensure the preservation of all tokens is to store a copy of the message on the server for a short period of time so that when it is reclassified, all of the data will be available in its original form. This is relatively easy to do with web-based and IMAP mail systems, since the messages are already on the server. Finally, other tools create a snapshot of the original training data instead of storing the original message to create a "signature."

Regardless of how the original data is retained, the retraining process will usually decrement one counter and increment the other. If the message is a spam that was classified erroneously, the innocent counters of all trained tokens pertaining to the message are decremented and the spam counters are incremented. This is essentially how the filter learns. As the mistakes are corrected, the dataset reflects these new values, which then directly affect the disposition of each token.

NOTE   *Depending on the features available in your chosen filter, there may be many different ways to implement error correction. The approach that is simplest for your users to understand while still providing pristine data for the filter may differ for each implementation.*

The Tokenizer and Calculating Token Values

When a message is processed, the tokenizer breaks it down into very small components (tokens) and assigns each token a value. A *token value* is a numeric representation of the token's disposition (good or evil), based on its appearance in previous emails. For example, if a word has appeared primarily in spam, it would be assigned a value reflecting a very strong probability of being spam (such as 99 percent).

Consider the following test corpus with exactly twice the amount of spam as legitimate mail.

Total Spam:	224
Total Legitimate Mail:	112

If we look at the number of occurrences of the word "the" in the corpus, we see that its appearance in spam is proportionately identical to its appearance in legitimate mail. That is, it appears just as often in spams as it does in legitimate messages. In our test corpus, the word "the" has appeared in 96 spams and 48 nonspams.

Feature	Appearances/Spam	Appearances/Ham
the	96	48

Common sense tells us that this word should be assigned a neutral value of 50 percent, since it appears in spam and nonspam equally. Now all we need is a mathematical formula that will give us the same reasonable results.

There are two popular mathematical formulas to choose from: Graham's and Gary Robinson's.

NOTE   *Some filters let you choose which of these two techniques (discussed next) to use. Selecting the correct option may be an exercise in trial and error, and may depend on the aggressiveness of your anti-spam policy. The first technique (Graham's) has been shown to be more aggressive in preventing spam, while Robinson's is more aggressive in preventing false positives.*

Graham's Technique for Computing Word Values

Graham provides a very simple formula for determining the probability that a given token is an identifier of spam. His approach takes into account the fact that many users will have an unbalanced collection of spam and legitimate email and computes a probability that factors in the total number of messages in each corpus.

In the following formula, *SH* and *IH* represent the total number of appearances in spam and innocent email for the token being computed. *TS* and *TI* represent the total number of spam and innocent messages in the user's corpus.

$$P = \frac{(SH)/(TS)}{((SH)/(TS)) + ((IH)/(TI))}$$

For example,

$$P = \frac{96/224}{(96/224) + (48/112)}$$

This calculation leaves us with *P*, a number between 0.0 and 1.0, where 0.5 is neutral (and the result of calculating "the" in our example). Tokens with a probability higher than a neutral 0.5 are considered guilty (or "spammy"), while tokens with a lower probability are considered hammy (or innocent). Tokens with a stronger disposition will be computed with a value closer to 0.0 or 1.0.

Robinson's Technique for Combining Word Values

Robinson improved on Graham's technique by factoring in a way to calibrate the value of a token probability based on the amount of historical data available for each token. Robinson believes that tokens with very few data points (historical occurrences) should have a weaker confidence than ones with many data points, and suggested a new way of calculating individual token probabilities.

Robinson adds onto Graham's existing calculation by applying a confidence factor. The resulting formula weakens the value of a token if it has very few data points. His function uses three variables:

N The total number of times a token has appeared in the dataset—in either spam or legitimate mail

X The assumed value of a token when *N*=0. A good starting value is 0.5000

S A constant that is tuned for performance, with a reasonable default value of 1

"In cases where there is very little information to work with," Robinson states, "we have some data, but we don't really have enough to be confident. In reality we should do something when *N* is any low number—0 being the most extreme case."

We first calculate the probability of a word using Graham's techniques. Call this $p(w)$ for word w, then calculate as follows.

$$F(W) = \frac{SX + N(P(W))}{S + N}$$

Robinson's approach yields results similar to Graham's, except that it is calibrated based only on the information available for a specific token. By taking into account cases in which very little data has been collected for a particular token, Robinson's technique yields a slight improvement in accuracy for many types of hard-to-classify messages. It is particularly useful in improving the identification of legitimate mail, thereby reducing false positives.

Single-Corpus Tokens

Some tokens are such strong indicators that they will appear in only one particular corpus of mail (spam or nonspam). These are referred to as *single-corpus tokens*. One caveat when assigning values to tokens is that no token should ever have a probability of 100 percent or 0 percent, because these are absolute probabilities (and more important, break our math). For example, because email evolves, there is no guarantee that messages containing the word "offer" have a 100 percent chance of being spam.

To solve this problem, a static value is assigned to single-corpus tokens. If a token appears in only one corpus, we assign it a hard-coded value. For example, most filters will assign tokens that appear only in our spam corpus a probability of 0.9900, and they will assign a probability of 0.0100 to tokens appearing only in legitimate mail. If Robinson's technique is being used, this value is assigned to the $p(w)$ value used in his formula.

When we apply these calculations to our test corpus from earlier in this chapter, we end up with a list of probabilities for each token.

Feature	Spam	Ham	Probability
fun	19	9	0.5135
girlfriend	4	0	0.9900
mariners	0	7	0.0100
tell	8	30	0.1176
the	96	48	0.5000
vehicle	11	3	0.6470
viagra	20	1	0.9090

A Biased Filter

Graham notes in his research that by doubling the occurrence of tokens in legitimate messages we can help to prevent false positives. Since spam filters typically err on the side of caution, Graham chooses to classify a message as spam only if there is an overwhelming amount of supporting data. The following is a modified version of Graham's approach that multiplies the number of innocent occurrences for a token by 2.

$$P = \frac{(SH)/(TS)}{((SH)/(TS)) + ((2IH)/(TI))}$$

NOTE *Many spam filters allow bias to be turned on or off. In many scenarios, applying bias has resulted in up to 50 percent fewer false positives, with only slight drops in the identification of spam.*

Hapaxes

Another thing to consider when assigning values to tokens is how we handle new tokens that we've never seen before, or for which we haven't collected enough data. These tokens are referred to as *hapaxes*.

Filters based on Graham's original outline in "A Plan for Spam" implement a threshold of occurrence—a minimum number of appearances in historical email before the filter will assign a calculated probability to the token. If the token doesn't meet the threshold, it will be assigned a relatively neutral value, such as 0.4000 or 0.5000, known as the *hapaxial value*, which is applied to the Graham-derived probability of the token.

A hapaxial value serves two purposes. First, it prevents unknown tokens from directing the outcome of the classification. Since spammers frequently flood their spam with random junk words, treating words we've never seen before as innocent would have a dreadful effect on accuracy. It would also be a mistake to treat unknown tokens as spam, because unknown words will always be present in email as a user's email behavior changes. The only option, in fact, is to assign a neutral value to hapaxes. This prevents the token from being used in our calculation at all—at least, until enough data has been collected about it.

NOTE *This is why Bayesian content filtering cannot be compromised with unknown random words or jumbles of random letters, in spite of popular myth.*

The second reason a threshold is necessary is to ensure honesty in our statistics and to avoid a situation in which the lack of data skews the overall results. For example, if a token has appeared only twice, both times in spam, we don't want our filter to treat it with a spammy probability of 0.9900 just yet, because we still don't have enough data. We need at least a handful of messages using that word to provide a good indicator of its real disposition.

As the philosophy on erring on the side of caution goes, one occurrence in a legitimate message is treated as two occurrences. Therefore, if we were to use a threshold of five occurrences, a token would need to appear in either three legitimate emails (for a total of six occurrences), five spam, or a combination between the two in order to be assigned a real token value.

Final Product

Once we apply these concepts, including a bias toward innocent email and an occurrence threshold of five, the result is a table of data that is slightly different from our original example. Here are the probabilities for our tokens after applying all of our design rules.

Feature	Spam	Ham	Probability
fun	19	9	0.3454
girlfriend	4	0	0.4000
mariners	0	7	0.0100
tell	8	30	0.0625
the	96	48	0.3333
vehicle	11	3	0.4782
viagra	20	1	0.8333

Although it may not be obvious, our final table identifies not only which characteristics are present in email, but also which are the most useful to us. If we look at the values in the table, we can see which tokens have the strongest disposition of spam (closest to 1.0) and nonspam (closest to 0.0).

The Analysis Engine

The analysis engine processes data provided by the tokenizer and builds a decision matrix containing the information most relevant to classifying the message.

Recall that most Bayesian filters are based on a limited window of factors, meaning that only the strongest (and most useful) data must fit into a window of a certain size, typically 15 tokens.

Let's see how this works in practice, using the following email. We'll first tokenize the message and then use the 15 most interesting tokens to build a decision matrix.

```
Subject: FREE ORIGINAL STAR WARS CARDS Adv:
Sender: fork-admin@xent.com
Errors-To: fork-admin@xent.com
X-Mailman-Version: 1.1
Precedence: bulk
```

Star Wars - Empire Strikes Back
OWN A UNIQUE, ONE-OF-A-KIND PIECE OF STAR-WARS HISTORY!

Exclusively Licensed From Lucas Film Ltd.
This Innovative New Collectible is the First to Display an Authentic One of
Kind 70mm Film Frame From the Star Wars/Empire Strikes Back Movie containing a
One of a Kind 70mm Frame in a 7-1/2" x 2-3/4" Diamond Cut, Acrylic, Mint
Collector's Case.
FACT: NO TWO FRAMES ARE ALIKE
Each Film Frame Is A Unique Original and Will Never Be Reproduced
Each fully licensed original film frame is sealed and individually serial
numbered with identification codes tamper proof holographic seals to prevent
fraudulent duplication.
#50049 LIGHTSABER DUEL Special Edition:
Features the fantastic lightsaber duel between Luke Skywalker and Darth Vader.
This Special Edition #50049 LIGHTSABER DUEL was only available with the
Willitts premium package #50707, which sold in retail shops for $125.00.
Special, Internet offer!
Order now and receive the above Rare Special Edition #50049 LIGHTSABER DUEL
for this Special Internet price of only $19.95! Special Bonus with your order,
you will receive 10 Original 1980 Topps Star Wars/Empire Strikes Back
Collector Cards Absultely Free!</font> These are Original 1980 Topps Star
Wars/Empire Strikes Back Collector Cards from 22 years ago! Not reprints!
HURRY! Please, respond now before our limited supplies are exhausted!!
Your film cell image may differ from the above sample.
Click here http://www.zephers.com/SW/default.asp?e=fork@xent.com
You have received this email as an opted-in subscriber, if this is not the
case, please click on the following link to be permanently removed from our
database. http://www.nospam1.com/remove.asp?e=fork@xent.com
866-667-5399
NOUCE 1
6822 22nd Avenue North
Saint Petersburg, FL 33710-3918

Sorting

The tokenization process leaves us with several tokens with distinct values. The
filter uses a sorting algorithm to reorder the tokens so that the most interesting
ones are toward the top (since these give us the best information about the
subject email).

We sort by ordering our tokens based on their distance from a neutral
0.5 value (the absolute value of $0.5 - P$). The resulting value is known as
the *delta* of a token, or its *interestingness*. When we sort the message above,
we might end up with values as shown below, depending on what's in our
dataset. The following table lists the tokens with the highest level of interestingness at the top.

P	Token	Interestingness
0.999900	Url*e	0.4999
0.999900	order	0.4999
0.999900	offer	0.4999
0.999900	ONE	0.4999
0.999900	Click	0.4999
0.999900	here	0.4999
0.999900	Be	0.4999 – PEAK
0.019655	Precedence*bulk	0.4804
0.020136	case	0.4799
0.029545	respond	0.4704
0.033896	Original	0.4661
0.043163	following	0.4569
0.057395	Is	0.4427
0.058070	sample	0.4420
0.937506	Url*http	0.4375

NOTE *Header and URL tokens are included, as we discussed in Chapter 3. Tokens such as "Url*http" are meta-tokens identifying a URL with "http" present in the message. Tokens such as "Precedence*bulk" are also meta-tokens that reference the word "bulk" in the Precedence header of the message.*

The first seven tokens (Url*e, order, offer, ONE, Click, here, and Be) in this example are considered *peak tokens* because they represent the strongest disposition (either spam or nonspam) of all the tokens in this matrix. These are by far the most interesting tokens and the most useful for analyzing the message.

Statistical Combination

Now that we have a better understanding of how to read the decision matrix, let's revisit an example from Chapter 3 to see how the computer uses this information. Here's our earlier example:

```
From: "Julie Ellison" <gcgbswamlgqy@sbcglobal.net>
Reply-To: "Julie Ellison" <gcgbswamlgqy@sbcglobal.net>
Subject: Don't Pay For Name Brand Drugs
Date: Sun, 11 Apr 2004 10:21:05 +0600
Content-Type: text/plain

CANADIAN GENERICS NOW HAS VALIUM!
Know where to find discounted Prescriptions? Buy your personal prescr.iption
drugs on the internet and $ave! Allergies, Weight Loss, Muscle and Pain Relief
```

Men and Womens Health, heartburn, migraines, Impotence Get meds from Canada here:
http://$scribbleheterozygous.zzstrore2.com/gp/default.asp?id=gm03

Order Some HERE

Our decision matrix is populated with the 15 most interesting tokens in this message.

S	I	Probability	Token
35	0	0.999900	NOW
27	0	0.999900	drugs
32	0	0.999900	meds
37	0	0.999900	Loss
76	0	0.999900	Date*Apr
50	0	0.999900	here
25	0	0.999900	Relief
28	0	0.999900	Weight
71	1	0.938004	Url*http
129	2	0.932180	Content-Type*text
109	3	0.885617	and
13	19	0.127251	personal
28	1	0.856461	HERE
27	1	0.851932	Url*gp
23	1	0.830545	Pain

To the human eye, it is fairly easy to tell whether the message is spam or not simply by glancing at the token values, but computers require logic. In many cases there may be a lot of variation in the probabilities of the tokens.

Given all of these different token probabilities, we need a way to combine them. Enter *statistical combination*. We use statistical combination to solve a probability-based decision matrix. To implement it, we look at each token in our decision matrix as an independent test. Statistical combination provides a way to combine the results of many tests to create a single result.

We'll cover the four popular approaches in use today.

NOTE *Some filters are based on only one combination technique, while others support a wide range of options that can be enabled or disabled. The descriptions that follow will help you identify the best approach for your particular environment.*

Bayesian Combination (Paul Graham)

Bayesian combination uses Bayes' Theorem to combine statistics. We use Bayesian logic to combine individual probabilities to produce a single outcome.

Graham's approach uses a decision matrix with a window size of 15 tokens (the 15 most interesting tokens). Bayes' Theorem allows multiple probabilities to be combined in this fashion:

$$\frac{AB}{AB + (1 - A)(1 - B)}$$

The product of these 15 probabilities is divided by itself and its inverse. For example,

$$\frac{(0.93)(0.67)}{(0.93)(0.67) + (1 - 0.93)(1 - 0.67)}$$

This gives us the result 0.9642, or roughly 96 percent. When applied to a set of 15 probabilities, Bayes' Theorem expands to support any number of factors, as shown in the following. Although 15 tokens are most commonly used in a calculation, some implementations use more. Some even use every single token in the message.

$$\frac{ABC...N}{ABC...N + (1 - A)(1 - B)(1 - C)...(1 - N)}$$

This combination usually results in a very extreme final value—either very close to 0.0 or very close to 1.0—representing a probability (between 0 percent and 100 percent). Graham's implementation assumes that any result that is greater than or equal to 0.90 is an indicator of spam and anything less is an indicator of legitimate email. Since the results are rather extreme, it is very rare to find many results lurking in the middle. This means that there is usually very little gray area for uncertainty.

This approach is very effective at filtering out most types of spam. Because the results are generally very extreme, there is very little uncertainty.

Bayesian Combination (Brian Burton)

The author of SpamProbe, Brian Burton, analyzed Graham's approach and made several enhancements. He extended the window size of the decision matrix to 27 elements and allowed for a single token to populate two slots in the matrix if it appears at least twice in a message.

Burton discovered a basic problem in Graham's approach that caused filters to frequently require a "tie-breaker" when there was too much strong data to fit in the decision matrix. Depending on how the filter processed the data, some messages hinged on mere randomness—the first side to fill up that eighth slot would win.

Burton also found that it was possible to have too little information when processing smaller messages. The decision matrix would be starved, populated with unimportant information. By allowing tokens appearing multiple times within an email to take up two slots in the matrix, Burton essentially gave a heavier weight to such tokens.

This resulted in higher levels of accuracy as compared to Graham's standard approach. In our example, the decision matrix to support an alternative Bayesian algorithm would look like the following:

S	I	Probability	Token
50	00	0.999900	Url*e
50	00	0.999900	Url*e
50	00	0.999900	order
50	00	0.999900	offer
36	00	0.999900	ONE
50	00	0.999900	Click
52	00	0.999900	here
34	00	0.999900	Be
4	41	0.019655	Precedence*bulk
3	30	0.020136	case
4	27	0.029545	respond
7	41	0.033896	Original
7	41	0.033896	Original
9	41	0.043163	following
8	27	0.057395	Is
8	27	0.057395	Is
9	30	0.058070	sample
73	01	0.937506	Url*http
73	01	0.937506	Url*http
72	01	0.937503	in
12	30	0.075576	sample
4	9	0.083275	permanently
53	1	0.915487	Your
49	1	0.909215	Click
43	1	0.897841	ARE
11	18	0.111035	ago
117	3	0.888531	and

Because tokens appearing more than once in the message take up two slots in the decision matrix, tokens such as "Url*http" now have a heavier "weight" in the final calculation than those that appear only once.

NOTE *Some spam filters implement both versions of the Bayesian combination algorithms to avoid any chance of missing a message due to one algorithm's weakness. Graham's implementation has been proven to work with a majority of common-size messages, while Burton's implementation is stronger with messages having too much or too little data. Combined, these two algorithms generally result in a higher level of accuracy than any one algorithm alone, with no noticeable increase in false positives.*

Robinson's Geometric Mean Test

One of the complaints about most implementations of the Bayesian approach is that the result is generally very extreme—hovering right around either 0 percent or 100 percent. This leaves very little room to determine just *how* guilty the filter considered a message to be.

Robinson's geometric mean test measures both the "spamminess" and "hamminess" of the data in the decision matrix and also provides more granular results ranging between 0 percent and 100 percent. Generally, a result of around 55 percent or higher using Robinson's algorithm is an indicator of spam. The algorithm also has another nice feature in that it is able to express a gray "uncertain" area. It returns a wide range of values (unlike Bayesian combination, which usually returns 0.0 or 1.0), allowing the filter author to consider some ranges as a "maybe" result.

Robinson's approach dramatically changes the way probabilities are combined. His algorithm provides three outputs:

P The level of spamminess in a message

Q The level of nonspamminess in a message

S A combined indicator

$$P = 1 - ((1 - P1)(1 - P2)...(1 - PN))^{(1/N)}$$

$$Q = 1 - ((P1)(P2)...(PN))^{(1/N)}$$

$$S = \frac{1 + \left(\frac{P - Q}{P + Q}\right)}{2}$$

Robinson's geometric mean test has been made obsolete by Fisher-Robinson's inverse chi-square algorithm, discussed next. Although the algorithm is not as accurate as some other techniques, it is excellent for calculating something that Graham's Bayesian approach cannot: confidence.

DSPAM uses Robinson's modified algorithm for determining a confidence factor. The granularity provided by Robinson's algorithm allows the filter to evaluate itself and determine whether or not a decision was solid. If the result shows that the confidence of the decision wasn't very high, the filter can then perform additional calculations or other tasks to try to improve its guess.

Fisher-Robinson's Inverse Chi-Square

Robinson released the *chi-square* approach in 2003, using the research of another well-known mathematician—Sir Ronald Fisher. Fisher-Robinson's chi-square got its name from the use of Fisher's chi-square distribution of combining individual probabilities. The chi-square algorithm provides the added benefit of being very sensitive to uncertainty. It produces granular results similar to Robinson's geometric mean test, in which the result of a calculation may fall within a wide midrange of values to indicate a level of uncertainty.

The chi-square algorithm's decision matrix is different from that of Bayesian combination in that it includes all tokens within a specific range of probability (usually 0.0 through 0.1 and 0.9 through 1.0) and doesn't require sorting. What's even more different about the chi-square approach is the statistical combination used. Robinson's statistical combination uses the formula below. In this formula, the following variables are used:

N	The total number of tokens used in the decision matrix
F1F2...Fn	The product of the probabilities of all included tokens
H	C-1 (-2 LN (F1F2...FN), 2N)
S	C-1 (-2 LN ((1.0 – F1)(1.0 – F2)...(1.0 – FN)), 2N)

The result gives us two indicators, one of ham and one of spam. These can be combined to give us a Graham-like indicator having a probability between 0.0 and 1.0.

$$I = (1 + H - S)/2$$

In our formula, $C^{-1}()$ represents the inverse chi-square function, which is applied to derive a statistical probability. Chi-square is a very popular statistic because it is relatively easy to calculate and interpret. Tim Peters, the author of SpamBayes, implemented a very simple chi-square algorithm that was later adopted by Robinson to replace a more proprietary one, the library of which was not available to many languages (such as Python). The code sample below illustrates the $C^{-1}()$ inverse chi-square function in C.

```c
double chi2Q (double x, int v)
{
  int i;
  double m, s, t;

  m = x / 2.0;
  s = exp(-m);
  t = s;

  for(i=1;i<(v/2);i++) {
    t *= m / i;
    s += t;
```

```
    }
    return (s < 1.0) ? s : 1.0;
}
```

A full explanation of Fisher-Robinson's chi-square can be found at http://www.linuxjournal.com/article.php?sid=6467.

Many code examples can also be found in anti-spam tools implementing Fisher-Robinson's chi-square, such as Bogofilter, SpamBayes, Mozilla, and SpamAssassin's "Bayesian Element."

NOTE *Gary Robinson has continued his research into the inverse chi-square technique and provided many enhancements that make it even more accurate (such as* ESF, *or* effective size factoring, *to remove redundancy). As discussed in this book, the plain vanilla chi-square algorithm delivers levels of accuracy that are slightly higher than those of existing Bayesian algorithms.*

Improvements to Statistical Analysis

So far, we've learned only the basics of statistical language analysis. Many other improvements have been layered on top of these fundamentals to further improve our ability to correctly classify messages.

Improving the Decision Matrix

We've learned so far that the decision matrix used in most popular Bayesian implementations can be limited to a finite number of elements, with only the most interesting tokens. However, since some messages contain more than 15 interesting tokens, it would be beneficial to improve the way we deal with tokens of similar interest.

For example, a single-corpus token that has appeared in only 10 spams is given the same value as one that has appeared in 100 spams. This doesn't really make sense. If a token has appeared in 100 spams, it should probably be considered even spammier than a token that's appeared in only 10.

One way to solve this problem might be to adopt a more dynamic approach to assigning token values that uses a base value. For example, we might take our original base of 0.9900 for spam-corpus tokens, and add from 0 to 99 hundred-thousandths to the token's probability depending on its representation as a percentage of total spam. The idea is to give preference to more popular tokens without dramatically affecting the probabilities themselves. For example, if the token has appeared in 5 percent of all spam, assigning a probability of 0.9905 will move the token up slightly in the decision matrix, above one that has appeared in only 2 percent of all spam (which would have a probability of 0.9902).

Another way to enhance the quality of the final result is to give preference to tokens based on how frequently they appear in the message being classified. For example, if two tokens both share a probability of 0.9900, and one of them has appeared twice in the message, by giving preference to that token in the decision matrix ordering we allow the more heavily used tokens in the message to be considered first. We can do this by tweaking the actual probability or by assigning a priority when the tokens are sorted by interestingness without affecting the actual probability of the token.

Improvements to Tokenization

Filtering is like NASCAR. All racecars go fast—it's squeezing the last 5 mph out that makes it an artful science. The quality of the data is almost always more important than any of the algorithms used to combine it. Unless the filter is using an entirely primitive set of algorithms, it will most likely do a good job of performing some acceptable level of filtering. What sets good filters apart from great ones is the quality of data presented to these algorithms.

Finding ways to extract better data from a message will improve the quality of the final result. Graham's original tokenization plans were very vanilla—all tokens were case insensitive, certain types of punctuation (such as exclamation points) were considered delimiters, and header and URL-specific associations didn't even exist. The data was so common that Graham's second paper on spam, "Better Bayesian Filtering," introduced many changes to make the data stand out more, which quickly improved accuracy.

Further approaches to enhance tokenization have been implemented in many filters; these are discussed in Chapter 11.

Statistical Sedation

We've discussed establishing a dataset by either training an existing corpus of email or starting from scratch. The initial results for users with a high volume of spam are usually less than impressive. Because of the high volume of spam being trained and a lack of legitimate mail, some users may experience a certain number of classification errors during the first few weeks of training. Statistical sedation is an algorithm originally designed for DSPAM that is used to dampen statistical data in the absence of adequate training.

If the user doesn't have much (or any) training data, or has a very high rate of spam, any tokens in their dataset will be relatively concentrated—that is, the word "free" might have a significant number of hits in spam, but the user may not have received enough innocent mail yet to adequately represent this token. Dampening is designed to curb this phenomenon by watering down the concentrated data from their dataset.

Statistical sedation doesn't affect the probabilities of the individual tokens in the dataset, but rather raises the minimum number of occurrences required in the dataset for the token to be given a calculated probability in place of its neutral hapaxial value. Two thresholds are defined within the algorithm itself. The first sets a very aggressive form of sedation, indicating that the user's dataset hasn't received very much training data at all. An initial threshold of 500 to 1,000 (loThresh) innocent messages is a good default. The second threshold is much more passive and identifies that the user has had some training but may still experience false positives on occasion. This value normally hovers around 1,500 to 2,500 (hiThresh) innocent messages. Both thresholds take the total number of spams and legitimate mail in a user's dataset into account, and the algorithm itself does not instantiate unless the user has received more spam than legitimate mail. Four variables are used in the sedation algorithm:

minHits   The minimum number of token occurrences required

TI   The total number of innocent messages learned

TS   The total number of spams learned

S   A number between 0 and 10 specifying the level of sedation

```
if TI < loThresh and TI < TS then
 minHits = minHits + (S/2) + (S((TS - TI)/200))

else if TI < hiThresh and TI < TS then
  minHits = minHits + (S/2) + S( 5(TS / (TS + TI)) )
```

NOTE   *The value 5 used in this formula originates from first multiplying the calculation by 100 to yield a percentage value, and then dividing by 20 to sedate the statistic into fifths.*

In the example above, the *minHits* value is computed based on the number of legitimate mails and spams in a corpus and the level of sedation specified by the implementer. The level of sedation is like a knob allowing the implementer to decide just how much caution to use when applying this algorithm. A good value to start out with is 5, and acceptable values usually range from 0 to 10.

NOTE   *The level of statistical sedation can be tuned in DSPAM v3.x using the tb=N feature. For example, –feature=tb=0 will disable statistical sedation, and –feature=tb=10 will set the maximum level of sedation. The default value of 5 is generally acceptable; however, some systems may call for a more aggressive approach to filtering.*

Iterative Training

Finally, another attempt to improve on basic statistical filtering is to incorporate iterative training (or retraining). Iterative training is an approach used by many spam filters, including SpamProbe and DSPAM, in an attempt to learn faster and ensure that the original mistake isn't made a second time. This is often referred to as test-conditional training, as the message that was erroneously classified is learned and then relearned until the original erroneous condition is no longer met.

For example, if the filter misjudges a message as spam, the user will present the false positive to the filter for relearning. Iterative training will cause the message to be relearned until it is no longer classified as a false positive. Many filter authors impose a maximum loop of five or ten iterations to retrain a single message, in order to prevent too many changes being made to a user's dataset, which could ultimately generate even more errors in the future.

Since most authors still program their filters to err on the side of caution, this is a reasonable algorithm to implement. It does result in more than one small change being made to the data, but the data being changed remains the same throughout the entire iterative training process (that is, only the tokens present in the message are being changed). While this approach increases the likelihood of the data's polarity (overall disposition) being changed, it also limits the amount of data in the dataset that could potentially be altered by training. This is much safer than training ten different messages in which ten different sets of data are changed.

NOTE   *If this feature is available in the filter you are using, enable it. Iterative training has proven to speed up the training cycle in many cases and will prevent the same mistakes from being made repeatedly.*

Learning New Tricks

Spammers have been trying to evade statistical filters for a few years, to no avail. As spammers change their messages to evade the filters, the filters always seem to have an eerie way of detecting their new tricks—usually without the end user even noticing. For example, using "v1agra" in place of "Viagra" in an email does nothing more than train the filter—and then "v1agra" becomes an even better indicator of spam.

There is so much information embedded within an email that it's extremely difficult for a spammer to craft a message with a completely unknown vocabulary, and even if they manage to find a way to get a message past the user's filter, it won't get through a second time. Most spammers don't have the resources to evolve every spam distribution for each individual, and so filters efficiently detect the known patterns while catching any new permutations that happen to be present in the message. A spammer would have to be the first to use a completely unique combination of words in the entire message for it to be virtually undetectable as spam, including a set of normal-looking, average-Joe headers, and at best they'd get away with it only once or twice before the filters caught on. Also, the message would most likely be so obfuscated that it would be difficult to read.

Final Thoughts

By now, the basic blueprint of a typical filter has been covered. The remaining chapters in this section will focus on specific components of a filter and provide useful information for developing or deploying one. Topics such as storage, sizing, and message decoding will be covered.

PART II

FUNDAMENTALS OF STATISTICAL FILTERING

5

DECODING: UNCOMBOBULATING MESSAGES

Until now, tokenizing a message has been where the entire process began—a message was presented to our filter, and we broke it down into very small pieces for analysis.

But what if the message being presented was hidden so that tokenizing it would only give us junk to work with? Spammers aren't above doing this, sadly, and it's well within their ethical standards to force others to read their message, whether or not they want to.

In this chapter, we'll discuss the many different ways in which messages can arrive encoded, why special attention must be given to inbound email, and the different methods of decoding that can be used to ensure that a message tokenizes properly. This chapter is focused more on practical encoding mechanisms in use, rather than on how spammers exploit them (although we'll see a few examples of that too). Chapter 7 explains in detail all of the different tricks spammers are using with encoding and further emphasizes the importance of decoding the different pieces of an encoded message.

Introduction to Encoding

Spammers will go to great lengths to make you read their message. They do this because they know that, although the vast majority of savvy individuals aren't interested in what they're selling, if they can flash something of interest on the screen long enough before the user hits the Delete button, they stand a very remote chance of changing the user's mind. If shock value sells, every spammer wants to be Janet Jackson's wardrobe malfunction.

When we see a message as an end user, we usually see the plain-text or HTML representation of what was sent—the presentation format. While in transit, however, the message may contain several different types of encodings and may not even be readable by a human.

An RFC, or Request for Comments, is a document published online as a means of proposing and achieving a consensus on standards for the Internet. Message encoding was introduced as part of a group of extensions to email in RFC 1521, which built on the original specification for email, RFC 822. RFC 1521 was later superseded by RFC 2045. Collectively, these extensions are referred to as Multipurpose Internet Mail Extensions, or MIME. MIME provides, among other things, a way to transport different types of media across an email message (a feature that wasn't initially considered in RFC 822, as emails up to that point were sent in plain ASCII format). Some methods of encoding are legitimate implementations used for message transport—sending attachments, using alternate character sets, and so on. Spammers use other types of encoding maliciously in an attempt to fool unaware filters. The same technology which was designed to make our lives a little easier is being used by spammers to make them a little more annoying.

The encodings essentially provided a way to translate the data from its pristine format into a more machine-tolerant set of printable characters that would be understood by legacy mail servers (which didn't understand binary attachments) and back again. What the user ends up seeing on the screen represents the original message after it has been decoded, which may be different than what was actually transported from mail server to mail server.

MIME also allows for multiple copies of the same document to be sent in a single email and allows the mail client to choose the best presentation of the document based on the user's settings. For example, legitimate HTML-enabled mail clients usually include a plain-text version of each email so that mail clients without HTML readers can still display the message. Messages can also contain attachments that can be displayed in-line as part of the message or saved to disk as separate files. All of these components require a spam filter to decode the message before it is passed to the tokenizer. This allows the tokenizer (and the rest of the filter) to view the message in its original, human-readable form.

Decoding

Decoding is the process of converting a message from its encoded form into the human-readable form it was authored in. The decoding process is necessary for our spam filter to adequately read encoded messages, but this doesn't necessarily mean that we should throw away the encoded message.

Once our filter has finished analyzing the message, it's generally a good practice to relay the original *encoded* message to the appropriate destination. The philosophy behind this is that the spam filter shouldn't make any modifications to the email other than those necessary—necessary modifications usually only include adding a few headers to the message to add some information about the spam-filtering process.

Three primary types of encoding are used in spam: message body encodings (to encode the message body), header encodings (which encode portions of a message header), and HTML encodings (which can make malicious use of some conveniences in HTML). Let's examine these different types of encoding.

Message Body Encodings

Message body encodings convert the body of a message into a more transport-friendly format. They are normally used to encode messages with alternate character sets or binary attachments, which contain nonprintable characters. Spammers commonly use these types of encodings to hide their messages from now-obsolete spam filters. Let's take a look at an example of an encoded message. The filter sees:

```
Reply-To: <health104580m43@mail.com>
From: <health104580m43@mail.com>
Subject: Penile enlargement method - guaranteed !
Date: Thu, 22 Aug 0102 12:07:35 +0800
MIME-Version: 1.0
X-Priority: 3 (Normal)
X-Msmail-Priority: Normal
X-Mailer: Microsoft Outlook Express 6.00.2600.0000
Importance: Normal
Content-Type: text/html; charset="iso-8859-1"
Content-Transfer-Encoding: base64
```

```
PGhObWw+PGJvZHk+PGRpdiBpZDOibWVzc2FnZUJvZHkiPjxkaXY+PGZvbnQg
ZmFjZToiQXJpYWwiIHNpemU9IjIiPlRoaXMgbWVzc2FnZSBpcyByBzZW5OIHRv
IG91ciBzdWJzY3JpYmVycyBvbmx5IBGdXJOaGVyIGVtYWlscyBObyB5b3Ug
YnkgdGhlIHNlbmRlciBoaGlzIG9uZSB3aWxsIGJ1IHN1c3BlbmRlZCBhdCBu
byBjb3NOIHRvIHlvdS4gU2NyZWVuaW5nIG9mIGFkZHJlc3NlcyBoYXMgYmVl
biBkb251IHRvIHRoZSBiZXNOIG9mIG91ciBhYmlsaXR5LCB1bmZvcnR1bmFO
ZWx5IGloIGlzIGltcG9zc2libGUgdG8gYmUgMTAwJSBhY2N1cmFOZSSwgc28g
aWYgeW91IGRpZCBub3QgYXNrIGZvciB0aGlzLCBviB3aXNOIHRvIGJlIGV4
Y2x1ZGVkIG9mIHRoaXMgbGlzdCwgcGxlYXNlIGNsaWNrIDxhIGhyZWY9Im1h
aWxObzpoZWFsdGgxMDVAbWFpbC5ydT9zdWJqZWNOPXJlbW92ZSIgdGFyZ2VO
PSJuZXdfd2luIj5oZXJlPC9hPjwvZm9udD48L2Rpdj4gIDxxwPjxiPjxmb250
```

and so on.

Not very much to look at, is it? If we fed this message directly to our tokenizer, we'd end up with a few headers' worth of information and gibberish for the rest.

This type of encoding is known as *Base64 encoding*. Its legitimate purposes include encoding binary attachments, such as pictures and files, being sent via email. When the user's mail client receives the message, it is decoded, and the recipient sees the following.

This message is sent to our subscribers only. Further emails to you by the sender this one will be suspended at no cost to you. Screening of addresses has been done to the best of our ability, unfortunately it is impossible to be 100% accurate, so if you did not ask for this, or wish to be excluded of this list, please click here

THIS IS FOR ADULT MEN ONLY ! IF YOU ARE NOT AN ADULT, DELETE NOW !

We are a serious company, offering a program that will enhance your sex life, and enlarge your penis in a totally natural way.

---

and so on.

Had we processed this message without first decoding it, we would have missed every bit of the message's content, which turned out to be spam. That would have left only the message headers to base our filter's decision on, which, of course, would result in a high error rate.

The message header "Content-Transfer-Encoding" identifies the encoding used for a particular message (or part of a message). This field can be present in an email's top-level headers or in a particular part of a multipart document.

Six different encodings can be specified with this field, and all are case insensitive. The first three, 7bit, 8bit, and binary, aren't nearly as complicated as the remaining encodings, as they don't adversely affect the format of the data.

- *7bit encoding* means that the data is all represented as short lines of ASCII data. Only characters from the US-ASCII character set will be present in the message.

- *8bit encoding* means that the lines are short, but there may be non-ASCII characters, such as Unicode or nonprintable characters.

- *Binary encoding* means that not only may non-ASCII characters be present, but also that the lines are not necessarily short enough for SMTP transport.

The big difference between 8bit and binary encoding is that binary doesn't require the lines to be trimmed to a specific length. If the message is going to contain any type of data outside of the standard US-ASCII character set, one of these encodings should be used. That is not to say, however, that spammers will conform to RFC standards.

The remaining three types of encoding—quoted-printable, Base64, and custom encoding—can dramatically alter the data for transport. When a message is received in one of these encodings, the filter usually needs to perform some level of decoding before the data will be useful enough for the tokenizer.

Quoted-Printable Encoding

Quoted-printable encoding was designed for encoding message components that consist primarily of human-readable ASCII characters. The encoding algorithm encodes certain nonprintable characters, such as carriage returns and special characters, leaving most of the readable portion of the message intact (but possibly broken up). The RFC specification for this encoding lists five basic rules that are used to encode the message. The full specification can be found in RFC 2045.

NOTE *The RFC contains a few other guidelines and plenty of other useful information about this type of encoding. You can read RFC 2045 in its entirety online at http:// www.ietf.org/rfc/rfc2045.txt.*

The typical quoted-printable encoded message looks very similar to a plain ASCII message, but the differences are apparent after a closer examination of some of the characters.

```
From: "MR.DOUGLAS  AND PRINCESS M." <douglassmith2004@yahoo.co.uk>
Reply-To: princessmar001@yahoo.com
X-Mailer: Microsoft Outlook Express 5.00.2919.6900 DM
MIME-Version: 1.0
Subject: [SA] URGENT HELP.............
Date: Mon, 5 Apr 1999 20:38:02 +0100
Content-Type: text/plain; charset="us-ascii"
Content-Transfer-Encoding: quoted-printable

DEAR SIR=2C
URGENT AND CONFIDENTIAL=3A

Re=3ATransfer of $50=2C000=2E000=2E00 USD=5BFIFTY MILLION UNITED
STATES DOLLARS=5D=2E

WE WANT TO TRANSFER TO OVERSEAS=5B$50=2C000=2E000=2E00=5BFIFTY =
MILLION UNITED STATES DOLLARS=5DFROM A SECURITY COMPANY =
IN SPAIN=2CI WANT TO ASK YOU TO QUIETLY LOOK FOR A =
RELIABLE AND HONEST PERSON WHO WILL BE CAPABLE AND FIT =
. . . . .
```

and so on.

Base64 Encoding

Base64 encoding was originally intended as a means of encoding binary data such as music and graphics. In fact, it's used for any type of data that isn't in human-readable form. Since the encoding translates any of the possible 256 bytes into printable ASCII bytes, the resulting encoded data is usually around 33 percent larger than the original file.

The Base64 algorithm is quite simple but detailed. You can read the complete description in RFC 2045. We've already seen an example of a Base64-encoded message earlier in this chapter. Note how little useful information can be drawn directly from the message without decoding it. This is one of the many dirty spammer tricks we'll cover in Chapter 7.

Base64 encoding is generally used to encode attachments, and so an email with a Base64-encoded body is generally very suspicious—most likely spam in fact (but don't count on that). Many heuristic filters will even go so far as to automatically drop messages with a Base64-encoded body.

Eventually, mail servers will get smart enough to reject any mail with a Base64-encoded body, forcing the few legitimate users of this practice to conform. Until that happens, it's necessary to spend the processor cycles decoding the message body just to be certain it's spam.

Custom Encodings

Custom encodings are those determined by the implementer. They are generally reserved for future expansion or for situations in which two proprietary applications require a different type of encoding to communicate. The use of custom encodings is usually frowned upon, as no other mail client would know how to decode the message unless it had been explicitly written to handle the custom encoding type. Nevertheless, one can use a token pre-pended with "x-" to specify a custom type—for example, x-myencoding.

If you're developing applications that use Internet mail to communicate, consider one of the existing transfer encodings first, and create a custom encoding only as a last resort for extremely sensitive uses.

Message Header Encodings

Message header encodings are designed to support different types of character sets. Unfortunately, they too are abused by spammers to trick unaware spam filters. Ironically, this trick works on quite a few filters, primarily legacy filters without header decoding logic.

One of the big things heuristic filters look at is the subject line of a message to determine whether it is spam; most humans can determine whether a message is spam nine times out of ten just by looking at the subject line. If the filter sees words like "ADV:" or "Viagra" in the subject, it knows to can the message. Statistical filters are usually much more sensible and won't can a message just because it has a guilty-looking header. But even a statistical filter can fail if it can't decode message headers.

RFC 2047 outlines an encoding that can be used in message headers. For example, the filter might see:

```
Subject: =?iso-8859-1?b?SW1tZWRpYXRlIERlbGl2ZXJ5IG9mIFZpYWdyL2E=?=
```

but the recipient will see:

```
Subject: Immediate Delivery of Viagr/a
```

NOTE *The entire header doesn't necessarily have to be encoded, and there can be multiple encodings per message header. The subject field isn't the only field that can use this type of encoding either. Many spams have encoded To/From fields.*

When this type of encoding is used, the recipient sees only the original text that was encoded, not the encoded portion of the message. The problem is that an unaware spam filter may fail to decode the header and also may fail to see it.

NOTE *Unfortunately, the mere presence of encoded headers isn't enough to determine whether a message is spam; many individuals who converse with people using a different character set (especially of a wide-character persuasion) will also be sending email with encoded headers.*

Message header encoding is fairly simple to detect and almost as easy to decode. RFC 2047 outlines the basic rules for header encoding.

Message headers support two primary encoding methods, and you've already heard about both of them. The same algorithm described in RFC 2045 for decoding Base64 messages can be used to decode a Base64-encoded header phrase. The second encoding method is quoted-printable. The rules outlined in RFC 2045 also apply to quoted-printable encoded header phrases, except that new line characters are not permissible.

There are a few other rules to be aware of with regard to this approach. For details, download RFC 2047 from http://www.ietf.org/rfc/rfc2047.txt.

HTML Encodings

Until now, we've been discussing content encodings. HTML isn't considered a content encoding, but there are components within HTML that should be decoded by the filter. Some types of HTML encodings make it more difficult to read text, and some make it easier to identify spam. (We'll discuss the latter in Chapter 7, as we learn more about spammers' tricks.) This section will cover the basic components in HTML that should be decoded by a filter.

There are a lot of ways to hide text in HTML. One of the most basic is to use HTML character encoding. Character encoding allows the author to use ASCII values, which then display as actual characters when viewed by an HTML-capable mail client. For example, the filter might see:

```
&#67;&#65;&#76;&#76;&#32;&#78;&#79;&#87;&#44;&#32;&#73;&#84;&#39;&#83;&#32;&#70;&#82;&#69;&#69;&#33;
```

but the recipient will see:

```
CALL NOW, IT'S FREE!
```

This encoding isn't particularly useful to the legitimate email sender, but it works wonders for spammers. And because it's supported in the web-browser world, email clients recognize it (at least until mail clients become smart enough to detect this type of abuse). Fortunately, the encoded characters can easily be decoded, after which the message can then be tokenized.

URL encoding is another type of encoding frequently used in HTML. It allows hexadecimal characters to be used in URLs to maintain continuity—that is, to prevent URLs from having spaces and other weird characters. For example, the filter sees:

```
http%3A//www.somedomain.com/%69%6e%64%65%78%2e%68%74%6d%6c
```

but when the recipient clicks it, they go to:

```
http://www.somedomain.com/index.html
```

Again, not a very complicated encoding, but nevertheless the filter could miss some very guilty data if it doesn't properly decode it. Encoded chunks of text like this usually contain the guiltiest tokens in an email, which is why they're hidden in the first place.

One of the tricky things about HTML encoding is that it can easily be layered underneath a Base64-encoded message part, so not only do you have to first decode the Base64 component, but you must then perform the necessary HTML decoding.

As you'll see in Chapter 7, a number of additional optimizations can be made to thwart obfuscation attempts by spammers. The good news is that encodings and obfuscation techniques have a finite number of variations. Mail clients support only the standard types of message encoding, and therefore a spammer can't simply make up a new encoding.

HTML gets a bit trickier, however, because there are many creative ways to hide text. Fortunately, as of this writing, spammers haven't been able to find too many new ways to hide text on top of the approaches that have already been counter-programmed by filter authors.

Message Actualization

Message actualization is the process of converting a message into components that can be managed by a computer program. If you're attempting to write software designed to parse an email, you'll do well to find a way not only to parse it, but also to actualize the message into objects the software can actually work with. DSPAM is one example of a filter that uses this approach to interact with the email while it is being processed by the software. The message is read in, and individual components, such as headers, message parts, and MIME delimiters, are cataloged and organized into a series of objects. Key pieces of information, such as the encoding type and media type, are stored as variables for each message part. This approach works remarkably well and allows the software to access different parts of the message as needed, rather than serially.

Supporting Software

A number of implementations of decoding algorithms are available on the Internet. Rather than attempt to roll your own, you may find it more beneficial to use one that's already written and that has a compatible licensing scheme to support your software. Here are some places to start.

- Zeegee Software has a set of PERL modules for MIME processing:

    http://www.zeegee.com/code/perl/MIME-tools

- Mimetic is a GPL MIME library written in C++:

    http://mime.codesink.org/mimetic_mime_library.html

- ripMIME is a C tool for ripping out MIME attachments:

    http://pldaniels.com/ripmime

- Hunny JMIME is a commercial set of Java classes for MIME extraction:

    http://www.hunnysoft.com/jmime

Final Thoughts

We've covered some of the basics of content encoding in this chapter. Chapter 7 goes into more detail on this, as part of our discussion of all the dirty tricks spammers use. There is a lot of room for abuse with these particular encodings, which is why it's necessary to identify and decode them.

Encoding has its practical uses, so it's hard to hate it completely, but modern-day spam filters should at least be aware of these encodings and have routines for managing them.

6

TOKENIZATION: THE BUILDING BLOCKS OF SPAM

Unlike older spam filters, in which the author programs the characteristics of spam, statistical filtering automatically chooses the characteristics (or "features") of spam and nonspam directly from each email. Two years from now, when spam has evolved in content, statistical filters will have learned enough to continue doing their job. This is because unlike older spam filters, in which the author programmed rules to identify spam, statistical filters automatically identify damning features of a spam based on message content.

Tokenization is the process of reducing a message to its colloquial components. These components can be individual words, word pairs, or other small chunks of text.

Data generated by the tokenizer is ultimately passed to the analysis engine, where it is interpreted. How the data is interpreted is important, but not necessarily as important as the quality of the data being passed. In other words, the way that a message is tokenized is more important than what we do with it later; even a simple change in tokenization can affect the accuracy of the filter. From a philosophical point of view, this raises the question, "What is content?" If content were just words on a page, then tokenizing only complete alphabetical words should be sufficient—but content is much more than that, as we'll see throughout this book.

Tokenizing a Heuristic Function

The one heuristic aspect of statistical filtering is tokenization. Even though the process of identifying features is dynamic, the way those features are initially established—how they are parsed out of an email—is programmed by a human. Fortunately, languages change slowly, and only a few minor tweaks are necessary to adapt the tokenization process to handle some of the wrenches thrown at it by spammers. Tokenization is the type of heuristic process that is usually defined once at build time and rarely requires further maintenance. In light of its simplicity, many attempts are still being made to establish tokenization through artificial intelligence, to remove all sense of heuristic programming from the equation. Within a few years, filters should be able to efficiently perform their own type of "DNA sequencing" on messages, determining the best possible way to extract data. In fact, this is already being researched as a solution to filtering some foreign languages that don't use spaces or any other type of word delimiter.

Basic Delimiters

Besides deciding how best to break apart a message, there are many other issues to consider when tokenizing. For example, we need to determine what constitutes a delimiter (token separator) and what constitutes a constituent character (part of the token). Do we break apart some pieces of a message differently than others? What data do we ignore (if any)?

The fundamental goal of tokenization is to separate and identify specific features of a text sample. This starts with separating the message into smaller components, which are usually plain old words. So our first delimiter would be a space, since spaces commonly separate words in most languages. This makes it very easy to tokenize a phrase like the following:

```
For A Confidential Phone Interview, Please Complete Form & Submit.
```

which can be broken up into the following words:

For	A	Confidential	Phone	Interview,
Please	Complete	Form	&	Submit.

As we've learned, each word typically is assigned one of two primary dispositions—spam or nonspam. The example above will cover a lot of text, but we're left with a few punctuation issues. For example, is the word "submit" on its own likely to have a different disposition from the word "submit." with a period after it? How about "interview" and "interview," containing a comma? In these cases, it makes sense to add some types of punctuation to the set of delimiters, as punctuation suggests a break in most languages. The following are some widely accepted punctuation delimiters:

- period (.)
- comma (,)
- semicolon (;)
- quotation marks (")
- colon (:)

Some other punctuation, such as the question mark, is a bit more controversial. Some authors believe that "warts" and "warts?" should be treated the same, in most cases as spammy tokens.

Including too much punctuation in the makeup of tokens could result in five or ten different permutations of a single word in the database. This can very rapidly diminish their usefulness. On the other hand, not having enough tokens can cause the tokens to become so common among both classes of email that they become uninteresting. The trick is to end up with tokens that would stick out in one particular corpus. If there were 100 spams about warts in the user's corpus, but only one posing a question in which "warts?" was used, the filter is likely to overlook this feature in the one message.

NOTE *I've found that treating a question mark as a delimiter results in slightly better accuracy (on the order of a few messages) in my corpus testing, as opposed to treating it as a constituent character. This could likely change in the future, however.*

Redundancy

Some types of punctuation are very useful; for example, the exclamation point makes a remarkable difference between "free" and "free!" and so you want to use some punctuation marks as constituent characters. One of the problems a filter author might run into when allowing these types of characters, however, is redundancy. Most would agree that there's no real difference between "free!" and "free!!!!" in a message, as both are equally condemning characteristics of spam. On the other hand, messages in which symbols are used to b!r!e!a!k up a word may behave a bit differently.

Some authors will view punctuation as part of a token only if it appears at the end of the token. If an exclamation point appears elsewhere, it will be treated as a delimiter in most cases. So for those punctuation marks that are permitted, we should consider working some method of de-duplication into our tokenizer, where only the first occurrence of the punctuation is used. We essentially look at "free!!!", "free!!!!!!!!!!", and "free!" as the same token by truncating the extra chaff. I've found that using the exclamation point as a constituent character slightly improves accuracy, which is the opposite effect that question marks appeared to have. This is probably because more spams use an obnoxiously loud used-car-salesman type of pretense rather than actually posing questions. Perhaps one day, spammers will become more philosophical, and then question marks will become just as useful as exclamation points.

Some filters permit a certain window size before the token is truncated; for example, tokens may be allowed to have up to three exclamation points before being truncated, giving the filter three different meanings for "free!", "free!!", and the extremely guilty and shameless "free!!!" One of the advantages to doing this, other than measuring the three levels of unbridled fervor, is that it allows a really obnoxious message that uses all three tokens to fill up more slots in the decision matrix.

It's important to truncate extraneous characters at some level because spammers could easily use *not* truncating them as a way to hide very spammy tokens; for example, a spammer wanting to hide the word "porn" could send "porn!!!" in the first spam and "porn!?!?!" the next time, so that in both cases the token would be considered a new token. Truncating will reduce both of these tokens to "porn!" or even "porn" if exclamation points are ignored all together. Tokens should generally be limited to only one acceptable punctuation mark at the end, or to an *N*-sized window of homogeneous punctuations at the most.

Other Delimiters

Other delimiters used by many applications include the following:

- brackets [ ]
- braces { }
- parentheses ( )
- mathematical operators + - / * = < >
- special characters | & ~ `
- the at sign @
- underscores and other rare characters

These delimiters frequently prevent the duplication of several different permutations of tokens, such as "when" and "(when". Other characters, such as the new line character, are also treated as delimiters. The nice thing about the way text is delimited is that it's going to result in unique tokens, even if the tokenization isn't perfect. This can be good or bad, but most of the time it's good. Even a token that isn't in human-readable format may be machine-readable and may occur with enough frequency to be a good identifier. In fact, Bayesian antivirus filtering uses an entirely different set of delimiters, because antivirus analysis involves the cataloging and analysis of several different binary sequences.

Exceptions

Some exceptions to the basic delimiters we've mentioned involve one-off instances where we actually want to preserve certain complete tokens. For example, IP addresses make for good spam markers, as do certain HTML characters like © and . If you're reading this book, there is most likely no shortage of spam in your inbox (or quarantine). Often the best way to discover new approaches to tokenization is to take a look at some of the text spammers are using in their samples. It's very important that the tokenizing approaches being used aren't biased against present-day spam.

The tokenizing algorithm should be generic in such a way that it can easily break down any kind of natural language or new type of message style, but it shouldn't be so plain vanilla that the features it generates are likely to appear as common in all email. It would be relatively easy to tokenize a message into individual characters, but that wouldn't be very useful, since the token "v" could occur in "viagra" or "violin." All-numeric tokens are generally not very useful on their own, but when combined with the proper punctuation (such as a dollar sign or exclamation mark) can make a significant distinction between "19" and "$19" or between "95" and "95!". Provide enough information to allow the token to be set apart from the rest, but not so much that it is unlikely to show up only a handful of times.

To some degree, this anal-retentive exercise is overrated. Any reasonable level of tokenization will most likely yield levels of accuracy above 99 percent, but making a mistake could cost a few misclassifications on occasion. I've found that using the question mark as a constituent character in my tests resulted in approximately 3 additional errors per 5,000. Experimentation and thorough testing is one of the best ways to decide on the tokenization approach that works best for the filter.

Token Reassembly

Occasionally, tokens will turn out to be a little too small due to attempts by spammers to obfuscate them (we'll go into more detail about the different obfuscation attempts in the next chapter). When this happens, reassembling individual letters into a token can help improve accuracy. Let's look at an example of obfuscated text:

```
C/A/L/L/ N-O-W -  I/T/S F_R_E_E
```

If the tokenizer we're using considers underscores, dashes, and slashes to be token delimiters, then instead of ending up with 4 one-word tokens, we'll end up with 14 single-character tokens. Many filter authors believe it's healthy to allow these individual characters to tokenize, while others believe that the resulting information is too generalized to be a good indicator of anything, at least without the risk of false positives.

Filter authors who share the latter philosophy can use token reassembly to join the original tokens back together. Token reassembly isn't a perfect science, but it provides more useful tokens to work with. The tokens "VIA" and "GRA" are much more useful than individual characters and are definitely more indicative of spam. Token reassembly basically concatenates single-character tokens that are adjacent to one another, looking for larger amounts of whitespace amidst the slicing and dicing to make an educated guess about what words go together. Since statistical filtering involves *machine* learning and not *human* learning, tokens like this are very useful to the computer, even though they may not make much sense to us. For example, the token "VIA" really doesn't mean much, which is exactly why it makes a great indicator of spam—you'd rarely see the word "VIA" in a legitimate message unless you were talking about motherboards. The word "GRA" is even more rare in legitimate mail. The fact that these tokens aren't necessarily comprehensible to a human makes it easier to identify them in spams. My dataset considers some of these fractional words to be extreme indicators of spam:

```
agra        S: 00030    I: 00000    P: 0.9999
eacute      S: 00021    I: 00000    P: 0.9999
prematur    S: 00020    I: 00000    P: 0.9999
```

Degeneration

Another solution Graham introduced into tokenization is called *degeneration*. Degeneration allows an token that hasn't been seen before to be reduced in complexity (location, case, and punctuation) until it matches a simpler token. If no tokens match a given token, we make it simpler until we find a match. For example, consider the use of the word "FREE!!!" in the subject. If it has never been seen before in the subject, degeneration has us reduce the phrase until it matches something we have seen before.

```
Subject*Free!!!
Subject*free!!!
Subject*FREE!
Subject*Free!
Subject*free!
Subject*FREE
Subject*Free
Subject*free
FREE!!!
Free!!!
free!!!
FREE!
Free!
free!
```

```
FREE
Free
free
```

Degeneration has a lot of room for customization, including the order in which the tokens decrease in complexity. At the very least, degeneration of punctuation is a wise move. If the word "free!" doesn't exist in the dataset yet, it makes good sense to use the value from a similar token.

Header Optimizations

Most filter authors agree that a token in the subject header is very different from a token in the message body, and that a token that appears in two different headers is unique enough to warrant keeping track of. Header tokens are usually processed differently from body tokens in order to maintain the origin of each token. Let's look at an example of an email with a lot of useful header information.

```
From: bazz@xum2.xumx.com
To: bazz@xum2.xumx.com
Reply-To: mort239o@xum2.xumx.com
Subject: ADV: FREE Mortgage Rate Quote - Save THOUSANDS! kplxl
X-Keywords:

Save thousands by refinancing now. Apply from the privacy of your home and
receive a FREE no-obligation loan quote.
http://211.78.96.11/acct/morquote/

Rates are Down. YOU Win!
Self-Employed or Poor Credit is OK!

Get CASH out or money for Home Improvements, Debt Consolidation and more.
Interest rates are at the lowest point in years-right now! This is the perfect
time for you to get a FREE quote and find out how much you can save!
```

In the spam shown here, several different tokens stand out. First, if my email address happened to be bazz@xum2.xumx.com, I wouldn't expect to be seeing it in the From: header, but it would be very normal in the To: header. Seeing my own email address in the From: header would be a clear indicator of spam, since most people don't usually send email to themselves unless they've had too much to drink.

Second, the word "Save" appears in both the subject line and the message body. I would expect to see it in the message body more frequently in legitimate mail—for example, "Save your files in the blue folder" or "Save me from this dreaded cubicle." Seeing the word "Save" in the subject header is much more suspicious, though, and it makes sense for me to have a different entry in the dataset for each of them.

The word "FREE" also shows up in both the subject line and message body, but in this case, they're both very guilty indicators of spam. The filter still benefits here because the tokens "FREE" and "Subject*FREE" now have the ability to take up two slots in my decision matrix, further condemning the spam. Header tokens are extremely useful for identifying both spam and legitimate mail.

Other types of header tokens are frequently found to be useful, and the set of delimiters used in the headers is usually slightly different from those used in the message body. For example, if I want to catch all of the IP addresses in the Received: headers, I would treat a period as a constituent character (part of the token) instead of a separator. If I wanted to tokenize the message-id, I'd also include the @ sign as a delimiter, as it is used to separate some pieces of the message-id.

Another advantage of including the header as part of the token is that it helps to create a virtual "whitelist" of users you trust. If I exchange a lot of correspondence with bobsmith@somedomain.com, tokens like "From*bobsmith" and "From*yourcompany.com" will start to appear in the dataset, usually with very innocent values. This works equally well in identifying the hostnames of trusted mail servers in the Received: header too.

URL Optimizations

Everyday innocent-sounding words like "order" and "cgi" often appear in the body of messages I receive from legitimate mailing lists. Seeing them appear in a URL, however, is much more suspicious. URLs are the spammers' preferred means of contact. It's much easier to run a scam using a website as your point of contact than it is to pay for the overhead of a phone system or mail processing department. Spammers also like their privacy, since the rest of the free world hates them, and they prefer that even customers not know how to contact them or the companies they spam for. Whether it's a link to click to visit a site or the URL of an image inside the message, URLs provide a lot of useful information specific to their own kind. Even non-sensible numbers will frequently stand out in URLs. This makes really good data for identifying not only spam but some legitimate mailing lists that use URLs in their unsubscribe tag lines. Users who are subscribed to some mailing lists that frequently include embedded advertisements (such as Yahoo Groups) will notice some specific characteristics of the URLs used in these advertisements that help the filter distinguish between advertising and real spam.

URLs are frequently tokenized differently than the rest of a message. The only delimiters usually used when tokenizing a URL are the slash, question mark, equal sign, period, and colon, although some filter authors perform the same basic type of token separation as they do in the rest of the message body. Tokenizing using URL-specific delimiters is done because the individual tokens are more frequently found based on their path in the URL, rather than on a specific context inside the URL. Regardless of how they are tokenized, URLs, when analyzed, can yield a lot of useful information. They can be categorized as places you want to go and places you don't want to go. A spam containing places you don't want to go is just as informative as a legitimate message containing places you do.

Url*getitrightnowwholesale	S: 00026	I: 00000	P: 0.9999
Url*thesedealzwontlast	S: 00026	I: 00000	P: 0.9999
Url*biz	S: 00008	I: 00000	P: 0.9998
Url*us	S: 00000	I: 00050	P: 0.0001
Url*java	S: 00018	I: 00000	P: 0.9999
Url*www	S: 00000	I: 00030	P: 0.0001
Url*com	S: 00000	I: 00033	P: 0.0001
Url*img	S: 00066	I: 00000	P: 0.9999

Ironically, legitimate URLs seem to be rare among spammers, while the wild and obnoxious names always pop up—with the exception of "java," of course, which appeared as spammy only because this user doesn't use Java (not because Java programmers were spamming). The appearance of certain naming conventions, such as the extensive use of "img," makes the task of identifying malicious URLs pretty easy. If we wanted to, we could probably determine the disposition of the message based on the URL information alone.

Ironically, URLs containing well-known web addresses are likely to appear as innocent or hapaxes. Not a single URL token containing the following words has ever appeared in my corpus as spammy:

- Url*microsoft
- Url*whitehouse
- Url*sco
- Url*linux
- Url*quicken
- Url*intuit
- Url*amazon
- Url*fbi

HTML Tokenization

One area that has plagued many filter authors is the decision as to what HTML to include and what other parts of the message to ignore—for example, should we ignore JavaScript? What about font tags? Most filters pay attention to all HTML tags except those on an exclusionary list—namely, a specific set of tokens that are common to all types of email. This approach works quite well, but there's still room for improvement. Ignoring data is always something to be concerned about, and you shouldn't do it unless you have good reason. The justification for ignoring some HTML data is that many people normally converse only with senders who do not use HTML.

This could cause any type of message with embedded HTML to be rejected as spam, which could be bad for the recipient if their boss suddenly started using an HTML-enabled mail client. The tags most filters ignore include

- td
- !doctype
- blockquote
- table
- tr
- div
- p
- body
- short tags, with fewer than N characters of content
- tags whose content contains no spaces

It is probably better to use an exclusionary list rather than an inclusionary one. You're more likely to miss a few tags or possibly to fail to name certain tags you never thought could be used in spam (for example, the object tag has recently become popular). If this happens, at worst the tag will sit and collect dust in the dataset with some neutral value or will fill up a decision matrix slot in error. If you fail to add a tag to an inclusive list, though, you're bound to ignore an important data point and may not even realize it.

Some of the HTML tags commonly used by spammers (which a filter should definitely be looking at) include the following:

APPLET	BGSOUND	FRAME	IFRAME
ILAYER	IMG	INPUT	LAYER
LINK	SCRIPT	A	AREA
BASE	DIV	LINK	SPAN
OBJECT	FONT	BODY	META

Some filters like to mark the tokens generated from HTML tags with an "HTML" identifier, while others go so far as to mark the particular tag the text belonged to (for example, "BODY:BGCOLOR=#FFFFFF"). Regardless of which tags the filter decides to keep and which get discarded, it's very important to handle HTML comments correctly. Spammers are using many tricks to obfuscate their text so that it's human readable, but not very machine readable. For example, the following may look like a complete mess in its machine-readable format:

```
Received: from 64.202.131.2 (h0007e9075130.ne.client2.attbi.com
[24.218.222.43])
Message-ID: <cp6-mh-rn-w$4pa2o965rl84@jn4yOhq1bcy>
From: "patsy stamm" <arthropathology71255@earthlink.net>
Reply-To: "patsy stamm" <arthropathology71255@earthlink.net>
Subject: Giving this to you
Date: Fri, 08 Aug 03 07:29:02 GMT
```

```
X-Mailer: MIME-tools 5.503 (Entity 5.501)
MIME-Version: 1.0
Content-Type: multipart/alternative;
        boundary="ADOE55.76_15.C"
X-Priority: 3
X-MSMail-Priority: Normal


--ADOE55.76_15.C
Content-Type: text/html;
Content-Transfer-Encoding: quoted-printable

Yes you he<!lansing>ard about th<!crossbill>ese weird <!cottony>little
pil<!domesday>ls
that are suppo<!=anabel>sed to make you bigger and of cou<!chord>rse you think
they're b<!soften>ogus snake potion. Well, let's look at the facts:
<strong>G<!eigenspace>RX2
has be<!waldron>en sold over 1.9 Mill<!audacity>ion times within the last 18
months</strong>...
With awe<!tapestry>some results for hun<!wield>dreds of thous<!locale>ands of
men all over the planet!  They all enjoy a seriously enhanced version of their
manh<!rescind>ood and <b>why shou<!seoul>ldn't you</b>?
```

But when the user clicks the message to read it, the HTML comments won't be visible, and the user will see this:

```
Yes you heard about these weird little pills
that are supposed to make you bigger and of course you think
they're bogus snake potion. Well, let's look at the facts: GRX2
has been sold over 1.9 Million times within the last 18 months...
With awesome results for hundreds of thousands of men all over the planet!
They all enjoy a seriously enhanced version of their manhood and why shouldn't
you?
```

A simple way to ensure that the message is tokenized correctly is to remove the HTML comments and reassemble the message.

Word Pairs

Using word pairs, or *nGrams*, has recently become very popular among authors of statistical filters and adds a lot of benefits to standard single-token filtering. Pairing words together creates more specialized tokens. For example, the word "play" could be considered a very neutral word, as it could be used to describe a lot of different things. But pairing it with the word adjacent to it will give us a token that will inevitably stick out more when it occurs—for example, "play lotto." This approach helps improve the processing of HTML components by identifying the different types of generators used to create the HTML messages. Each generator, whether it's a legitimate mail client or a spam tool, has its own unique signature, which joining tokens together can help to highlight. Tokenizers that implement these types of approaches are referred to as *concept-based tokenizers,* because they identify concepts in addition to content. We'll discuss the different implementations of nGrams in Chapter 11.

Sparse Binary Polynomial Hashing

Bill Yerazunis originally introduced the concept known as *SBPH,* or *sparse binary polynomial hashing.* SBPH is an approach to tokenization using word pairs and phrases. If it wasn't so effective at what it does, it would probably be a terrible idea—but Yerazunis has repeatedly astonished the spam-filtering community with the leaps in accuracy made by SBPH tokenization. Graham refers to SBPH with the same mixed feelings regarding its ingenuity and need for medication:

> Another project I heard about . . . was Bill Yerazunis' CRM114. This is the counterexample to the design principle I just mentioned. It's a straight text classifier, but such a stunningly effective one that it manages to filter spam almost perfectly without even knowing that's what it's doing.

SBPH tokenizes entire phrases, up to five tokens across, and allows for word skipping in between. It led the way in terms of accuracy for a long period of time, but it also created an enormous amount of data, which is one of the reasons it presently functions only in a train-on-error environment. SBPH provides the benefit of using the simplest, most colloquial tokens but giving special notice to more complex tokens as well—which are usually much stronger indicators of spam when they appear.

A few filters, such as CRM114, perform this type of word skipping, which will tokenize something like "manh+<!rescind>+ood" and also help the filter "see" the original token by performing the word skipping: "manh+ood." Since tokenization is an imperfect process, approaches like this generally provide more machine-readable tokens to deal with, without necessarily requiring much work. The more permutations of machine-readable tokens are created, however, the larger and more spread out the dataset will become, possibly affecting accuracy. The amount of data generated by SBPH generally turns a lot of filter authors off to it in favor of simple functions such as HTML comment filtering. We'll cover SBPH more in depth in Chapter 11.

Internationalization

The tokenization methods discussed thus far have covered only standard character sets. The issue of foreign languages will eventually require a solution. Most spam filters simply use wide characters as placeholders, such as the letter "z" or an asterisk. This functionality allows the filter to catch just about any messages written using a wide character set. Some users, however, may expect to receive email from others speaking such a language, and for them this approach won't function well at all, filtering only based on header data. The rest of the body will look (to the filter) like this:

ZZZZZ,

ZZ ZZZZ ZZZ ZZZZZZZ ZZZ ZZZ Z ZZZZZZ Z ZZZZZZ
ZZZZ Z ZZZ ZZZZ ZZZZZZZ ZZ ZZZZZZ ZZ ZZZ ZZZZZZZ

ZZ,
ZZZZZZZZ

Some filters implement i18n internationalization, which lets their filter support some additional languages. To make matters more complicated, however, some languages don't use whitespace, making it very difficult to identify words at all. This commonly calls for more advanced solutions such as variable-length nGrams, which we'll discuss in Chapter 11.

Final Thoughts

We've run the gamut of approaches to tokenizing in this chapter. We'll learn more about tokenizing phrases in Chapter 11, and in Chapter 13 we'll cover another type of prefilter that actually despeckles the noise inherent in tokens. Tokenizing strives to define content by defining the construct and, more importantly, what the root components of content are. This is a noble quest, but, as with other areas of machine learning, is a function that may eventually be better left up to the computer. As new types of neural decision-making algorithms surface, the analysis of unformatted text may become one of the next forms of AI. Until this happens, tokenizing remains one of the few heuristic components of a statistical spam filter. It should therefore be respected and kept somewhat simple, so as not to require any maintenance in the years to come.

7

THE LOW-DOWN DIRTY TRICKS OF SPAMMERS

The world wouldn't have a need for spam filters if spammers would just add "**SPAM**" to their subject headers. Unfortunately, we don't live in the kind of world where people play fair. We don't even live in a world where those who don't play fair are publicly flogged often enough. Since the invention of spam filters, spammers have employed the services of (usually mediocre) programmers to help them push their messages into our inboxes against our will and at our own expense. Spammers know we don't want to read their spam, and yet they make countless efforts to obfuscate their messages and gloss over the guiltiness of their advertisements. This chapter is dedicated to exposing many of the most common tricks spammers use to evade spam filters.

The good news is that none of these tricks are working on modern-day statistical filters. Despite some of the media hype about tricks like *word salad* (inserting arbitrary words into a message), the majority of people using modern-day statistical filters aren't seeing their filters crack under pressure. In fact, the more salad a spammer doles out, the better the job these filters are doing in identifying them as spam. Many of the algorithms discussed in this book have been implemented to perform advanced decoding of messages, enhancement of concept identification, and even data polishing to further enhance the effectiveness of filters. As spammers have invented new tricks to evade these types of filters, all statistical filters have needed is the occasional tweaking of code or turning of a knob by the filter author. Plenty of new tricks are being devised even today by spammers' programmers, but so far none have been found that actually work effectively enough to continue making money.

Successful Filtering

Being the anal-retentive hackers we are, we start to think that if a spammer has managed to get a single spam past our filter, the filter is a failure. It's a lot more work to get a message through to a hundred people (let alone a million) than it is to get it to one user, especially if each of those individuals has a different idea about what is and isn't spam. It's not going to be enough for a spammer to push their message past one user's filter—in order to make money, they have to get it through to tens of thousands of users, and get at least a handful of not-so-bright greenhorns to click their link. Many savvy filter users receive only one or two spams per month, or even less. This suggests that even though filters aren't 100 percent accurate, they are succeeding. Fortunately, there are dozens of different spam filters out there to choose from, and so spammers can't spend much time trying to find the weaknesses in any one filter. Because spam filtering isn't a monoculture, and because statistical filters are able to learn from their mistakes, spammers are delivering far fewer spams than they once did.

No More Headaches

During the time heuristic filters were popular, an arms race began between spammers and filter authors, in which spammers tried to evolve the features of spam faster than the filter authors could revise the rule sets. When statistical filtering came on the scene, things quickly changed, and spammers realized that they could no longer succeed in spamming simply by giving the developer a new headache. The playground quickly transformed, and statistical filters became the bully. Spammers are currently shifting their tactics to specifically target these new filters, and although there's a lot of media hype, the spam-*filtering* community now has the winning hand. We know we're winning, not only by the accuracy of our filters, but also by the fact that spammers are trying so many different tricks to target them.

The best way to beat a statistical filter is not to run one. It is to the spammers' benefit to continue the spread of misinformation about statistical filters—namely the misconception that they are ineffective. Any negative media hype or urban legends that can be propagated could turn people away from these types of filters, which is the only way spammers have found to evade them. Educating engineers about this misinformation is now a responsibility left up to, well, someone. Nobody wants to keep the spammers in business, and so convincing people that these approaches are futile is one way to help raise the overall accuracy of spam filtering (by getting more people involved in running the appropriate tools).

The nearsightedness of spammers gives us an advantage in our programming efforts. As we look at all of the common tricks spammers have incorporated, we'll see that they have been directed only at the present problem of the day—with absolutely no imagination invested in finding real ways to potentially beat a spam filter. Spammers still make basic, uneducated attempts to evade filters. Spamming is a slimeball business. You'd hardly find the best-of-breed hackers working for spammers; more often they're mediocre programmers looking for work. This fact has prevented statistical filtering from coming up against any intelligent counterattack. With the popularization of interpreted languages, CGI, and simple layout languages like HTML, a subculture has developed proclaiming the philosophy that reading a book about Perl or PHP, or learning how to do up a website in Microsoft FrontPage can make someone a real programmer. Talent is truly on our side in the fight against spam. No self-respecting, talented software developer wants anything to do with it, apart from using the Delete button, if necessary.

A Weak Link in Statistical Filters?

Statistical filtering has proven very unshakable, but our filters aren't made up entirely of statistical algorithms. Some heuristic-like algorithms are still used simply because we haven't yet trained our filters to learn *how* to learn on their own. Tokenization is one of the most common heuristic algorithms in these filters, and spammers are beginning to view them as targets. Since spammers can't shoot down the machine-learning pieces of the filter, they've found ways to make it more difficult to tokenize messages by using new types of encodings and trickery to hide text. The spammer will sometimes succeed in causing the tokenizer to tokenize junk, but this junk will then be a clear indicator of spam.

If there is one weak link in the spam filters of today, it is in the human-coded subroutines used to support this robust statistical engine. Heuristic algorithms have a much higher chance of failing, primarily because they do exactly what we've told them to do and nothing more.

Special care must therefore be taken in the design of our supporting heuristic algorithms, as they are clearly the weaker component of our unbreakable (to date) filters. We've already started to see these primitive operations as the ones more often under attack.

Attacks on Tokenizers

The most common attack in the past has been on tokenizers, the heuristic component of the filter that performs breakdown of the message's content. The responsibility for converting the message into meaningful data rests with the tokenizer. The most common approach spammers use is to obfuscate the message and try to confuse the heuristic functions so that they misinterpret the data. This approach could target not only the tokenizers but also the heuristic rule sets from the former generation of spam filters, as well as any other supporting algorithms used, such as data-polishing algorithms and even collaborative algorithms.

Encoding Abuses

As we discussed in Chapter 5, present-day Internet messages support a set of Multipurpose Internet Mail Extensions, or MIME. Part of MIME includes a series of encodings that can be used to convert non-ASCII data into ASCII data to support the existing mail transport infrastructure. MIME is frequently abused, however. Although it was originally intended to convert non-ASCII data, spammers have been using it for years to hide their message content.

The Problem

Obviously, if the filter can't read the message, it can't classify it as spam. The encoding most commonly used by spammers is Base64. This encoding is completely unintelligible to a human and doesn't even contain any delimiters to make machine analysis useful. A Base64-encoded message will be transported and will appear to the spam filter as a bunch of binary junk. The message will be decoded by the user's mail client back into its human-readable form, having never been read by and interpreted by a Base64-unaware spam filter.

The Solution

Fortunately, this problem has an easy solution: Just decode all Base64-encoded portions of the message. There are many public domain decoding tools that can be freely used to perform this decoding, or you can even write your own based on the encoding specification.

The Importance

This approach is still used today by many spammers as a last-ditch effort to push their spam through filters. It works only on the most primitive filters that are not Base64-aware, but that doesn't stop spammers from wasting the extra few processor cycles to do it. Some believe this is done to evade some outgoing-mail spam detectors, which may be encountered when spamming through an open relay. Even these types of filters are widely Base64-aware, but some may not be.

Header Encodings

Header encodings are just as easily abused by spammers as message body encodings. In Chapter 5, we discussed header encodings as a means of using alternate character sets and also provided a few examples of how spammers are using these encodings to conceal guilty text in the message headers.

The Problem

Filters that are unaware of header-based encoding are likely to miss key information embedded in the message headers. While the filter may be able to compensate for this omission of data by analyzing the rest of the message, some email that is starved for data (such as image spams), could be missed if this data is ignored.

```
Subject: =?iso-8859-1?B?U2lsZGVuYWZpbCBDaXRyYXRlICBTaGlwcGVkIFF1aWNrbHk=?=
From: "Cruz Maldonado" <cmaldonadosv@ccsg.tau.ac.il>
Date: Sat, 17 Apr 2004 22:13:28 +0000
MIME-Version: 1.0
Content-Type: text/plain
Content-Transfer-Encoding: 8bit
```

The human-readable data in these headers looks pretty innocent. When we decode the headers, however, we see that the subject is as guilty as they come.

```
Subject: Sildenafil Citrate Shipped Quickly
```

The Solution

The solution is easy—detect and decode portions of the message headers that are encoded. The encoding most commonly used by spammers is Base64, discussed in Chapter 5. Spam filters should be looking for these types of encodings in any of the message headers, not just in the subject. Spams use encoding in the From: headers, in the Subject:, and sometimes even in the To: headers. Multiple encoded blocks may be present in any one header, so it's important to be thorough.

The Importance

The importance of decoding headers is in finding the hidden content. Data that is encoded is likely to be some of the most guilty data in the spam. A majority of spam can still be classified without this information, but adding support for decoding will help whittle away at that annoying little 0.10 percent of messages that make it through most filters.

Hypertextus Interruptus

The term "hypertextus interruptus" was originally coined by Bill Yerazunis and cited in Dr. John Graham-Cumming's "The Spammers' Compendium" at http://jgc.org/tsc. HTML comments are a part of the original HTML specification and are designed to allow web page authors to insert miscellaneous comments about whatever it is they're coding in HTML. While these comments are present in the HTML source code of a document, they are not visible to the end user.

The Problem

HTML comments are abused by spammers to break up guilty-sounding words in spam. Since HTML comments are invisible to the end user, the original words will appear intact while the spam filter will see only a myriad of junk text.

```
Yes you he<!lansing>ard about th<!crossbill>ese weird <!cottony>little
pil<!domesday>ls that are suppo<!=anabel>sed to make you bigger and of
cou<!chord>rse you think they're b<!soften>ogus snake potion. Well, let's look
at the facts: <strong>G<!eigenspace>RX2 has be<!waldron>en sold over 1.9
Mill<!audacity>ion times within the last 18 months</strong>...
With awe<!tapestry>some results for hun<!wield>dreds of thous<!locale>ands of
men all over the planet! They all enjoy a seriously enhanced version of their
manh<!rescind>ood and <b>why shou<!seoul>ldn't you</b>?
```

At first glance, the text above looks like a bunch of junk with a few words here and there. That is how the spam filters would view the message and would likely end up delivering it. The end user would see the message entirely differently, once the hypertext comments were removed by their email client.

```
Yes you heard about these weird little pills
that are supposed to make you bigger and of course you think
they're bogus snake potion. Well, let's look at the facts: GRX2
has been sold over 1.9 Million times within the last 18 months...
With awesome results for hundreds of thousands of men all over the planet!
They all enjoy a seriously enhanced version of their manhood and why shouldn't
you?
```

The Solution

The solution to hypertext comments is to remove them, reassembling any words that they might have broken up. HTML comments can be identified by a leading <! symbol. Comments that span multiple lines usually end with –>, while short HTML comments end with just a single bracket >. Another thing spammers are doing to try to confuse filters is adding legitimate-sounding text to the HTML comments. Since the text inside HTML comments will never be viewable to the end user, the best practice is simply to ignore any data in comments. Finally, the hypertext being used to separate tokens doesn't have to be in the form of HTML comments. Nonexistent HTML tags containing random words can be used in the same way to split up guilty tokens. A tokenizer should be aware of HTML tags without spaces, or with a length that is too long to possibly be a legitimate HTML tag.

Spam filters using multiword tokenizers may end up identifying the individual tokens even without HTML comment filtering. For example, if the window size of the tokenizer is three, the tokenizer might recognize "manh<!rescind>ood" as three separate tokens, "manh," the comment, and "ood." Tokenizers such as SBPH, which we'll discuss in Chapter 11, will reassemble this using word skipping, but this approach is still imperfect.

Filtering out the HTML comments seems to be the easiest and best practice, as it both eliminates the fake legitimate data and puts an emphasis on the guilty data.

The Importance

Data loss could occur if some type of filtering isn't used to remove these HTML comments. Since these comments can be used anywhere in the message body, an entire message could be lost if the filter fails to assemble these tokens. On the other hand, an unaware filter will begin to learn these token fragments, such as "manh" and "ood" instead of "manhood," and eventually these will be clear identifiers of spam. This is a somewhat slower learning process, as spammers can break up guilty words in a number of different ways: "m," "ma," "man," "manh," "manho," and "manhoo." This increases the size of the dataset and takes longer, but once these tokens are trained they are usually very clear markers of spam.

ASCII Spam

Believe it or not, the first ASCII spam was actually detected about six months before this book was written. The idea behind ASCII spam is to provide nothing but junk data to the tokenizer so that it will pass the message through. ASCII spam uses ASCII art to draw pictures of concepts rather than spell them out or use images, which have a consistent framework. Fortunately, ASCII spams don't appear correctly in every mail client, and they are also not very good at providing the much-needed teasers spammers rely on to attract middle-aged men to click a pornographic link (as you can see in Figure 7-1).

The Problem

The tokenizer approaches we discuss in this book don't include any provisions for managing ASCII spam and will end up providing only the intelligible part of the message body and the message headers to the filter. ASCII spam generally consists of many different types of text, commonly a large percentage of characters that a filter would consider delimiters.

The Solution

There are many potential solutions for dealing with this kind of spam. Fortunately, many of the characters in this type of spam are normally treated as delimiters. This results in much of the message content being ignored, which will help whatever guilty data there is to stick out. The rest will be tokenized as garble, but it's useful garble. I've seen only a few different ASCII spams, but many of them use the same types of garble to construct words and objects (primarily naked ladies, which generally have the same artistic detail as the mud-flap girls on semi-trailers—mama sita!). One thing spammers just can't get around is that they have to provide a link to click on or some other way to contact them. It's possible for this link also to be an illustration of ASCII art, but then the spammer would lose their instant-click or copy-paste feature. The URL itself, which is the spammer's only means of contact, becomes more prominent in the absence of any other message body data and that helps to detect them.

Since these URLs are important, the tokenizer should include URL-specific tokens as part of its implementation. Header tokens are also important. Finally, if all else fails, collaborative algorithms such as message inoculation are very effective at inoculating the other users in a group with certain types of ASCII spam. This usually isn't necessary, though. My filter doesn't seem to have any trouble identifying the few ASCII spams I did receive, based on all of the other information in the message. I suspect that if things get worse and ASCII spams start to pop up everywhere, filters will easily adapt to identify them. ASCII spams are also cheesy, and spammers appear to realize this. The "teaser" effect is pretty much lost when using ASCII, so it behooves the spammer not to use it. Still, should a spam get through it's much better than letting a raunchy picture spam through and might even give you a little giggle at what a corny spammer you're dealing with.

Figure 7-1: An ASCII spam

The Importance

ASCII spam hasn't been used enough to determine whether or not it will affect the accuracy of filters, but it is believed it will do so to some small degree. Messages like this are commonly evaluated based on their message headers and any plain text included in the message body. Some commonly used constructive text may also help not only to identify the message as spam but also to categorize these types of spams by artist. This is an area on which filter developers will definitely be focusing in the future, as the approach becomes more popularized.

Text-Splitting

We've already discussed how spammers use HTML comments to break up guilty-sounding tokens. Another approach they are using is *text-splitting*. Text-splitting is designed to degenerate guilty tokens into mere characters, making them indistinguishable from legitimate uses of the letters.

The Problem

Text-splitting uses a series of known delimiters to break up guilty-sounding tokens into single characters. For example,

```
From: Alicia Johnson <Alicia_Johnson___r-vtgzcjtkgcakvb@wholebargain.com>
Reply-To: Alicia Johnson <Alicia_Johnson___r-vtgzcjtkgcakvb@wholebargain.com>
Subject: Get your F/R/E/E 10 Day Supply N/O/W!
Mime-Version: 1.0
Content-Type: multipart/alternative;
        boundary="_----------=_2656431139258145356951"
List-Unsubscribe: <mailto:unsub-vtgzcjtkgcakvb@wholebargain.com>
```

In this message, the subject includes guilty text that was split up using delimiter characters. This approach isn't limited to a message's headers; it can be used in the message body as well. If the filter doesn't compensate for this, the data could become lost or wind up as degenerate in the dataset.

The idea behind this type of attack is to prevent the filter from seeing the words "FREE" and "NOW!" and instead to make it see only letters, which may leave it uncertain about the disposition of the message.

The Solution

Fortunately, this approach backfires most of the time. There is plenty of other guilty data for the filter to work with, and most filters have no problem identifying spams that use this technique. Even heuristic-based filters have coded additional rule sets to identify the extensive use of obfuscation. Statistical filters may or may not use the individual characters that result in the dataset. Some data is just as guilty in its single-character form as it is in a whole-word form. For example, the letters "S" and "X" by themselves are extremely guilty in my dataset.

To compensate for text-splitting, some filters have applied a form of token reassembly that will search for single-character tokens adjacent to other single-character tokens and attempt to group them together. For example,

```
F-R-E-E  V/I/A/G/R/A
```

can easily be reassembled into "FREE" and "VIAGRA" just by looking for adjacent single characters.

Since there are a lot of different ways to split up text in this fashion, tokens don't always reassemble perfectly. They are usually accurate enough for the filter to identify anyway, such as the token "AGRA." A multiword-capable tokenizer can also identify the different components of partly reassembled tokens and form joined tokens such as "VI+AGRA."

There are only a finite number of different ways to split up individual words. By the time they've seen a few spams, most filters have learned what they need to know to successfully identify the different permutations in future messages.

Other ways that spammers split up text include the use of non-commenting HTML tags. For example,

```
V<FONT SIZE=0> </FONT>
I<FONT SIZE=0> </FONT>
A<FONT SIZE=0> </FONT>
G<FONT SIZE=0> </FONT>
R<FONT SIZE=0> </FONT>
A
```

These types of approaches are futile, because they provide even more interesting data than the original guilty word. The different font tags and other types of HTML junk inserted between characters are an easy identifier of spam. Implementing multiword-capable tokenizers, such as chained tokens (which we'll discuss in Chapter 11), can greatly improve the ability to identify these types of attacks, although it is rarely necessary to do so. One advantage these advanced tokenizers have is the ability to associate each letter with an HTML tag to generate a very guilty token used exclusively by spammers.

And that's the catch—spammers can use whatever obfuscation techniques they want to obscure text, but they leave plenty of trace evidence that the filter is capable of learning. Filters have a way of performing their own "email forensics" to detect these subtle attempts.

The Importance

Just like other approaches to obfuscation, text-splitting can potentially cause data loss. Also like other approaches, the degenerated data may be more interesting than the original data. Text reassembly is one of those areas where a self-evaluating algorithm could be used to determine if certain texts should be reassembled.

Table-Based Obfuscation

A rarely used approach to breaking up guilty text involves using a table to break words up into individual characters for each line. When the message is displayed to the user, the characters are reassembled, making the message appear as if it were a whole text. John Graham-Cumming first identified this approach in "The Spammers' Compendium."

The Problem

Text that is split up using tables is difficult to reassemble. As a result, much of the data could possibly be lost, leaving the filter with a limited amount of data to classify the message.

```
<table cellpadding=0 cellspacing=0 border=0><tr>
<td><table cellspacing=0 cellpadding=0 border=0><tr><td>
<font face="Courier New, Courier, mono" size=2>
 <br>U<br> <br>O<br>a<br> <br>D<br>u<br>a
<br> <br>N<br> <br>B<br>d<br> <br>N<br>
<br>C<br> <br>C<br>w<br> <br>1<br> <br>
<br> <br>1<br> <br>C<br>S<br></font></td></tr></table></td>
<td><table cellspacing=0 cellpadding=0 border=0><tr><td><font
face="Courier New, Courier, mono" size=2>
   <br> N <br>   <br>bta
<br>nd <br>   <br>ipl<br>niv<br>nd <br>
   <br>o r<br>   <br>ach<br>ipl
<br>   <br>o o<br>   <br>onf<br>
   <br>ALL<br>ith<br>   <br> -
<br>   <br>   <br>   <br>
 - <br>   <br>all<br>und<br></font></td></tr></table></td>
<td><table cellspacing=0 cellpadding=0 border=0><tr><td><font
face="Courier New, Courier, mono" size=2>
   <br>I V<br>   <br>in <br>the
<br>   <br>oma<br>ers<br>lif<br>   <br>equ
<br>   <br>elo<br>oma<br>   <br>ne <br>
  <br>ide<br>   <br> NO<br>in <br>
  <br>3 1<br>   <br>
<br>   <br>2 1<br>   <br> 24<br>ays
<br></font></td></tr></table></td>
<td><table cellspacing=0 cellpadding=0 border=0><tr><td><font face="Courier
New, Courier, mono" size=2>
  <br> E<br>   <br>a <br> a<br>
<br>s <br>it<br>e <br>   <br>ir<br>   <br>rs<br>s
 <br>   <br>is<br>   <br>nt<br>   <br>W
<br>da<br>   <br> 2<br>   <br>   <br>
 <br> 2<br>   <br> h<br> a<br></font></td></tr></table></td>
```

What looks like a garble of text actually appears in the recipient's mail client looking like a legitimate whole message (shown in Figure 7-2). This approach is particularly devious but requires a bit of work and isn't guaranteed to succeed.

```
UNIVERSITY  DIPLOMAS

Obtain a prosperous future, money earning power,
and the admiration of all.

Diplomas from prestigious non-accredited
universities based on your present knowledge
and life experience.

No required tests, classes, books, or interviews.

Bachelors, masters, MBA, and doctorate (PhD)
diplomas available in the field of your choice.

No one is turned down.

Confidentiality assured.

CALL NOW to receive your diploma
within days!!!

1 - 3 1 2 - 6 8 3 - 5 2 3 3

              OR                       (U.S.A)

1 - 2 1 2 - 4 7 9 - 0 8 7 0

Call 24 hours a day, 7 days a week, including
Sundays and holidays.
```

Figure 7-2: A mail client's rendering of a table-sliced message (courtesy of "The Spammers' Compendium," http://jgc.org/tsc)

The Solution

As is the case with many approaches like this, the amount of HTML code it takes to generate this kind of attack is itself a very detectable marker of spam. The use of many different combinations of HTML tags, such as table identifiers, often gives away the message as spam. The degenerated data itself can even provide useful evidence for the filter. Message headers can also be dead giveaways. All of the typical bogus information used in headers can't be avoided using this approach, and ultimately most filters can still effectively identify these types of messages.

Filter authors could code a rather complex "pre-filter" to parse this information. The parsing would first break up the table column by column and assemble individual column cells together. In most cases, however, this is too much work. Since this approach is used only rarely and is easily detectable without parsing the table, most filters don't need to do anything special to detect these messages.

The Importance

Most filter authors prefer to allow the tokenizer to grab all of the useful HTML that this spamming approach uses, which then becomes a clear identifier of spam. It's not necessary for a filter to directly implement any type of table disassembly or token reassembly, and many believe that doing so even hurts accuracy. As long as approaches like this continue to leave an HTML signature of what they're doing, it won't be necessary to counter these types of attacks.

URL Encodings

Previously, we've discussed the use of encodings to translate different parts of a message. Another type of encoding that is frequently abused is *URL encoding*. It's still unclear why web browsers incorporated some types of URL encoding, as they appear only to promote misdirection. For example, some older versions of browsers support the 32-bit representation of an IP address, or even a hexadecimal representation. This support has been removed in some newer versions of browsers to prevent malicious use but still exists in many mainstream web browsers. Unfortunately, the more important encodings are necessary to prevent special characters such as spaces and such in URLs.

The Problem

URL encodings that use hexadecimal codes can be used to break up guilty tokens inside a URL. For example,

```
http://127.0.0.1/%69%6e%64%65%78%2e%68%74%6d%6c
```

is actually an encoded representation of

```
http://127.0.0.1/index.html
```

Other types of encoding can include the use of HTML ASCII values to create characters. The same URL could be represented as follows:

```
&#104;&#116;&#116;&#112;&#58;&#47;&#47;&#49;&#50;&#55;&#46;&#48;&#46;&#48;&#46
;&#49;&#47;&#105;&#110;&#100;&#101;&#120;&#46;&#104;&#116;&#109;&#108;&#0;
```

The actual URL isn't clickable but could easily be embedded in an HTML message for show.

The Solution

Filters should be aware of these encodings in URLs and perform decoding on them. Although there is most likely a significant amount of other information in the email to qualify it as spam, it's possible that microspams (spams containing very little data) containing only a single encoded URL could pass through the filter if they aren't first decoded. URL-specific tokens can also make the identification of these microspams easier.

The Importance

The encoded portions of the URL are usually the guiltiest. If a tokenizer were to leave the URLs encoded, it would generate tokens such as "105," "110," and so on, which correspond to the decimal codes for individual characters. This by itself *may* be useful information, but the guilty words in URLs are often believed to be even more revealing. Some filters also ignore whole numbers unless they are mixed with some other punctuation, such as a dollar sign. If the filter doesn't decode these types of URLs, it should at the very least use a pound sign in the token to set them apart from other types of numeric tokens.

Symbolic Text

The use of special characters and numbers to replace certain characters in guilty tokens has been seen in the wild since around the end of 2002.

The Problem

Guilty tokens are obfuscated with numbers and special characters to prevent spam filters from detecting them.

---

wõrk fr[]m hOme
v1agrá

The Solution

These types of attacks are actually beneficial to identifying spam, because they set the text apart from legitimate text. Since these tokens are different from their plain-text counterparts, filters usually look at them as a completely different token—one that no legitimate user would ever use. Tokenizers can be made aware of these types of tricks, although in most cases no action is required to cause this attack to backfire on spammers.

The Importance

No special dispensation needs to be made for these types of tricks. In fact, spammers are doing us a favor by using them, as they are clear indicators of spam. No legitimate message would use the word "v1agrá." One of the biggest mistakes spammers can make is using approaches that generate unique identifiers of spam.

Just Plain Dumb

Plenty of approaches to obfuscating the message are just plain dumb and not worth even considering in the coding of filter. In spite of popular myth, the approaches in this section are generally ineffective and lack in imagination. Some of these include the following.

Breaking Up URLs (Dumb)

Spammers will break up the URL to their website so that the spam filter doesn't consider it to be a URL-specific token. For example,

```
type http://www then the following URL into your web browser:
.somewebsite.com/somepage.html
```

It's true that this will prevent somewebsite.com from ever being treated as a URL-specific token, but the spammer will be able to get away with this only once before the token is learned. On top of this, the spammer generates more guilty-sounding text by giving the user instructions for typing in the URL! It's unlikely that such a message would ever get past a trained filter, even the first time.

Embedded JavaScript (Really Dumb)

Some spam has been cleverly devised to include the entire message contents in JavaScript. The JavaScript will then populate the message window when the user opens the document. This type of trick may fool some unaware heuristic filters but is ultimately useless against statistical filters because it leaves so much trace evidence. Any email with embedded JavaScript is suspicious, and the fingerprint many spams provide is easy to identify. On top of this, many mail clients have moved away from allowing JavaScript to run inside an email, so the email would appear blank to the end user.

Removal of Whitespace (Stupid)

One of the more idiotic ideas spammers have had includes removing AllTheWhiteSpaceFromAMessage. The idea is to trick spam filters by making the text unintelligible without delimiters. This approach works all too well and makes the message undecipherable—even to humans! Since this affects the spammer's message itself (not to mention making the spammer look stupid), this approach is very rare and is found only among the dumbest spammers.

Attacks on the Dataset

There have been a few attacks on the actual data in the dataset. The ultimate goal is to either poison the filter with guilty data it thinks is legitimate or neutralize existing data that the filter thinks is guilty. Dataset attacks aren't as widespread as other types of attacks, but they can be effective for sending out one specific distribution targeting a small group of users. Since these types of attacks require dedicated work and attention, spammers are unlikely to use them, and only a limited number of attempts has been seen.

Mailing List Attacks

Mailing list attacks have recently become popular as a last-ditch effort to get spam through. The purpose of abusing a mailing list is that many statistical filters learn over time to trust all messages originating from such lists, putting confidence in messages with the list's headers, subject markers, and embedded taglines.

How It Works

The spammer subscribes to a mailing list and begins harvesting addresses from the list. Usually the spammer will spend a month or two just listening in to acquire a list of valid email addresses and will possibly even use a Bayesian algorithm to determine the most likely candidates for legitimate tokens among mailing list users. The attack begins in one of two ways. First, the spammer could easily just send a spam to the list. If the list is unmoderated, the spam will go out to all mailing list members with the headers, markers, and taglines specific to the list. Any users on the mailing list whose statistical filters have learned the particular characteristics of the list will be at risk of having the message misclassified as a legitimate message. Since this approach generally works only once per mailing list, the spammer will attempt to forge as many of the headers as possible and send out several spams at once from their own mail server. Even though some of the list's headers won't be present, such as the IP address of the list's mail server, enough information can usually be copied from the original list email to spoof a legitimate message from the list.

Why It Doesn't Work

Fortunately, this technique typically works only once or twice, as the statistical filter will then correct itself and learn not to trust the list based on its identifying marks alone. Not all filters train on every message either, and these are less likely to be tricked by this type of attack. Nevertheless, it can work once or twice. Since this approach requires work on the spammer's part, you don't see it very often. Also, spammers are able to target only individuals who are actually on the list (it won't work at all to send a spoofed message to a nonmember). Since they are used to sending mass messages to millions of individuals per day, putting them in a box where they may reach only a thousand certainly cuts back on their ability to profit. In addition, most individuals on a mailing list are likely to be savvy users; they are not generally interested in spam, and therefore the response rate should be even lower for spamming a list.

The Importance

The lesson in mailing list spam is that there are many sources of email out there that our filters have trusted implicitly. Many people debate the wisdom of trusting individual sources, but everyone agrees that a mailing list should never be considered a trusted source, even if it's moderated. Statistical filters do a good job of distrusting lists that spam has originated from, and so this error is generally dismissed as a process that is worked out by the user's training loop. Filters that wish to implement some type of specific counter-action for this type of attack can refuse to assign extreme values to header tokens, although this generally isn't necessary.

Bayesian Poisoning

Bayesian poisoning can be employed in many different ways, although the most common is through a mailing list or series of blank probes (email with an empty message body, usually sent for the purpose of detecting the existence of your email account). Bayesian poisoning is designed to trick the dataset into thinking that several different pseudo-tokens are legitimate. These pseudo-tokens are usually random strings made up by the spammer. Random strings of text on their own are meaningless and have no chance of evading a statistical filter, because unknown words are generally given a very neutral probability. In order for these random words to be successful in evading a filter, they have to be programmed into the filter as legitimate words. On top of this, they have to be interesting enough that they're likely to appear in the decision matrix, and they must appear in enough abundance to flood the decision matrix with so much legitimate data that there is no room for the spam.

How It Works

Bayesian poisoning is a covert operation. The spammer will usually subscribe to a mailing list or find other ways to send innocuous email to a large group of users—email that has a very low chance of being reported into the system as spam. Apart from mailing list messages, this could potentially include blank messages or bogus mailer-daemon notifications. These emails will appear legitimate but will have several hidden tokens embedded in the message—usually in the headers. Over a period of time, these tokens will be learned by some statistical filters. It is beneficial for the spammer to send messages that are likely not even to be read but just deleted. What's most important to this operation is that the target user remain unaware of what's going on. One of the simplest ways to do this on a mailing list is to reply to an existing thread without saying anything of much importance.

```
To: <full-disclosure@lists.netsys.com>
From: ross9917@Flashmail.com
Subject: Re: Cross-Site Scripting Vulnerability
Date: Wed, 10 Jul 2002 04:09:18 -0700
MIME-Version: 1.0
Content-Type: text/plain
X-Wajdf0ief: wlekfjlwefk lkjfewln l fwekl ewfkj l1eoi1e02 21e 0e1j 0j

Wow, thanks for this information!
```

Over a period of time, several different subtle tokens are created in a user's dictionary as the spammer continues to insert hidden headers. The random tokens would need to be repeated several times in order to adequately train the user's dictionary. In addition to this, the spammer would most likely choose alternating sets of tokens so as to build a larger corpus of data in the user's dataset.

```
To: <full-disclosure@lists.netsys.com>
From: ross9917@Flashmail.com
Subject: Re: Vulnerability in Linux Kernel v2.4
Date: Wed, 10 Jul 2002 04:09:18 -0700
MIME-Version: 1.0
Content-Type: text/plain
X-q0djq0dw9j: lkej lwk23 01 0fwj0 w0j 9 09jr320 j09jr32lnfdlkn lkf wef

Wow, thanks for this information!
```

Over a short period of time, these random tokens have trained TOE filters of all of the users on the mailing list. Ideally, the spammer would train 30 to 45 tokens minimum, to attempt to flood the decision matrix with data that now has a very low probability in the dataset. When the spammer decides to send the spam, they'll usually send a microspam with as little guilty information as possible. What ultimately leads to the spammer's success, however, is these once-unknown tokens, which have been trained as innocent. The spam gets sent, either through the mailing list or with forged headers.

```
To: <full-disclosure@lists.netsys.com>
From: ross9917@Flashmail.com
Subject: Enjoy!
Date: Wed, 10 Jul 2002 04:09:18 -0700
MIME-Version: 1.0
Content-Type: text/plain
X-q0djq0dw9j: lkej lwk23 01 0fwj0 w0j 9 09jr320 j09jr32lnfdlkn lkf wef
X-Wajdf0ief: wlekfjlwefk lkjfewln l fwekl ewfkj l1eoi1e02 21e 0e1j 0j
<10 other poisoned sets of header data>

<html>
<head>
<title>Dietary Supplement</title>
</head>
<body link=3D"#FFFFFF" alink=3D"#FFFFFF"  vlink=3D"#FFFFFF">
<table width=3D525 cellpadding=3D5 border=3D0><tr><td><p>
<img src=3D"http://www.hebalist.com/m1.jpg"></p>
</td></tr></table>
<table width=3D525 cellpadding=3D5 border=3D0><tr>
<td  valign=3Dmiddle><p>
<img src=3D"http://www.hebalist.com/m3.jpg"><br>
<a href=3D"http://www.hebalist.com?id=3D610">
<img src=3D"http://www.hebalist.com/m2.jpg"></a></p></td>
</tr></table>
<table width=3D525 cellpadding=3D5 border=3D0><tr><td><p>
```

```
<a href=3D"http://www.hebalist.com/service.html">
<img src=3D"http://www.hebalist.com/m4.jpg"></a></p>
</td></tr></table>
</body>
</html>
```

Another way to poison users' databases is to do just the opposite—to feed some would-be guilty tokens into innocent messages to deprogram the filter. Just a few words at a time is all the spammer can get away with, but if they're able to dumb down words in the filter that they plan on using in future spam, they'll have a much better chance of making their message through the filter.

Why It Doesn't Work

Fortunately, once users receive the spam and train their filters with it, the tokens become useless to the spammer. The tokens also require more than a single message to train on—filters originating from Graham's research generally require a minimum of three innocent occurrences before the tokens are considered "real." The forged mailing list headers are also useless, as the data no longer favors the mailing list. The data from the Received: headers, which is not easily forged, has also been trained, marking the origin of the spam distribution.

All in all, this approach is not very beneficial to the spammers as it takes time and resources, and usually results in a very low success rate. If the process is spread out over too long a period of time, the spammer risks having the tokens purged from users' datasets. The spammer has truly worked for their one spam in time and computing power. The approach is effective but is not lucrative for the spammer. Nevertheless, as statistical filtering continues to become mainstream, spammers may use desperate attempts like this more often.

Statistical filters that want to protect themselves against these types of attacks can take several precautions to avoid allowing the dataset to be poisoned. First, the filter could be designed to detect unknown headers and make sure they're brought to the attention of the user (or administrator). Injecting unknown headers into a collaborative tracking system could easily identify these types of attacks before they became useful for the spammer. Even invisible ink is somewhat detectable in the message body, more so than headers that nobody looks at. *Invisible ink* is the process of hiding tokens by making them the same font color as the background. They alone are a good indicator of spam.

```
<FONT COLOR=WHITE>lwefkj lkjfe lkwfjlwekf</FONT>
```

Some filter authors prefer to ignore any text in invisible ink, while others don't see it as enough of a statistical problem to worry about.

The second way of protecting against this type of attack is to change the training modes so as not to allow extreme data that would permit mailing lists and other tokens to become implicitly trusted. If your filter isn't training on every new word, then it's not likely to be poisoned by this kind of data. In order for a spammer to poison a dataset protected by TOE-mode training, for example, they would have to convince the spam filter to quarantine the message as spam and then convince the user that the message was a false positive. This is quite an ambitious task, however, and is improbable in most cases as even dumb users aren't about to mark a suspicious message as a false positive—and the message would have had to been made suspicious in order to be quarantined in the first place.

Finally, some filters have experimented with giving preference to guilty tokens over legitimate tokens when the probabilities are tied. This will ensure that decision matrices don't get flooded with bogus data but that the guilty data will always be considered first. Other implementations attempt to interleave the dispositions of tokens with similar probabilities.

The initial philosophy when statistical filters were designed was to give bias toward legitimate mail. As filters have become more and more accurate, this bias has started to tip in the other direction, and ideals that were once rejected for fear of false positives are now feasible solutions that actually improve the accuracy of filters. This makes perfect sense, as the average user's email is now upward of 85 percent spam. Some unfortunate souls out there receive 90 to 95 percent spam.

The Importance

Bayesian poisoning warrants some concern, but because it requires a lot of work on the spammer's part, it isn't something filter authors should be overly paranoid about. It's important to find ways to counter Bayesian poisoning to avoid the possibility for this approach to become widespread in the future. Decommissioning this type of attack by implementing training modes other than TEFT or by finding other defenses will help prevent Bayesian poisoning from becoming mainstream. Mail client authors should also become aware of better ways to alert the user to unorthodox headers to expose innocent looking poisoning attempts. Ultimately, Bayesian poisoning could be used successfully to circumvent some filters, and therefore it's important to consider training, collaborative filtering, and other approaches for fighting it before it's an issue.

Empty but Not Empty Probes

Lately, a flood of emails with empty message bodies have been circulating around the Internet. Many of these messages have been simple probes by spammers to figure out what email addresses are valid—some implementing a form of web bug hidden in HTML code and others using exclusion lists based on the bounce messages returned. A *web bug* is an HTML object embedded in an email, such as an image or other resource, that loads automatically when the email is previewed or opened. When the user's email client makes a connection to the spammer's server to acquire the resource, a special piece of data embedded in the URL "phones home" telling the spammer which recipient is requesting the object. This confirms the validity of the email address and also confirms that the person received the probe. Most newer email clients have a feature to prevent the loading of external images (and other objects), but this feature is usually disabled by default.

How It Works

The philosophy behind empty message probes hinges on the presumption that the user will simply delete the message rather than train their filter on it. Since many filters are still cumbersome in training, users generally prefer to train spams only when they receive one. Because most users don't realize that many of these empty messages are spam, they're more likely to just delete them rather than insert them into whatever type of training cycle is available for the filter.

The empty messages can contain invisible headers, just as they do in Bayesian poisoning attempts. As the user continues to delete these messages, the tokens will eventually train in the user's dataset. Finally, a single spam is sent, using these tokens as "keys" to fool the statistical filters. Spammers know they can use these tokens only once before they have to be reprogrammed, and so it is more beneficial to try to perform this type of training on a mass crowd of millions of users. Empty messages are one of the only vehicles for doing this.

Why It Doesn't Work

There are some obvious problems with this approach. We've already discussed the problem that tokens become useless once the first spam is sent, after which they become only a marker for additional identification of the spams. Another problem with this approach is that a series of blank messages is far less likely to make it through an individual's inbox without raising some suspicion—after a few, someone will undoubtedly begin to examine the messages and either discover what's going on or automatically punt them into the spam bucket. The third problem is that many spam filters (among other tools) will dump any messages containing an empty body. Finally, as we discussed previously, empty messages don't necessarily train every filter out there, only TEFT-based filters. If the tokens that the spammer is attempting to deprogram have already matured, this approach won't work in TUM-based filters any more than it will in TOE-based filters.

In conclusion, all attempts to poison a user's dataset are potentially effective only with filters that perform TEFT-mode training. Although filters that perform this training are susceptible to these types of attacks, the attacks themselves are very tricky and require a lot of resources that most spammers just won't find profitable. Too many people make the mistake of thinking that spammers are motivated by sending spams; they're not—they're motivated by how much money they can make. While in many cases, sending email does equate to making money, most spammers do realize over long periods of time that attempts like this are mostly futile and not nearly as lucrative as blindly sending out ten million messages.

The Importance

Probes should be trained into the spam filter for all of the reasons just discussed. Since they could be used to train new tokens and exploit some training modes, empty messages could become more widespread if users aren't educated in the proper handling of these potential probes.

Attacks on the Decision Matrix

The decision matrix is another area that is frequently attacked by spammers. The goal of attacking the decision matrix is to flood it with a significant amount of either meaningless or legitimate-sounding data, so that it doesn't see the more guilty data in the message, or to starve the decision matrix of enough information to make a useful decision.

Image Spams

Image spams are one of the ways in which spammers attempt to starve the decision matrix of information. This type of spam is also used to try and circumvent heuristic-based filters by providing so little data that it's difficult to determine whether the message is spam or not. Unfortunately, a heuristic filter can't simply filter out any messages containing images, as many legitimate senders include these. Many legitimate senders also have the annoying habit of sending a message whose entire content is a single image—and others like it!

The Problem

Image spams frequently provide very little data to work with, but they still contain more than enough for a statistical filter to accurately identify the message. These types of spam usually consist of a small amount of HTML to include a remote image in the message.

```
X-Sender: offer888.net
X-Mailid: 3444431.13
Errors-To: report@offer888.net
Complain-To: abuse@offer888.net
From: Trimlife <trimlife@offer888.net>
Subject: Lose Inches and Look Great This Summer!
X-Keywords:
Content-Type: text/html;


<html>
<head>
<title>Untitled Document</title>
<meta http-equiv="Content-Type" content="text/html; charset=iso-8859-1">
</head>
```

```
<body bgcolor="#FFFFFF" text="#000000" leftmargin="0" topmargin="0"
marginwidth="0" marginheight="0">

<a href="http://track.offer888.net/cgi-bin/trimlife?e=3444431.13"> <img
src="http://www.freeze.com/snow/standalones/images/Creative--003.gif"
width="450" height="300" border="0"></a>
</body>
</html>
```

One of the side effects of this approach is that it gives the spammers an opportunity to create what Graham-Cumming refers to as a *feedback loop.* Since the image has to be loaded from one of the spammer's servers, it's easy to embed a unique identifier into the URL of the image so that the spammer can keep track of who views (or previews) the message. When the user's email client receives the spam and either highlights it for preview or opens it at the user's request, the image will be loaded from the server and will most likely confirm to the spammer that the recipient's address was valid. It also confirms to the spammer that whatever lexical data was used in the spam was successful in evading whatever filter may have been protecting the user's mailbox, helping them devise a directed attack (discussed later).

The Solution

Many recent versions of email clients have been outfitted with an option to disable the loading of images embedded in HTML. This is a wise move, as it both prevents the spammer's web bug from working and prevents the user from having to look at what could potentially be objectionable material— especially if you happen to be sitting down with one of your kids.

Apart from client-side filtering, spam filters can easily identify these types of messages based on content. It takes a certain amount of HTML to construct a message like this, and many of the frequently guilty tokens include the content headers and different combinations of HTML tags.

Token	SH	IH	Probability
img+src	00050	00000	0.9999
Url*http	00087	00003	0.8530
img+border	00050	00000	0.9999
Url*image	00051	00001	0.9137

On top of this, web bugs and other types of markers work to our advantage. For example, the presence of my email address in a URL yields a probability of 0.9999. The same goes for unique identifiers, such as long numbers, that can be used to track you over a long period of time. Even the simplest HTML conventions used by the spammers' generators are a clear indicator of spam. The phrase "Untitled+Document" also yields a probability of 0.9999 in my dataset.

Essentially, the solution to catching these types of spam is to implement machine learning in your spam filter, which is what this entire book is designed to teach you to do. Additional accuracy can be achieved by using a concept-based tokenizer, which we'll discuss in Chapter 11. Finally, tokenizing header and URL-specific tokens will provide additional data points to analyze.

The Importance

Image spams starve the language classifier for information, and although there is generally still enough information to classify the message, this technique, combined with additional approaches, could potentially hurt accuracy in some filters that use primitive tokenizers. Implementing concept tokenizers or taking other steps to counter these types of approaches is important, to ensure that the filter has enough data to work with. If it doesn't, it could degenerate into an image tag classifier, which could create false positives in some legitimate newsletters and such.

Random Strings of Text

Nobody's quite certain who initially came up with the concept of injecting random strings of text into emails to confuse filters, but the myth that this approach helps to circumvent statistical filters about as credible as the lone gunman theory. A typical random-string spam will contain the spam payload and then a series of random pieces of junk text somewhere in the message—usually in an unreadable portion of the message. It was originally thought that these unknown words would help messages score a more innocent probability, since they would include several words the filter knew nothing about. Possibly some of the earliest naive Bayesian filters could have been vulnerable to this approach, but any window of opportunity for it is long since past.

The Problem

Spammers will embed a long series of random junk text into spams in an attempt to evade filters.

```
From: "alvin" <swbeetp08@hotmail.com>
Sender: swbeetp08@hotmail.com
Subject: Never have a hangover again! bernie isaacPill that cures hangovers!
Content-Type: text/plain;

Come and play at the world's PREMIPill that cures hangovers!ERE ONLINCure your
hangover with just a pill!E CASCure your hangover with just a pill!INO!
We are happy to offer you, in an elegant atmosphere, a 50% BONUHangover pills
are finally here!S for YOUR FIRST DEPOCure your hangover with just a pill!SIT
as a New Player.

Sign up now! Don't wait!

http://www.virtualcasinoes.net/_e4faa55afa1972493c43ac8a3f66f869/
```

```
wlefk lkwejf 2l3fj 2l3klew fhewlf jhewlk jewflk jfelkfew j
lfewjnbwlkfejlewkjfwelfkjh lkjhfelkj hewflkjhlk kljw hfelkjew lf hlkj
alflo2lkjl  qweoijwfe0923 oiv09juwflk32 fjnhoijn fewkjn43
wfeoi2j329f8hj 29f8 h29f hwfiu hfew98wh fohjnkjnld nbzpwefwef poewf
```

The Solution

The only necessary solution, which is implemented by just about all modern-day filters, is to assign unknown words a fairly neutral value so that they won't influence the decision of the filter. The standard among most filters is generally 0.4000 or 0.5000. Since these unknown words have never appeared before in the user's dataset, they will be assigned this neutral value, with the result that the more guilty-sounding text will rising to the top of the decision matrix.

Quite ironically, these types of random text are sometimes very clear indicators of spam. Spammers are usually too lazy to rotate the random text often enough to keep it new to the filter, and as a result, the filter learns them as clear markers of spam. Some believe that the random text doesn't always change because it is the tail end of a Bayesian poisoning approach. If this is indeed the case, the spammers have done us a favor by leaving these identifying markers for our filters to see.

The Importance

Being one of the dumber ideas spammers have come up with, this approach isn't particularly important, except for the need to understand that all the media hype about it is false.

Word Salad

Injecting random words into a message is a little different from injecting random text. The goal of the spammer in launching *word salad* attacks is to make the filter think that the content is legitimate by hiding the more guilty-sounding tokens. In this case, the spammer will proceed to pick several different words out of a dictionary, from a list of last names, or from other lists, with the goal of hitting on words that may have an innocent disposition in the recipients' datasets.

The Problem

Spammers embed hundreds of dictionary words in their spam in an attempt to flood the decision matrix with innocent tokens. The tokens used will range from common household words to more specific words that may be more likely to generate hits on some users' datasets (for example, "Quebec" or "Marvin").

```
From: "Frank Mansfield" <rynzoten@oddpost.com>
Reply-To: "Frank Mansfield" <rynzoten@oddpost.com>
To: jonathan@networkdweebs.com
Subject: Please her like never before
Date: Sat, 10 Aug 2002 02:57:07 -0400
```

```
14613317844455311
```

```
Did you know That the normal cost for Super vi@*gr@ is $20, per dose?
We are running a hot special!! TODAY Its only an amazing $3.00
Sh1pped world wide!
http://conserve.dryydd.com/py/a
```

```
repetitious stoke hartford floodlight can't nab capitulate millenia resusc=
itate bela eden drone countywide pi cerebral toccata siemens blackberry co=
ntusion bedtime deflater cambridge phenomena teresa syntax bum astraddle c=
onvoke decor argive guesswork menelaus litigant andromeda intent trigonome=
try dixon polygonal=20 abetted discrete franz scripture amplitude boeing t=
ype eeoc belt crafty warhead bosch transcendent earnest africa protrude ed=
wardine crest crossway carey saturnalia warwick plug aerospace marksmen cr=
aftsmen show matinal hexameter advisable kodiak horatio infight jaime=20
```

These tokens can be anywhere in the message. They are sometimes hidden in one of the many ways spammers use to hide text, such as inside a separate part of the message, in form variables, or even inside HTML tags. The text can also be right out in the open, usually appended to the end of the message, as in this example. Since the goal is to flood a decision matrix, the spammer knows they have to have at least 15 to 20 solid hits, and so several different words are used. Some messages have used up to a thousand or more random words.

The Solution

This approach rarely works in modern-day statistical filters, because the filter is smarter than the spammer. Graham-Cumming provided an excellent presentation about word salad spams at the MIT Spam Conference in 2004. To prove that these types of spams had no effect on spam filters, he took several microspams (also known as *picospams*), which contain very little data, and added hundreds of random words from his dictionary, websites, and even Wikipedia (an online encyclopedia; http://www.wikipedia.org). He then sent the messages through his filter, which in the very worst case allowed only 0.04 percent of the messages through. Achieving an error rate this high required that the recipient be sent over 10,000 spams and that each message increase in size by 300 percent from the last one! Since spammers aren't doing this, the error rate of spams like these is very small, well below 0.01 percent.

The reason these types of spams rarely work is that they use too many obscure tokens, at which point they are learned as spam. As spammers continue to use many obscure words in such emails, the tokens that *are* known become more likely to have been found to be guilty than innocent. For example, if I never use the word "disassociation," but a spammer does, my filter's much more likely to can a message containing the word. While the spammer may hit two or three innocent tokens, they've also hit several guilty ones. The more this approach is used, the less effective it becomes, since there are only so many different types of random words to use.

In order for this approach to work, the spammer must use primarily words that the recipient is using in their correspondence and must use fewer unknown or spammy words. Any words that the user isn't using—no matter how innocent sounding—are likely to become guilty tokens in the user's database.

The Importance

Word salad is not something to be concerned about, since the approach doesn't work very often, but it is important to consider the effects it may have on a user's dataset. It generates a great deal of data, which will need to be purged from the system at some point to avoid having large amounts of junk data taking up disk space. This approach may be ineffective at evading spam filters, but it does create a very slow denial of service attack if the data isn't kept in check.

Directed Attacks

Directed attacks can, in theory, work, but require so much work on the spammer's part that the spam-filtering community hasn't seen a true attempt of these in the wild. The idea behind a *directed attack* is for the spammer to create a profile for each recipient of the message. This profile contains a list of the most innocent words in the user's database, so that they can be used in a spam distribution specifically for that user or group. This requires inner knowledge of the user's spam filter data—knowledge that is difficult to come by and constantly changes.

The Problem

The spammer will use one of several different approaches to attempt to build a profile on the targeted recipient. In most cases this involves sending several thousand messages to the target. The spammer will include a web bug— perhaps through the use of embedded images—to create a feedback loop. This feedback loop will tell the spammer which messages made it through the spam filter. The spammer can then take the messages that have gotten through and feed them into a similar Bayesian classifier to generate tokens that are most likely to be considered legitimate by the target—just like the old card trick, where you pick the card you're thinking of out of five decks. Over time, the spammer will be able to develop a short list of very innocent tokens.

Now comes the spam. The spammer sends their spam to the user with the list of very innocent tokens deduced from the previous profiled analysis of the target. The innocent tokens used in the spams will then make their way into the decision matrix and trick the filter into thinking that the message is legitimate.

Why This Doesn't Work

This approach *can* work, and work quite effectively. Fortunately, it requires a significant amount of resources. Spammers don't have the time or resources to perform massive analysis of millions of users—yet. It is much more lucrative just to send out millions of blind emails a day. This approach could possibly work its way into the standard operating procedure of spammers in the future—what is too expensive today can become feasible as spammers learn to adapt. Presently, many are relying on spammers not to use this approach in the future, but an infrastructure to support this type of profiling already exists as computing power and available bandwidth increase.

This approach has two inherent flaws, which filters with the appropriate logic can take advantage of. First, more complex tokenizers generate more data to fill up the decision matrix with guilty data, forcing the spammers to come up with more innocent data to counter it. Legitimate email will usually generate innocent individual tokens as well as innocent token pairs, but since the spammer is sending a hodgepodge of innocent tokens, the token pairs will be, for the most part, unknown to the filter. While a primitive tokenizer would identify only some of the spammer's tokens, such as "Free" and "Viagra," a more complex tokenizer would also be able to come up with tokens like "Free+Viagra," which will most definitely show up in the decision matrix. Not only is it more difficult to circumvent filters that are using these types of tokenizers, but once the first distribution referencing these innocent tokens gets sent, the innocent tokens will no longer have their extremely innocent disposition and will be outweighed by the guilty tokens.

The second flaw inherent in this type of attack is that the patterns of words used aren't consistent with the patterns used in legitimate mail. This creates a type of contextual anomaly which can be detected using advanced algorithms such as Bayesian noise reduction (discussed in Chapter 13).

There's been a lot of speculation about these types of attacks becoming mainstream, which is why it's important to incorporate some of these additional functions into a filter. The most basic concept tokenizer can avoid much of the heartache that will be created when these types of attacks begin to be launched.

This approach was not invented by a spammer, mind you—it was invented by a very gifted spam filter author who also happens to have a doctorate and is vice president of a technology company, the author of many books, and the holder of two U.S. patents. These types of individuals don't hang around spam slums working for the spammers. Most spammers' staffs are generally lacking in skills and education. It will therefore take a significant amount of time for spammers to figure out ways to even understand these types of attacks and incorporate them into their spam tools. Once they do, however, it's possible that primitive tokenizers will become obsolete or will at least cause a drop in the accuracy of the filter that doesn't employ conceptual filtering.

The Importance

Directed attacks are an important type of attack to consider when developing spam filters. They can be very effective, and if the spammers devise a system to perform real-time user profiling, this approach could be detrimental to filters that don't use more advanced analysis approaches. The more complex tokenizers discussed in Chapter 11, Bayesian noise reduction, and smarter mail clients are all ways to fight a directed attack successfully. This approach will certainly smash naive filters that don't at least take the possibility of an attack of this type into consideration.

Final Thoughts

We've taken a look at many different types of attacks in this chapter. Aside from minor tweaks that are required to put the data into a machine-readable format, filters are getting better day by day without any additional maintenance.

There is a buffer between spammers and those who hire them. A spam that receives only half the number of expected responses won't necessarily cost the spammer money, but it will hurt the spammer's reputation. Over the long haul, spam filters make spammers look less intelligent and less effective, which hurts their credibility. Once the companies hiring them see that spammers aren't getting the results they're used to, they'll consider dropping them. It's not about stopping one message; it's about stopping many.

In just the past year, filters have increased in accuracy by a factor of 10. In 2003, many filter authors wondered whether they would ever reach 99.9 percent accuracy and in 2004 passed the four-nines milestone. Five 9s accuracy is just a matter of time, and the ideal recipe for a complete anti-spam solution is being implemented already by many Internet service providers. If filtering based on pure content alone has gotten us this far, imagine the level of accuracy that we can reach when incorporating other technologies, such as statistical blackhole lists and collaborative engines.

As our spam filters reach new levels of accuracy, spammers are undoubtedly trying to come up with new tricks to fool them. The ideal defense against spammers is to develop intelligent learning machines capable of identifying these new types of attacks and adjusting the filter's own computations to accommodate them. That is what the next generation of statistical filters will be about.

Even though spam filters aren't yet 100 percent accurate, we can take solace in the fact that the spams that do make it through our filters have been toned down to the point that they don't even look very spamlike anymore. I'd prefer not to receive any spam, but if I must receive some, I would rather that it were boring and not the raunchy pornographic variety.

8

DATA STORAGE FOR A ZILLION RECORDS

Language classifiers are great at making decisions, but in order to make a decision, they have to have a lot of information. This leaves the question of what to do with all the data created by the tokenizer. We're not terribly concerned with the amount of data, although that's important in a large-scale environment. The data may take up only around 10 MB to 25 MB per user. However, the number of records can be considerable. Primitive tokenizers usually create around 150,000 records, or as many as 300,000 for a very high-volume user. Concept-based tokenizers are even worse, with nGram (chained tokens) or *SBPH (sparse binary polynomial hashing)* tokenizers peaking at up to half a million records.

With this enormous amount of data comes the challenge of how to manage it. Filters have implemented many different approaches to manage storage. In this chapter, we'll take a look at some of the most popular mechanisms used for storage and what the benefits of each are.

Storage Considerations

Managing storage is a trade-off. There are many different factors that will ultimately determine which storage implementation is the best for a particular project. Depending on whether the filter is running on an end user's machine or on a mail server protecting 100,000 users, certain aspects may be less important.

Disk Space

Some implementations use up more disk space than others, even though the information being stored is the same. There are two general factors that affect the amount of disk space used with any implementation. First, some implementations reserve a certain amount of extra space for performing their operations. An implementation may also use up more disk space than another depending on its ability to reclaim *free space* (disk space that was originally used to store a record that is now deleted). In spam filtering, you're dealing with hundreds of thousands of very small records. The record size, if optimized, can sometimes be only a few bytes. Implementations that poorly maintain free space, or don't offer any type of housekeeping to maintain the database, may end up leaving a lot of stale data just taking room up in the file system.

Speed

A spam filter will generally need to read and write between a few hundred and a few thousand records in storage at any given time (depending, of course, on your training mode), including a fair number of inserts for new data. During a user's training phase, nearly half of the tokens found in a message may never have been seen before and will need to be inserted into storage. The algorithms behind many storage implementations are just as important as how efficiently they store data to disk. *Asymptotic analysis* is the process by which we measure the growth rate of an algorithm. Many algorithms perform differently depending on the number of data points presented to them. Algorithms also have a cutoff point where they become less efficient than others.

Things like key size will also play a role in the speed of a particular approach. A record's key is a unique identifier used to access the record. *Variable-length keys* are keys whose length may vary. This can happen if you're using the plain-text names of the tokens, for example. These are likely to create additional optimization issues, taking longer to query than fixed-length keys (such as numeric keys). Implementing hashing algorithms (such as CRC32 and CRC64) to create numeric keys can help many storage mechanisms run faster.

Algorithms that are too slow won't be able to keep up with the load of email coming in. If you're designing your filter as a client-side tool, this may not be as big a concern, but if you're designing it for a server-side implementation, in which you'll need to deal with hundreds or possibly thousands of messages per second, processing time will be critical.

Locking

How the data is locked is another important consideration. Many operations are likely to be occurring simultaneously. These range from multiple processes to possibly multiple threads inside a process, all analyzing data. The method the storage implementation uses to lock records could be detrimental to the filter. A storage implementation will undoubtedly need to handle locking very efficiently. Some storage implementations have very poor locking, which can lead to lock contention, data corruption, and massive delays in processing. Other implementations require no locking from the application programming interface (API), but perform their own internal locking as requests are processed. These are generally easier to use and less likely to fail in many cases.

Portability

If you plan on having other people use your software, it will need to be portable to many different platforms. What good is the perfect solution if it can only run on Amiga? If you're developing an open source filter, you'll need a storage solution that will function on a large number of different operating systems.

Wherever you take your software, you must also take all of your dependencies. This is one reason that building a storage driver interface is very beneficial. We'll discuss supporting multiple storage mechanisms using a driver interface later on in this chapter.

Statefulness

Statefulness refers to the need to run a process in the background to service requests. A background process maintains important information about the database's running environment, or *state*. Some storage mechanisms, such as Oracle, require a stateful (persistent) process to be running in order to use them. Others, such as Berkeley DB and SQLite, don't require a background process but will manage the entire environment in a set of files. Some support both (such as MySQL). Stateful solutions generally run faster because the running process(es) offer the benefit of services available on demand, and they also perform many housekeeping functions in their idle time. State*less* solutions can be useful for some installations, as they don't require a background process to be running—which may be impossible to do on a hosted machine or may require more work than the user is willing to put in (adding another process to baby-sit).

Recovery

Systems crash, and when they do, many realize that they chose the wrong storage implementation. The type of recovery options and safeguards offered vary from tool to tool. Recovery is typically one of the considerations that apply to just about every possible filtering project out there. If you're developing a client-side filter, the system will likely be powered up and shut down many times a week, with a high probability of system crashes from end-user applications running on the machine (such as Microsoft Office or Internet Explorer). If you're developing a server-based application, crashes usually occur less frequently but are much harder when they do. Sometimes the file system itself will need to be recovered, and any dirty data could be lost if the recovery mechanism isn't solid. If there is no recovery mechanism, you risk having data become corrupted at the first sign of a crash, and your users may end up having to start training their filters from scratch again.

I/O Contention

The training behavior of your filter will play a role in determining what storage implementation is more optimized for your particular needs. Filters that train on error (TOE) generally perform a significant number of reads but only a few writes, as they train only when the filter has made a mistake. On the other hand, TEFT (train-everything) filters, which train on every single message sent to the user, will perform a significant amount of reading *and* writing simultaneously. The storage implementation could adversely affect the filter's performance and create a bottleneck if not optimized for this type of behavior. The architecture of the typical installation will also play a role in determining I/O contention. A desktop Windows-based user will not fare well with an Oracle process running in the background. At the same time, a large-scale server-based solution with a massive storage array probably won't run at peak performance using a flat file for storage. The storage approach should complement the implementation.

Random-Access Features

With millions of records in storage, the spam filter is bound to require a good bowel movement every so often. How difficult this is to do can depend on the random-access properties of the storage solution. SQL-based storage solutions provide Structured Query Language (SQL), which is a very easy-to-use language designed to access specific data on demand. Solutions without such features may require the filter author to code a routine to iterate through the entire dataset and perform analysis of each record. Whatever access features the storage approach doesn't support will undoubtedly be ones that you'll have to code yourself.

Different tools have very different levels of random-access functionality. Since you'll need to pull a few thousand records, out of potentially a million or more, it's a good idea to find a solution that provides a selection of very fast algorithms for accessing the right data.

Ease of Use

If you're considering a third-party storage approach, you've also got to consider how easy it is to use the API. The API is the set of routines written by the author of the storage mechanism for anyone to use when interfacing with it. A simple, understandable API will generally save you many hours of development work, whereas an API that's more complicated just for the sake of being complicated will likely leave you sitting at your desk for hours hacking "write-only" code. Complex APIs are useful if there is a certain level of granularity, but in most cases a less complex API will provide for a quicker development cycle.

Storage Framework

A *storage framework* is a design architecture allowing one of many different storage solutions to be used with the filter. This approach is generally beneficial for open source projects, as it caters to the needs of many. It also helps to identify a set of standard functions the filter will need to perform on storage, which results in cleaner code. Not implementing a storage framework usually results in many different pieces of storage code being spread throughout the project, which can cause problems when changes need to be made (or if a different storage solution needs to be supported).

If you plan on authoring a spam filter that is going to be used in many different environments, it may be a good idea to develop a framework that supports multiple storage solutions. Writing a multistorage-capable filter will allow the implementer (your software's users) to choose the best storage approach for their particular environment.

As an example, the DSPAM project includes a storage driver framework. The framework allows for the implementer to select any single storage approach from many at compile time, and to have the chosen approach built into the software. The project presently supports the following drivers:

- Berkeley DB 3.*x* and 4.*x*
- SQLite 2.*x* and 3.*x*
- MySQL
- PostgreSQL
- Oracle

Supporting multiple storage solutions has several advantages, the most obvious being that it allows additional drivers to be coded with ease without having to touch the filtering code itself or affect any existing installations of the software that are using a different driver. The other advantage is that a storage driver framework helps to better modularize code. If all of your storage read/write routines exist in one place, you won't have to worry as much about quality control. If the storage functions were sparsely distributed throughout your entire filter's code base, you would have a much greater likelihood of making an error somewhere, which could result in the loss of data or, even worse, in spam getting through.

A framework also caters to individuals who already have legacy software running on their infrastructure. For example, if your filter implemented PostgreSQL, but the network administrator was already using MySQL, he may not be as inclined to use your software, as it adds yet another tool to learn and baby-sit. Many companies also incorporate standard practices forbidding them to use any software that hasn't been sanctioned for the infrastructure. Being able to integrate the filter into the user's existing infrastructure is more often than not a perk for systems administrators who are evaluating different solutions.

A storage driver framework is easy to implement. The first step is to compile a list of all the different operations the filter will need to perform on the data. This is fairly standard for most filters:

- Retrieve a list of tokens
- Store a list of tokens
- Insert a new list of tokens
- Delete tokens based on certain criteria

Depending on what supporting tools are written for the project, it may also be necessary to perform additional functions, such as obtaining a list of users on the system or retrieving a complete list of tokens in a particular user's dataset. These functions are frequently used to display information about a user, or to provide verbose debugging data. Systems administrators and savvy geeks will also want to tweak a little and play around with your filter; this kind of data gives them something interesting to look at.

Now compile a list of all the basic operations any particular storage driver will need to perform:

- Establish a connection to the database
- Terminate a connection to the database
- Open a file
- Initialize an environment
- And so forth

All of these operations have one thing in common—they are all either initialization functions or shutdown functions. A good storage driver implementation will provide at least one type of initialization function and one type of shutdown function, so that the various drivers are capable of setting up the initial environment they work in.

Once you have a set of common operations, you'll want to decide on the standard arguments of the functions and on what data is going to be passed into and out of each function. For example, how are you going to provide a group of records to your group functions? What types of data will a function return? It will most likely be necessary to declare a few standardized structures for all storage drivers to use when implementing these functions (such as structures containing lists of tokens and their values). One thing all storage drivers need is a place to store information that will remain stateful during the execution of the process—for example, open file handles, a database, a handle, and cursors for a particular query. This usually calls for a type of *storage context* structure.

Once you have your structures defined, you can use them to define your functions. If you're using an object-oriented language (such as C++ or Java), you'll probably create a storage class and implement the operations as member functions of the class. If you're using a procedural language (such as C), these functions may simply be global functions available to the rest of the software.

Finally, once you have all of your functions and data types laid out, the next step is to determine how you're going to select a particular driver. Some tools may compile in the correct driver statically. Other approaches may use dynamic linking to load the appropriate driver module at startup or even at run time. Now all you need is a storage solution to wrap your code around.

Third-Party Storage Solutions

There are a lot of different third-party storage solutions out there, and chances are good that one of them will meet your needs. In this section, we'll discuss some of the more popular solutions available and describe their individual benefits.

Stateless Database Implementations

A few standard stateless database implementations are available to developers, including Berkeley DB (BDB) and Gnu DBM (GDBM). Both are stateless data management libraries used by many popular open source applications. Most stateless database implementations support a few different types of databases, including hashes and binary trees. One of the benefits to using one of these implementations is that they are simple. In addition, just about every flavor of Unix is distributed with some implementation of them. Filters using stateless database implementations don't need to worry about precon-figuring a database server or performing other types of preinstallation tasks. While these tools are very popular, they are also, unfortunately, infamous for problems, at least in the setting of spam filtering. Many filter authors started out using BDB or GDBM at one point and have since switched due to some of the problems they've encountered. One more promising stateless imple-mentation is known as SQLite (http://www.sqlite.org). SQLite is a SQL-based stateless database implementation providing many advanced features and enhancements over the old-school databases.

Stateless database implementations are very useful for simple, small-scale implementations, particularly for end users or small server installs. They are usually available in the form of a shared library that the software developer can link into their application.

Disk Space

Your mileage will vary, usually on the low end, when it comes to disk space efficiency with a stateless database implementation. Berkeley DB does appear to have some functions for reclaiming unused space, but many databases have still managed to grow up to a couple hundred megabytes per user. The only *effective* way to optimize the database and reclaim all free space is to read the entire database in and rewrite it to a fresh file on disk. One advantage to most implementations of stateless databases is that they allow you to store any type of object you like—structures, numbers, characters, and so forth. This can help the disk space issue by allowing the author to develop very small structures to store data in.

Performance

Most stateless systems suffer from only marginal performance, far slower than stateful SQL servers (discussed next). This, of course, depends on the size of the database. Smaller databases appear to be much faster, but as they grow over time they'll become slow. An occasional dump and rewrite of the database will help keep it optimized, but it may be necessary to do this on a nightly basis, depending on the amount of mail traffic.

While testing drivers for the DSPAM project, I found that the Berkeley DB implementation initially ran as fast as a SQL-based solution, but once the dataset began to grow, it took at best 10 to 20 times longer to process a message than it took a SQL-based solution.

Dynamic linking is also somewhat expensive, and so if you're implementing a tool like this you may want to consider statically linking it to your application.

Locking

Most stateless databases do support different locking functions, but most filter authors have found themselves with corrupt data or deadlocks because they're not designed to lock between multiple processes. Stateless databases don't appear to have very good support for deadlock management—for handling locks of crashed processes or multiple processes fighting over a single lock—and so some authors attempt to code around it. A full recovery is sometimes found to be required in the event of a bad deadlock scenario.

Portability

Berkeley DB is available on just about every major platform. It is therefore the ideal choice for applications that require a high level of portability.

Other types of databases are generally available on a wide range of Unix platforms, but some of the more popular ones have ports to Windows and other operating systems as well (such as SQLite). Since a lot of Windows software isn't released as open source, many of these tools are restricted from use by license.

Recovery

Basic recovery functions are usually supported but are lacking in most practical senses of usefulness. Many users have complained that the recovery function doesn't always work quite well enough, or they complain of corrupt data or even "loops" in which a cursor iterating through a set of records will indefinitely repeat the same records over and over again.

BDB's recovery function destroys any locks held on the database, whether they are legitimate or not. This can frequently lead to corruption if recovery is performed while other processes are attempting to access the database.

I/O Contention

Usually, these types of simple database libraries perform fairly well under the pressure of concurrent reads and writes, but only due to their locking mechanisms (or additional layers of locking added by the filter author). Since these databases don't support relative update functions (e.g., total = total + 1 functionality), the records must be locked between a read and a write. Filter authors will frequently lock the user's database upon instance startup and unlock it upon shutdown, meaning that at any given time only be a single process will be accessing the data. This avoids many of the I/O contention issues but raises the issue of queued processes. If locking is implemented on a per-user basis, this generally provides an acceptable level of performance before lock contention occurs.

Random-Access Features

Most stateless database implementations don't offer any advanced indexing or query functions like those of SQL-based solutions. In order to purge data, each record must be inspected through the iteration of a cursor. Candidates for deletion must be deleted individually. SQLite is, of course, one exception to this.

Ease of Use

While a lot of libraries are somewhat cumbersome, they are extremely easy to use. A few lines of code are all that's required to create, open, and begin working with a database. The API is simple, yet flexible enough to support user-defined data types.

Stateful SQL-Based Solutions

SQL-based solutions have become very popular and fill in most of the holes that other solutions, including Berkeley DB, leave wide open. Solutions such as MySQL, PostgreSQL, and Oracle all provide an optimal, feature-rich environment for managing millions of records.

One of the nice features of SQL-based solutions is that SQL servers are generally very tunable and can handle an enormous server load. Large-scale implementations experiencing performance issues can be tweaked and prodded, replicated and tuned to dedicate more memory to a particular part of the process, increase certain thresholds, and so forth.

Disk Space

SQL-based solutions are designed for online transaction processing and therefore have very good algorithms for cleaning up unused space. Some additional functions provide added optimizations that can be run once in a while to clean up anything that doesn't normally get reclaimed by standard processing. Like stateless databases, many SQL servers do rebuild their datafiles from scratch when optimizing them, but they're also capable of doing it much faster.

There is a trade-off between disk space and performance. Variable-length records can be used to conserve disk space, but fixed-length records will improve performance. The flexibility provided by this allows the implementer to choose what is best.

Performance

All well-written SQL-based solutions provide indexing functions to find data without performing a full table scan. This provides exceptional speed, even in an environment with millions of tokens in the database. A few bottlenecks exist, however. Because these solutions use indexes, insert and delete operations are much slower than select and update operations. This is because all new or deleted records must be updated in each index created. Some tables may require two or more indexes (for example, to index user id and token id), depending on the implementation, and therefore will require both indexes to be updated on record insertion.

This can result in slower performance during a user's initial training period, when several new inserts are being performed for every message. It can also cause purges to run a bit slowly. Overall, the slowdown of inserts and deletes isn't very noticeable, and it appears to affect only the largest implementations.

Locking

SQL-based solutions support the use of relative updates—for example, setting a value to the value + 1. Since direct updates are not necessary, most implementations don't need to perform any type of locking, other than the locking that the solution performs internally. This low-level locking is also tunable by implementers to support their particular needs—for example, MySQL supports both table-level locking and row-level locking. The software need not worry about which type of locking is used, but the systems administrator can switch between the two flawlessly to see if one provides better performance.

Portability

SQL-based solutions are generally available for all major platforms, allowing the applications to also be developed on these platforms. Another advantage to using SQL-based solutions is that they are designed with a client/server architecture. The filtering software doesn't necessarily have to be running on the same machine—or the same operating system—as the SQL server.

Recovery

Most SQL-based solutions incorporate many advanced recovery approaches. Oracle, among other tools, incorporates the use of a redo log, in which each transaction is prewritten before any changes are made to the database. This allows for better recovery by ensuring that any corrupt data in the database is already accounted for in the redo log, and that any corrupt data in the redo log hasn't yet been written to the database. It also allows for archival logs, point-in-time recovery, and other advanced functions.

Because of this capability, it's extremely difficult to kill a database. The server could crash hundreds of times before any data was lost, other than what had not yet been written to disk at the time of the crash.

I/O Contention

Many databases have problems with I/O contention, and because of this, filters that operate in TOE (train-on-error) or TUM (train-until-mature) training modes will generally experience much better performance than those using a TEFT (train-everything) training mode. The recommended *small* Oracle installation itself requires the use of several disks just to avoid this issue. I/O contention can also be fought off by a savvy database administrator who is able to lay out disks properly, partition tables based on volatility, and perform other types of DB fu.

Random-Access Features

SQL-based solutions come with a suite of useful features for indexing and querying data. For example, instead of writing a purge function to iterate through every token in the database, the implementer can write a simple script to purge bulk data. These extra tools mean code that the developer doesn't have to write.

Ease of Use

Ease of use will vary from solution to solution. Many APIs, such as the MySQL and PostgreSQL APIs, are extremely programmer friendly. Other APIs, such as the Oracle Call Interface (OCI), are much more complex and difficult to use.

Peter Graf's PBL ISAM Library

After experiencing many problems with Berkeley DB, Brian Burton, the author of SpamProbe, decided to implement an alternative solution. He came across Peter Graf's PBL ISAM library, which provides the same stateless database functionality as Berkeley DB, but with many nice additions. The library is released under the LGPL license and has many impressive features, including:

- Ultrafast B-tree implementations
- Transaction handling
- A footprint so small (less than 75 kilobytes) that it can be embedded
- Support for files up to 4 terabytes in size
- Support for up to 2^{48} records
- Advanced key compression

This was Burton's third attempt at a storage solution for his filter. He describes his experiences as follows:

> SpamProbe has used three different database libraries in its brief history. The original implementation used GDBM for its storage. Unfortunately, GDBM did not scale well for a large number of terms.
>
> Next I adopted Berkeley DB. This had the benefit of being open source and widely known. While BDB had significantly better performance than GDBM, we quickly ran into problems with the library. Growth of the data files quickly outpaced the number of terms being added. The growth seemed to be boundless. This led people to periodically compact their BDB databases by performing an export/import operation. Another, more serious, issue we ran into with BDB was reliability. BDB files had a nasty habit of becoming corrupted over time. Specifically, the indexes would develop cycles that led to infinite loops when traversing the database.
>
> While looking for a replacement for BDB I discovered a lesser known alternative called PBL. Thus far, PBL has proved itself to be vastly superior to BDB (for my purposes).

The PBL library can be downloaded from http://mission.base.com/peter/source. Brian Burton graciously provided his evaluation of PBL in the following categories.

Disk Space

Disk space usage with PBL has been acceptable. When initially created, PBL files tend to be somewhat larger than equivalent BDB files. However PBL's data files tend to grow significantly less over time.

My personal SpamProbe database contains 1.7 million records and occupies 88 MB on disk. For comparison, a text export file containing all of the records in text format occupies 49 MB. This implies that the index occupies approximately the same amount of space as the raw data.

Performance

Performance of PBL has been comparable to that of BDB in my tests. Initial database imports seemed to be slower with PBL; however, tests under load conditions (using formail to run 20 to 30 SpamProbe instances simultaneously) tended to be somewhat faster than PBL.

Locking

PBL does not provide locking. SpamProbe uses its own lock file (fcntl) to provide synchronization, so this has never been an issue. (Filters implementing PBL will need to manage their own locking.)

Portability

I have personally compiled PBL on Linux and FreeBSD. Some users have reported problems compiling it on Solaris, but I have never tried, so I don't know if their complaints have merit. PBL uses a simple makefile for compilation rather than autoconf, so it probably works best on Linux-like platforms.

Recovery

PBL provides in-memory transaction processing only. Updates are cached in memory until the commit function is called. This allows rollback while the program is running but does not provide for recovery if the process exits abnormally (such as a program crash or sudden reboot). In practice, I have never encountered data corruption with PBL.

I/O Contention

I have not measured the I/O load of PBL. Since PBL does not provide any specific concurrency control features, programs have to provide their own. SpamProbe uses a simple multiple-read/single-writer locking scheme that is adequate for its target usage (personal email filter) but is not as viable for extremely high-load servers (Yahoo email server).

Random-Access Features

PBL does not have any SQL syntax. It provides fairly basic file access features and reliable storage and retrieval using a straightforward C API.

Ease of Use

Integrating PBL with SpamProbe was fairly straightforward, since its API operates in a manner similar to BDB. The documentation was spartan and made selection of the proper API (PBL offers several) and feature set somewhat difficult. The author graciously contributed code for the proper API and helped to shrink the size of the data files SP produced.

SQLite

SQLite is a lightweight, embeddable SQL-based database engine that has recently been put to good use in DSPAM, POPFile, and many other filters.

It is robust without the anarchy of running your own SQL server. It has many of the properties of a stateless database engine in that it is a shared library that links directly into an application. Since it doesn't require a server process to be running, it can be implemented without any preinstallation tasks.

One of the nice things about SQLite is that it's completely public domain. It can be downloaded from http://www.sqlite.org.

Disk Space

SQLite shares the same inherent flaw as most stateless database engines in that the file size of the database doesn't shrink. It does support a VACUUM command that will rebuild the data file, but this process generally takes a little bit of time (a half second per megabyte, according to the documentation). SQLite does maintain a free list, so that the disk space will be reused when more tokens are added. If efficient, this can be ideal for a spam filter implementation.

Performance

A significant amount of useful information about SQLite's performance is available at http://www.hwaci.com/sw/sqlite/speed.html, including a comparison with MySQL and PostgreSQL. In many tests, SQLite outperformed both databases, sometimes by up to a factor of four.

Locking

SQLite performs all the transaction support available in other SQL servers and can handle incremental updates. It is thread-safe and can handle multiple simultaneous database calls.

Portability

SQLite is available both for Unix and Windows implementations and appears to work well on any platform it compiles on.

Recovery

SQLite performs transactional recovery and crash recovery. The recovery unit test simulates a thousand sequential crashes on the database. Overall, SQLite is quite robust at recovering from typical spontaneous reboots and the like. Since SQLite doesn't require the extensive locking management that other stateless database engines need, risk of corruption is fairly minimal.

I/O Contention

There is no official data on I/O contention, but it is believed to be similar to that of most SQL servers. Based on the performance benchmarks, SQLite can perform much faster than most SQL servers but is susceptible to the same delays on insert. In testing, SQLite took less than half the time to perform 2,500 UPDATEs.

Random-Access Features

SQLite provides all of the same SQL-based features as other SQL servers, making purges and other types of mass updates/deletes very easy, so not a lot of code needs to be written.

Ease of Use

SQLite is brain-dead simple to get running in your application. In fact, the shared library is so simple that it can be invoked from a shell script with minimal coding. The primary functions used in SQLite involve one to open the database, one to execute a query, and one to close the database. No complicated statement handles or allocations are necessary. SQLite is truly a lightweight SQL engine.

Proprietary Implementations

Of course, if you don't feel like using a third-party product, you can always build one yourself. That's what Bill Yerazunis did to support the large amounts of data powering his SBPH tokenizer. Bill's proprietary implementation proves that home-brew solutions can get the job done right.

Yerazunis's implementation consists of a series of files ending in .css, although they shouldn't be confused with cascading style sheets. Each .css file is exactly 1 MB in size plus 1 byte. Presently, CRM114 has been modified to use 64-bit hash values as keys. These numeric keys are then used to create a modulus based on the file size. The modulus determines the exact spot in the 1 MB file where the token belongs, and therefore no traversal or complex indexing is necessary. Each record is exactly 12 bytes in size, making the average database approximately 25 MB.

Yerazunis's latest implementation of this storage solution has resulted in very fast execution time, much more acceptable than previous versions of the software. The average classification cycle uses approximately 0.10 seconds of real time, 0.03 second user, and 0.02 second system—much more impressive than many other filters available today. On top of speed, CRM114 is considered one of the most accurate language classifiers freely available today. Disk space is cheap, so supporting 10,000 users won't cost too much. CRM114 is presently being used on some large-scale implementations in Spain, and many optimizations are available for the software. The storage implementation continues to improve, and with the software under an open source license, it's bound to get a significant amount of attention.

Final Thoughts

We've explored many different third-party storage solutions in this chapter and looked at one home-brew implementation done right. Many different tools are available to meet many different types of needs. We've also covered the primary concerns when choosing a tool, and provided a basic outline for how to build your own storage driver interface.

The concepts covered in this chapter, applied well, will allow you to create a flexible storage facility capable of handling millions of records. Implementing an efficient storage mechanism is one of the most critical steps in creating an efficient spam filter. If the data can't be accessed with enough reliability, the spam filter will become unreliable. Locking, recovery, and concurrency are all important aspects of creating a reliable storage implementation. Speed and performance are both important to the practical usefulness of it.

9

SCALING IN LARGE ENVIRONMENTS

One basic requirement for any server-side spam filter is to be scalable enough to support large installations. Large corporations, universities, and ISPs with tens or even hundreds of thousands of mailboxes are among the potential users of spam filters. The cost involved in implementing a filter for this number of users can sometimes play a dramatic role in the choice of software. If a filter can produce five 9s accuracy but is incapable of supporting more than a handful of users, it will likely be too expensive to implement on large systems.

Most administrators of large-scale networks aren't nearly as demanding as the developers of the filtering application. While the developer may struggle to catch that last 0.10 percent of annoying spam, many large-scale administrators are quite happy with filtering rates of 99 percent. Accuracy is only one important balancing factor to most ISPs. Many are also concerned about deployment cost. If the cost of inaccuracy plus the cost of deployment is greater than the cost of managing spam, an ISP might opt to just manage it (with the delete button).

This chapter highlights the important aspects of scalability introduced in the previous chapter and discusses many ways that filter authors and systems administrators can make their filters more scalable.

If you're looking to implement a spam filter on your network, this chapter will also help you plan, size, and deploy it. It includes many questions you will need to consider, as well as discussions of some popular distributed network approaches.

Requirements Assessment

In Chapter 8, we discussed the key considerations for a storage driver. These considerations were primarily focused on internal design of the filter:

- Disk space utilization
- Performance
- Locking
- Portability
- Recovery
- I/O contention
- Random-access features
- Ease of use

However, these properties extend into the topics many institutions consider when evaluating different solutions on their network. These concerns will need to be taken into account in the development of the entire filter, as they will play a role in whether or not a filter may be usable in certain size networks. We'll discuss the basic questions that get asked when looking at a filter and provide a little bit of foresight into the different answers that may be suitable for a particular network based on its size, budget, and methodology. These issues can be broken up into the following categories:

- Total disk space requirements
- Total processing power
- Parallelization
- Operating system requirements
- High availability requirements
- I/O bandwidth requirements
- Feature requirements
- End-user support

Large-scale spam-filtering projects usually have considerable budgets, but these budgets are likely to remain within the boundaries of managing spam (that is, without filtering). The goal in developing a scalable spam filter is to strike a balance between meeting the requirements just listed while keeping the cost within the confines of a typical budget. Return on investment is the biggest requirement managers have (or should have) when considering whether to deploy a new tool. Everyone agrees that spam is annoying, and everyone would like to filter it—unfortunately, if the management is unable to justify an actual return on their investment, it may be cheaper to let spam run rampant on the network.

Total Disk Space Requirements

The amount of disk space used to service an individual user versus that needed for a network of 100,000 users is usually seen as a linear problem. In global environments, in which a single dataset is shared, this generally isn't an issue, and since a lot of institutions prefer cost over accuracy, many are willing to settle with the mediocre 99 percent accuracy levels a global dataset would offer.

Providing greater accuracy for a large number of users requires more disk space, however, and while many companies are happy with mediocre levels of accuracy, there are some interested enough in the problem to bite at a better solution. Customer support and even customer satisfaction are sometimes driving reasons to deploy a "spam filter that learns" on the network. Users are going to receive spam from time to time (and a lot of it if the system is filtering only 99 percent), but whether they call up the tech support department or simply click a button labeled "Report Spam" may determine how much money the company is willing to invest in managing inaccuracy. Politics may also drive this decision, as many universities and ISPs face privacy and user-control issues.

Greater accuracy requires personalized learning, and usually additional data. While it may be trivial to dedicate 25 MB of disk space to each user on a 10-user system, 25 MB of disk space per user on a 100,000-user system would require more than 2.5 TB of storage! Clearly, 25 MB per user is far too much for such a large-scale implementation. There are a few ways of reducing this amount, the biggest of which requires converting the issue of storage into a nonlinear problem.

Establishing a Purge Policy

An aggressive purge policy is your first defense in keeping the size of the dataset down. A majority of the data created by a tokenizer is never seen again in other messages—especially if you're using a complex tokenizer that recognizes word pairs and lexical data. Nightly purges can help to

- Remove data that has been stale for a period of time
- Remove hapaxes that have been stale for a period of time
- Remove uninteresting data that has matured

Data that has been stale for a period of time is likely not to appear in future messages. Since spam evolves, it's possible that much of the data from two or three months ago will not be seen again in future distributions. It's also likely that as users change their email behavior, much of the data from their old behavior will become obsolete. All that meaty data collected from mailing list headers stagnates indefinitely when a user unsubscribes from a list.

Hapaxes are likely to be in significant numbers in any dataset, representing data that has been seen only once (or few enough times for a real value to actually be assigned to the data). Data that has appeared only a few times over a period of a month is unlikely to play any significant role in effectively filtering messages.

Finally, uninteresting data is data that is unlikely to show up in a decision matrix. As we discussed in Chapter 4, most decision matrices used today are sorted based on a token's distance from a neutral 0.5. This results in many tokens whose probability hovers around this neutral value never showing up in a decision matrix. Purging data with probabilities between 0.3 and 0.7 is a generally acceptable method of reducing the size of the dataset.

The important thing to consider in purging all of these types of data is that we want to allow enough time for the data to actually establish some type of value. On very large systems with high-volume users, this may be only a few days. The general philosophy is that if the data isn't interesting after a certain period of time, not enough messages are coming in for the data to be useful, and it will appear in only a very small number of decisions.

Using Merged Global Datasets

The use of an exclusive global dataset is generally frowned upon because it diminishes accuracy. A merged global dataset, however, not only can provide the out-of-the-box functionality most users appreciate, but can also help keep the size of individual datasets down.

A *merged global dataset* is a feature used in some spam filters to provide a common set of training data to all users on the system while still allowing them to correct learning mistakes and maintain their own personal set of important tokens. The approach involves the creation of a global dataset in much the same way that one would be created for an exclusive global system. This global dataset should be populated enough to cover a wide range of data for many users, but should also be generic enough to avoid a significant number of false positives. The global dataset then provides a training base for the user and is merged with the user's personalized training data at run time. As the filter begins to learn the specifics of a user's behavior, the user's data reflects only the necessarily corrections *(diffs)* to the global data. When the data is loaded into memory, the individual user's data will adjust the value of the global data and yield a customized dataset for that user. The amount of training required by the system's users in a merged group is in direct relation to the quality of the global database, meaning if you can create a high-quality global database then each user will require less disk space to correct it.

In a situation like this, all users benefit. Users who experience almost no classification errors continue to depend more on the global dataset without building much of their own training data. Users who experience a significant number of errors build more data to offset the global data, but this is still very trivial compared to the amount of training that would be necessary had the user been required to build a dataset from scratch. Merged groups don't usually leave the user with long-term levels of accuracy as high as those of users who have built their own dataset from scratch, but they are usually close enough to make it a feasible solution in light of the disk space savings.

The ultimate goal of a merged global approach is to place as much common data as possible in the global space, so that it needs to take up disk space only once. A 100 MB global dataset with 5 MB training sets for 100,000 users will require only about 488 GB of storage, which is much more feasible than 2.5 TB and will still yield very accurate results in the range of around 99.9 percent.

Implementing Global Ingress

Another approach that can be layered on top of merged groups to improve the accuracy of a merged group is to maintain a tentative global ingress. A *global ingress* keeps track of the number of unique users whose filters discover new and useful data. This data can be used to season a global database with new and interesting data found. If a token remains interesting after being merged with the data from several other users, it is clearly a very specific and useful piece of data. After inserting this data into the global dataset, we can then delete it from all of the users' individual datasets, freeing up space. This converts our problem of storage from a linear one to one of contextual similarities among users.

Total Processing Power

Processing power is generally thought to be much more expensive than disk space. Processing power is usually measured in terms of CPU and memory resources.

Many different variables play a role in the amount of processing power required to support a large number of users, and there are always ways to further optimize the software to run with a lighter footprint. Some factors to consider include the following:

- Choice of programming language
- Sorting and other algorithms used
- Design paradigm and process instantiation

Choice of Language

The language that the filter is written in can play a significant role in how fast the application starts up and executes, and could ultimately mean the difference between supporting 5,000 users per machine or 20,000 users per machine.

There are two general types of languages to choose from: compiled languages and interpreted languages. Compiled languages such as C and C++ compile the source code into assembly language, from which it is assembled directly into machine code. Compiled programs are run as executables by the operating system and generally run much faster than interpreted programs, with a much lighter footprint as well. Interpreted languages, instead of compiling the source into machine code, will compile it into a proprietary bytecode that is then interpreted at execution time. These languages typically include just-in-time compiled languages as well, such as Java and Perl.

Interpreted languages aren't actually executed by the operating system but rather are interpreted, evaluated, and then executed by an interpreter. Because interpreters are charged with the responsibility of evaluating the program and executing it themselves, the target program will usually have a slower execution time and require additional resources. The interpreters themselves have a considerable amount of bootstrap in that they require the loading of their own language libraries and other objects at startup. If each process requires its own instance of an interpreter, each process will use up a certain amount of memory and processor resources over and above what the program itself requires. This could range from a few hundred kilobytes of memory and a few hundredths of a second of execution time to megabytes of memory and full seconds of execution time.

Both types of languages have their strengths. Interpreted languages provide additional safeguards to prevent one's code from being compromised by exploiting buffer overflow vulnerabilities and other programming errors caused by humans, so development with an interpreted language can be faster and require less care. The opposing point of view is that programming in interpreted languages takes less discipline, creating bad habits along the way that will ultimately lead to poor code anyway. Compiled languages run faster because they are executable machine code and generally provide more granular control over the software and access to more low-level functions. And without the additional overhead of bootstrap or interpretation, the execution runs at processor speed.

It's very possible to write a successful, scalable spam filter in either type of language. Some upper-class spam filters today, such as Death2Spam, are written in interpreted languages and can handle reasonable loads. There are plenty of poorly written spam filters in either type of language, so the bottom line is that much depends on the skills of the programmer. Given two identical programs, one compiled and the other interpreted, the compiled execution will have a clear advantage over the interpreted one when implemented in a setting of 100,000 users. How much of an advantage this provides depends on the implementation—on very large-scale implementations (such as those for several hundred thousand users), it may mean the difference between purchasing 15 machines versus 50 machines.

If the goal of your project is to make the filter scalable enough for many large implementations, consider a compiled language for the added performance, but emphasize writing good code.

NOTE *Look for a well-written tool in a fast language. The generally accepted execution time for a spam filter is approximately one-tenth of a second of real time per message on small- to medium-sized implementations. Many filters outperform this and can achieve speeds of even one-hundredth of a second per message.*

Sorting and Other Algorithms

It is entirely possible to write an application in BASIC that can outperform an assembly language program, depending on the techniques used in writing the program. Sorting algorithms and other types of looping and recursion can make a noticeable difference between an execution time of one-tenth of a second versus one of several seconds.

Asymptotic analysis involves the study of the growth rate of algorithms. Two goals of this type of analysis are to determine the worst-case running time for an algorithm and to identify the threshold for optimal performance. Depending on the type of tokenizer being used, there will be a certain threshold in the number of data points for the best- and worst-case scenarios. These values can be used to help determine the best algorithms for the particular implementation.

All algorithms have their worst-case scenarios. Some will perform exceptionally well with 50,000 data points but will run much slower than another with only a few thousand. Asymptotic analysis helps identify the best sorting algorithm for a given situation. Since the number of tokens could potentially reach millions, it's difficult to ascertain the worst-case scenario. There are plenty of algorithms to consider. The parsing and tokenizing of a message can itself take up a fraction of a second, or several seconds. Avoiding unnecessary loops and finding alternative methods of parsing can greatly improve performance. Using profiling tools such as gprof can help to identify problem areas of code. Don't guess what code is slow; know what code is slow and fix it.

The book *Introduction to Algorithms* by Cormen, Leiserson, Rivest, and Stein (MIT Press) is an excellent introduction to the basics of asymptotic analysis and also provides a volume full of existing algorithms to use in your applications. There is also a series by Donald Knuth titled *The Art of Computer Programming*, which consists of several books on understanding basic and advanced algorithms, with many examples. Either of these choices should provide excellent insight into the use and development of algorithms that perform optimally for a particular project.

Design Paradigm and Process Instantiation

The number of processes used in the solution, and how these processes communicate with other processes (such as a mail server) can affect performance as well as the licensing of the software.

Most filters fall into two general paradigms. The first, a client/server model, involves running the filter as a daemon process and allowing clients to communicate (usually the mail server or a lightweight piece of middleware) via TCP or a domain socket. The other involves starting a new filter process for each message and passing data across a pipe.

Client/server designs running as a dedicated server process can generally improve efficiency by reducing the amount of bootstrap code that's executed, caching configuration data and database connections, and by performing housekeeping during idle periods, to keep the data optimized for longer periods of time. These designs also allow for more seamless integration with mail servers using protocols such as local mail transfer protocol (LMTP), a protocol designed for local mail system communication.

Instantiating a new filter process for each message directly from the mail server is another approach that yields acceptable results but may not scale quite as well as a the client/server model. This approach involves the mail server starting a new filter process and then passing data to the process via a pipe. For large systems processing hundreds of messages per second, this can mean that over one hundred filter processes are running simultaneously.

Parallelization versus Serialization

Whether or not messages are processed serially or in parallel will make a noticeable difference in the performance of the application. Many filter implementations use some form of locking in order to prevent data from being corrupted by two different filter instances changing it at the same time. If the filter uses extensive locking, lock contention may not only result in processes having to queue, but could create additional delays in overhead while waiting on locks or executing a back-off protocol. Designing the filter to use as little locking as possible while still maintaining data integrity will help avoid these situations. Parallelizing processes so that multiple messages can be processed simultaneously will greatly improve performance—this can be done by partitioning the data so that each user has their own set of locks or by implementing storage mechanisms, such as a SQL-based server, that perform their own *row-level locking* (locking only data that is being changed).

One of the common problems with serialization is the amount of delay in process execution, which can lead to a significant number of processes waiting on the system. If the number of processes exceeds the system's capabilities, the result may be unpredictable. If each message takes half a second of real time to process, a serialized system will not be able to process more than that rate of inbound email over a sustained period of time. Wherever possible, implement efficient locking to allow muliple filter instances to run simultaneously.

Operating System Requirements

Companies have different requirements for the operating systems they support. As we touched on in the last chapter, the choice of storage driver implementation and other variables can directly affect which operating systems the software will compile on. Other considerations to take into account are any optimizations in the code for a particular operating system, and the use of any additional dependencies that may be available only for specific operating systems. It's generally considered good practice to write software that follows a particular set of compiler standards—for example, use of the POSIX interfaces.

Taking advantage of operating system—specific functions, such as low-level kernel calls and the use of proprietary libraries (such as the Solaris thread library), can provide added optimization but can also make the software more proprietary. If you plan on adding these features to your software, it's a good idea to code them in such a way that they can be disabled or replaced with more generic optimizations when a different operating system is being used.

High Availability

Disaster recovery depends largely on the operating system, but several routines can be coded into the software to ensure that it is tolerant of interruptions and failures.

Creating a diagram of the process flow for your project can help identify all of the different components that could potentially fail. In the case of a server-side filter, there are many potential points of failure, including:

- The mail server
- Delivery agents
- Back-end database components (if any)
- The file system (full, read-only, or corrupt)
- Remote sockets (if using LMTP or similar protocols)

A good server-side filter will have a fail-over mode that will attempt to deliver the message or otherwise recover if any internal components fail. If an external component fails, it's important to return the correct error codes so that the mail server can then requeue the message for later processing and delivery.

Transactional processing is also important in a large-scale environment. If your filter processes part of the message and writes it to disk, but then a failure causes the process to fail as a whole, the changes written to disk must be rolled back so that they aren't made again when the system attempts to redeliver the message. SQL-based storage solutions do a great job of providing transactional support.

Mapping out a worst-case scenario via a flowchart is one of the best ways to establish all of the possible points of failure for the project; a subroutine can be written to handle potential failures, roll back transactions, and perform any other types of cleanup that may be necessary. The following layers cover the process flow for most implementations:

Internal layer
   The internal components of the filter software itself.

Dependency layer
   The external components that the filter software directly relies upon for processing, such as a MySQL database.

Service layer
   The different services communicating with the filter, including the mail server, delivery agents, virus scanner, and any other pieces that directly touch the software.

Device layer
   The different devices communicating with the filtering server and other components related directly to filtering.

Network layer

The potentially failing network paths, which could result in timeouts or connection failures.

I/O Bandwidth Requirements

The amount of bandwidth needed to communicate with the storage mechanism or other parts of the system (such as any pass-through components) can affect the decision as to whether a distributed cluster of servers can be configured to manage spam or whether it will be necessary to design a storage area network to handle the load of the software. In implementing I/O, many factors, such as the I/O needed to load and store data, should be taken into consideration. Using SQL-based solutions again appears to be the best way to optimize this type of I/O. Designing the data model and writing queries so that only one or two queries are necessary to perform certain tasks can help optimize the amount of bandwidth required.

Additionally, the training mode used will play a key role in the amount of bandwidth required, as well as in I/O contention issues. The train-everything (TEFT) mode of training requires the greatest number of simultaneous reads and writes to a system, while the train-on-error (TOE) mode requires the fewest.

A majority of SQL-based servers provide support for caching commonly used information to be immediately available for future queries. Most large-scale implementations use the TOE or train-until-mature (TUM) training modes to compensate for I/O issues.

NOTE   *Implementing RAID devices and fiber-channel controllers can help increase the amount of bandwidth available to an application, as well as help avoid I/O contention by adding more disk heads.*

Finally, the operating system can play a large role in the amount of I/O contention on the system. For example, the maintainers of the Linux 2.6 kernel recently overhauled many of the disk access components, resulting in less moving of a drive's head back and forth and increasing performance. Finding a good systems administrator to implement a large-scale solution can make it much easier to support hundreds of thousands of users without having to make further coding optimizations or leave out features that would otherwise be useful. Identifying the right operating system to deploy the solution onto is an equally valuable asset to the fine-tuned performance of a large-scale filter.

Features

In order for an application to be truly scalable, it must be able to support a diverse set of feature requirements. Support for multiple training modes, storage interfaces, and other types of features can make the difference between a company choosing one solution over another. When we first code our projects, we usually design them to solve our own problems. To counteract this urge, visit some customer sites or discuss your project with others in the field to analyze what areas your project should address.

Required features may end up having less to do with individual training modes and more to do with the different knobs and whistles available on a particular piece of software. Some companies desire the ability to customize their software to meet new needs as they arise, while others require notifications and reports to be generated automatically and certain types of intelligent handling of particular events to be configurable.

End-User Support

The amount of support that the company implementing the software will need to provide to its own customers or end users also plays a role in just how scalable the application is. There's no point in investing to save $50,000 of lost bandwidth every month if the company's also going to have to spend $50,000 to provide help to the filter's users.

A filter should be designed so that grandma can use it and understand it fairly quickly. Chances are, a large corporation will develop its own documentation to teach its employees and customers how to use the software, but having some prewritten generic documentation can expedite this process. Smaller businesses may have to depend on the documentation you provide. The software should be well documented but should also be easy enough to explain in a two-minute conversation. Ultimately, the software should be simple enough for even the most computer-illiterate person to use.

In addition, the filter should work with as many mail clients as possible. Not all mail clients support features such as bouncing or redirecting a message. Other mail clients may not support the client-side plug-ins that may be required to use the software. The design of the software must be global enough for everyone to use but should have enough features to do its job well and require little support.

Sizing Machine Capacity

We've discussed the major concerns many companies have when looking at implementing a new filtering solution. As you may have guessed, supporting 100,000 users may not be something that a single machine can handle by itself. Designing the filter to handle a distributed cluster of machines will make it much more scalable in these environments.

One of the factors to consider in deploying a filter on a large network is the approximate number of users a single machine can handle or, alternatively, the number of messages per second it can process. Depending on how the system is designed, a series of processing agents may be distributed on multiple servers, with actual user data residing on another layer of machines behind them, or there might be only one layer of machines, with a certain number of users stored on each machine. We'll discuss all of these scenarios later in this chapter.

Sizing the machine is important in determining how scalable the filtering software will be. In cases in which there is no data on which to base a hypothesis, this can be determined only through predictive analysis or trial and error. Other times, mathematical formulas can be applied to determine execution time, peak processing, and other variables. Considering some of the general questions a systems administrator will ask is a good way to begin sizing a machine for use on large networks. After we take a look at the general questions, we'll discuss the scientific factors, which are also necessary and designed to provide answers for a specific sizing model.

General Resource Planning

General resource planning involves answering several practical questions to discern the realistic issues involved in a deployment model. General questions focus more on political and financial constraints than on scientific hardware sizing. Some of these questions include the following:

- What type of hardware is available?
- What operating system should the software run on?
- How many individual machines are available?
- What is the company's methodology?
- How many administrators are available?

What Type of Hardware Is Available?

Sometimes companies are bound by specific financial agreements with vendors and have a set of hardware they deploy on the network. As a result, only specific hardware with one of many configurations is available. Depending on the number of users at each location, the cost of the hardware, and the operating system, the beefiest box may not necessarily be the best box.

What Operating System Should the Software Run On?

The operating system may play a role in the number of users the hardware is capable of supporting. Some operating systems are built to handle heavier loads than others, and some are designed to run as fast as possible but can handle only a certain load. The networking limitations of the operating system (such as the TCP stack) and other variables may also play a role in which operating system is best suited for the particular implementation.

How Many Individual Machines Are Available?

If there's an initial limit on the number of machines available, each machine will have no choice but to support a specific number of users. Five machines for 100,000 users create a minimum requirement of 20,000 users per machine. If a limited amount of hardware is available, what optimizations will be necessary, and what features will need to be dropped in order to support the requirement?

What Is the Company's Methodology?

Sometimes the company's methodology may play a role in the type and size of hardware that is chosen. If the company has a very strict methodology with regard to testing, staging, and production, *X* number of machines will be needed to develop a test lab. If the methodology calls for a specific amount of redundancy, it may be necessary to deploy many small machines rather than a few large ones, and a certain level of fail-over resources will need to be planned.

How Many Administrators Are Available?

If only a single administrator is available, having fewer machines will help avoid a maintenance headache. When new updates are available and additional systems have to be deployed, one or two administrators will be required to carry out these requests. Since people are more expensive than machinery, in cases where staff is limited, beefier boxes will sometimes be necessary.

Assessing Resource Utilization

A resource-planning matrix takes the factors of present-day utilization of the mail system into consideration. It is important to identify the following:

- The peak hour of processing
- The overall volume
- The concurrent workload
- The target CPU utilization
- The estimated fail-over

Identifying the Peak Hour of Processing

The peak hour of processing is the time period during which CPU utilization on the machines is at its highest. This will be when you receive the most mail into the system. The peak hour of processing will identify the amount of load for consideration in a deployment. In identifying this peak, consider the volume of email throughout the year. If you're uncertain as to what your peak capacity is, it may be necessary to implement some graphing utilities, such as MRTG (the Mullti-Router Traffic Grapher).

Identifying the Volume

Once you've determined the peak processing capacity, it's necessary to identify the different components of the mail system that use a significant load. This can not only help to determine if additional hardware will be required, but may play a role in determining how much of the filter's work will be necessary. For example, many users may opt not to be enrolled in a spam-filtering solution. Other companies may choose not to pass internal company email through the filter to conserve load. If a virus scanner is present on the network, what percentage of inbound messages will be caught before they make it to the filter? Determining the overall volume can help to identify the overall peak demand of the filter.

Identifying the Concurrent Workload

The concurrent workload takes into account the total number of operations running in parallel on a system. If the mail server is processing 3,600 messages per hour, this load could be calculated as 1 concurrent operation per second, or it could be as many as 10 concurrent operations over a period of ten seconds. Identifying the concurrent workload will help to identify areas of need in the storage implementation (such as locking) and will also help estimate I/O contention to better size the required storage hardware.

Identifying Target CPU Utilization

Based on the peak hour of processing, determine the desired level of CPU utilization during this time period. This should take into account unexpected spikes in load, total capacity, and whether or not it is appropriate for performance to degrade during a fail-over.

Estimating Fail-Over

Based on the peak hour of processing, determine the number of machines that can be allowed to fail while still meeting the requirements for desired CPU utilization at the time of the peak. A minimum of two machines in a distributed environment should be allowed to fail simultaneously. What resources will be required in order to manage this failure? Will fail-over take place instantaneously, or will the systems administrator need to perform other tasks in order to establish fail-over?

Building a Distributed Model

In many large-scale implementations, it makes sense to build a distributed cluster of machines capable of performing independently of one another in the event of fail-over. It's also sometimes necessary to run the spam-filtering software on a machine other than the mail server itself. There are countless hodgepodges of distributed networks powering the Internet on eggshells, but only a few that can provide reliable, incremental scaling. Depending on how the target network is already configured, some implementations may work better than others. This section covers some of the most common distributed networking approaches for spam-filtering installations.

Round-Robin Distributed Networking

A *round-robin distributed network* comprises a series of nodes capable of servicing any user on the system (see Figure 9-1). The term "round-robin" is used to denote a DNS round-robin or another type of implementation (possibly using a layer-4 switch) that is capable of sporadically directing requests to different machines.

The round-robin approach is commonly used to balance other types of network traffic such as web traffic. In a spam-filtering environment, this approach requires that one or more static systems reside behind the round-robin servers to store user data. Otherwise, users would experience a different result depending on which machine the inbound message hit. Systems employing a static global dataset don't need to worry about this extra layer.

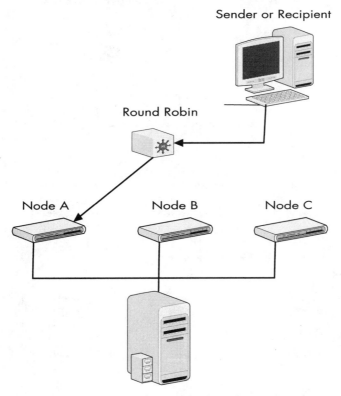

Figure 9-1: Round-robin configuration with single storage node

In configurations like this, the bottleneck is usually the per-user storage system. The more nodes and users there are on the network, the higher the load average of the storage facility. For this reason, some like to take a modified approach to distributed networking by installing the primary filter software on each node and clustering an independent set of storage devices together. The storage devices are generally kept independent of one another to reduce the amount of disk space and load for each device. One way to do this is to split up the storage devices based on user-id or username.

In Figure 9-2, we see the same series of nodes in a round-robin filter cluster, but the storage is now distributed based on the first letter of the username. This approach works reasonably well in a setting where the growth rate of users is very static, but there is a drawback in systems with a faster growth rate. In order to add more nodes, the naming scheme for the distributed storage must be changed, which results in an overabundance of work. A much better alternative for systems that grow rapidly is to use the numeric user-id to distribute the storage cluster. As more users are added to a network, the user-ids only increase or replace older users who are no longer on the system. As new ranges of user-ids start to become utilized, it becomes much less work to configure a fourth or fifth storage machine and make a minor update to the filtering software installed on each node.

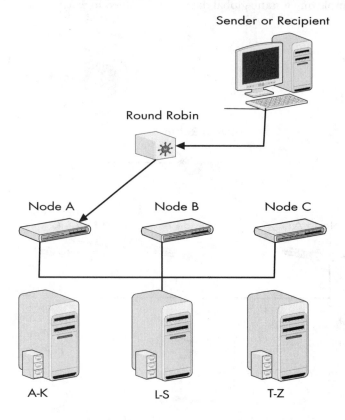

Figure 9-2: Round-robin configuration with distributed storage

Distributed BGP Networking

Nationwide networks have the burden of managing not only server resources but also internal bandwidth from leased lines or their own physical networks of dark fiber buried in cow pastures. It's inefficient to retrieve data from a server in Virginia for a user who is primarily connected to Palo Alto, California. A distributed border gateway protocol (BGP) network provides for an inverselike filtering (and mail distribution) approach for networks with many points of presence (see Figure 9-3).

By placing a machine at every major point of presence and having that machine handle a specific subset of users who are connected to that location, systems administrators can have inbound mail routed to the local mail server at the POP and stored in the vicinity of the destination user. When the user connects to receive email, they point their mail client at an IP address that the network has ghosted across every major point of presence. The server that is closest to the user will, by default, answer the request and should hopefully have the user's data located on the local storage facility at that POP.

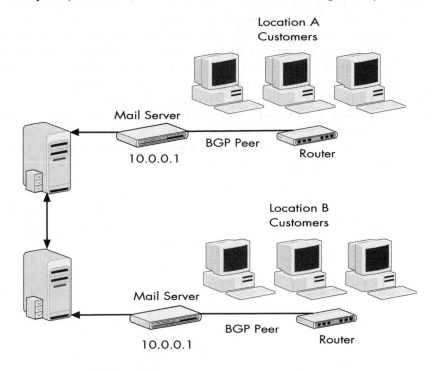

Figure 9-3: Distributed BGP networking

If the user travels out of town, the individual storage servers (or the mail servers themselves) must be configured to communicate with one another for retrieval of the data. This is done by configuring each machine with an internal IP address of its own, while using the same public-facing IP address at each point of presence so that the user can move around without having to change mail settings. This commonly requires two network interfaces in each machine. BGP takes care of most of the issues with regard to ghosting IP addresses on a large network, so the user will end up hitting the closest server to them.

The obvious advantage of this approach is not only to prevent extraneous traffic from traveling over the network, but also to distribute the filtering (and mail server) network based on location, providing a level of redundancy. If a main trunk from California to Virginia goes down, it should affect only users who are not within their local service area who want to check their mail. If storage is being mirrored at the two closest locations to a user's service area, then even the primary location failing wouldn't result in a complete loss of service. Much of the success of this approach depends on the appropriate sizing of the machines to provide a level of fail-over capacity.

Final Thoughts

We've looked at many different approaches to scaling for a spam-filtering solution. There's much room for further optimization, including performance tuning, intelligent purging, and even the possibility for neural declustering, as we'll cover later in this book. All of these approaches require the right amount of human resources and skill. Large nationwide networks have these resources to dedicate to implementing high-performance, distributed solutions on the network. For a filter developer, the key to developing a scalable tool is foresight regarding the many different types of scaling these large providers may require. Including support for different types of scaling, such as user-id distribution and peak hour statistics, can make life easier for the systems administrators installing and maintaining the software on their network.

PART III

ADVANCED CONCEPTS OF STATISTICAL FILTERING

10

TESTING THEORY

Statistical filtering is unlike any other spam-filtering approach we've seen, and because of this, it tests differently than any other beast. The testing approaches used to measure heuristic spam filters are frequently and erroneously applied to statistical filters, which produces poor results. The intricacies of machine learning require a more scientific approach than simply throwing mail at the filter, and even the most detailed approaches to testing such a tool only barely succeed in accomplishing a real-world simulation. In this chapter, we'll discuss some of the best practices put into place by filter authors for testing the efficiency of language classifiers. We'll also take a look at several common tests used to measure different areas of filtering and address some common problems testers make.

The Challenge of Testing

Modern-day language classifiers face a very unique situation—they learn based on the environment around them. The problem in testing them, therefore, involves the need to create an extremely controlled environment. When heuristic filtering was popular, there were many different ways to test it. Since the filter didn't base its decisions on the previous results, an accurate set of results would accommodate just about any type of testing approach used.

The state of a statistical language classifier is similar to that of a sequential circuit, in that the output is a combination of both the inputs and the previous state of the filter. The previous state of the filter is based on a previous set of inputs, which are based on a previous set of results, and so on. Think of it in terms of going to the supermarket every week: what you buy from visit to visit is based on what you have in your refrigerator. A single change in the environment (such as an impending snowstorm) can easily affect the contents of your refrigerator by many Twinkies. Similarly, a change in the filter's environment can affect a filter by many messages. With this in mind, the challenge of testing is to create an environment that simulates real-world behavior as closely as possible—after all, what we are trying to measure is how accurate the filter will be in the real world. This means that testing a statistical filter is no longer a matter of testing but of *simulation*. Simulating a real-world behavior takes many factors into consideration that obsolete heuristic testing doesn't.

Of course, when you're not testing to measure accuracy, this type of simulation isn't always necessary. Chaos in message ordering and content may be appropriate when testing to compare features for a particular filter or for any other kind of blind test for which accuracy isn't as important as deviation.

Message Continuity

Message continuity refers to the existence of uninterrupted threads and their message content, specifically in the set of test messages used. Many test sets are based on older testing approaches and consist of nothing more than a random selection of emails from several users. This is ideal for static filter tests, such as those of heuristic filters or even blacklists or tests for which the accuracy of a filter isn't being measured (such as the feature comparison test we'll discuss later).

However, such test messages don't take into consideration the importance of supplying complete threads or continuity of headers, and they are therefore not very useful sources of data for conducting tests involving accuracy. Unfortunately, many individuals make the mistake of using these types of message corpora to test statistical filters, which results in extremely unreliable conclusions.

Because the results of a statistical filter depend in part on the state of the filter, every single message that is learned plays a role in the results. If the message is from an unknown individual, the filter will begin to learn the individual's distinct signature. The sender's message headers, grammatical pretense, and other characteristics of the learned message all play a role in identifying the sender as either a legitimate user or a spammer. When future messages are received from the same sender, the original information learned will play a role in determining the outcome of the classification. Senders who have sent several legitimate messages to a recipient and are well known to the filter are trusted more than unknown users. As a result they have slightly more flexibility in the content of their message. Another common problem in maintaining message continuity is the order in which the messages are arranged in the corpus. In some cases, the original thread ordering will be preserved. The tests that do not preserve the ordering will generally provide poorer results than ordered tests.

A test corpus that doesn't take message continuity into consideration will likely have several types of *hard ham* messages for testing but won't provide a historical thread of data from the original senders. Statistical filters therefore will see more of these messages as spam, never able to take into consideration whether the topics discussed in the message are familiar to the user. This is also true of spam, in that the same spammers will generally be invading a user's inbox. Presenting a filter with a random set of spams with may not provide an accurate representation of real-life results, because the same spammers generally spam a user over and over again, giving themselves away by, among other things, their message headers (and, ironically, a lot of the junk text they use to try to fool spam filters).

In designing a simulation for a language classifier, it's generally acceptable to use several corpora of actual users' mail and spam. Establishing a test group of about 10 to 20 users who are willing to build a corpus of mail will provide the most accurate simulation because the message contents and ordering will both be preserved.

An ideal training corpus should capture between three and six months' worth of messages. One additional month should be captured to produce a set of testing messages. More advanced tests may even extend this to nine or ten months, measuring the accuracy of each month throughout the testing process. This will ensure both message continuity and the contextual differences between the types of spam. Although the continuity of the messages is important, many users make the mistake of presenting the same messages they used to train as candidates for classification. This usually results in wonderful but terribly dishonest results. The test corpus should be contiguous from the training corpus, rather than a repetition.

Training corpora aren't necessarily trained directly into the filter. Depending on the recommended training mode, messages may be trained only upon misclassification. This is especially true with filters using train-on-error (TOE) mode, in which training every single message would result in poor levels of accuracy.

Archive Window

The archive window is a frequently overlooked area of test simulation. As we've learned through Terry Sullivan's research, spam evolves over the course of several months. The seas change every four to six months on average, and in building a test corpus, many users overlook this. Some will archive several thousand messages captured over a few weeks' time. The resulting simulation provides only short-term accuracy, as the filter has not yet learned the different permutations that gradually take place in spam over a longer period of time.

Using the corpus exclusively as an archive and using fresh spam for the test will further impair results. The quantity of messages isn't nearly as important as the time period over which the messages were captured. The difference is between having six months of experience with spam or having one month of experience six times.

Similarly, the window for building an archive shouldn't be too much older than four to six months if the testing will be performed on a more recent archive of mail, as spam (and likely the user's own legitimate mail) will have evolved beyond the characteristics learned by the filter. The spam from six months ago is dissimilar to the spam of today. The spam from a year ago is virtually useless when classifying the spam of today. Only by learning recent messages and their permutations can a filter accurately learn the patterns it will need to classify new text. Ideally, a real-world corpus of mail should be captured for training and another one for testing. The corpora should be established during similar sequential time periods.

The exception to this is when measuring several concurrent time periods. If a year of messages has been archived, the first six months can be used as training data and the remaining six months can be treated as six different tests. If a corrective training approach is implemented during the testing, the filter can learn from its mistakes during each training period and provide enough learning continuity to be able to adequately classify each message. As long as there is no gap between the training corpus and the test corpus, the messages will permute gradually enough to be measured adequately.

Purge Simulation

Another area that is frequently disregarded in a statistical learning simulation is the purging of stale data. When the training corpus is learned, each message is trained within the same short period of time (usually a period of several minutes or hours). The usual purging a filter might employ doesn't take place because all of the data trained is considered new.

The purging of stale data can very frequently affect the polarity of many tokens in the user's database. In most cases, the conventional purge tools can't be used because they fail to see the data as stale. If the data that would normally be considered stale is not purged, the less volatile data will fail to reflect the same results as a real-world scenario. This is because the legacy data left over will still affect the tokens' polarity. In extreme cases, this could cause guilty tokens to take on an innocent probability and uninteresting tokens to become erroneously interesting.

To establish a true purge simulation, it may be necessary to make actual changes to the software to use the time stamp represented in the message headers to set the actual time period for data. It will also be necessary to simulate the purge tool running at its standard intervals—usually nightly or weekly. This can be done by parsing the time period from the message headers and treating it as a *virtual* time period. The purge should run and remove any stale data it finds in the dataset based on the virtual time stamps extracted from the messages.

Interleave

The interleave at which messages from the corpus are trained, corrected, and classified can play a dramatic role in the results of the test. Many people erroneously perform tests by feeding in two separate corpora—one of legitimate mail and one of spam. Some tests use a 1-to-1 interleave, while others try their best to simulate a real-world scenario. The original ordering of the messages in the corpus will generally yield the most realistic results.

The interleave should, if possible, include both legitimate mail and spams in the order they were received, and the original interleave should be recorded.

Corrective Training Delay

The delay in retraining classification errors is probably one of the most difficult characteristics to simulate. When a misclassification occurs, the user doesn't report it immediately—several other messages are likely to come in before the user checks their email and corrects the error.

If a user receives 20 spams overnight and the first of these is erroneously classified, the other 19 messages may have been affected by the error. In most cases this plays against the filter and can risk generating additional false positives or spam misses, but sometimes this can also err in favor of the filter. A corrective training delay plays a role in the decisions of all the messages between the time that the error was made and when it was corrected. Without simulating this, the snowball effect frequently experienced in real-world scenarios doesn't occur, leaving the results somewhat skewed.

Establishing an average message count between errors occurring and being corrected can help to simulate such a delay. Log files from the filter reporting on the number of messages processed during this period of time can help to create a reasonable message count to use as a corrective delay. Filters that perform their function at MTA (mail transfer agent or mail server) time (that is, when the message is received by the MTA) are likely to experience a much longer corrective training delay than ones that perform their function at MUA (mail user agent) time (that is, when the user downloads their email).

Types of Simulations

There are many different reasons to perform a testing simulation. The following types of simulations are the most common; we'll provide some examples of these in this chapter.

- Testing to measure the range of accuracy for a specific filter
- Testing to measure the speed of adaptation in chaotic environments

- Testing to compare the effectiveness of multiple filters
- Testing to compare features in a single filter

Not all simulations require the strict quality assurance discussed in the previous section. Tests in which the results themselves are not as interesting as how the results change between tests generally permit a more lenient test simulation (and sometimes a chaotic one). However, these types of tests are usually effective only at measuring features in a homogeneous environment (that is, where the same filter is being tested against itself). Since all filters react differently to the data, the only true way to compare filters or to measure the real-world accuracy of a filter is to use data that takes all test challenges into consideration.

Measuring the Accuracy of a Specific Filter

This test is designed to measure a range of accuracy for a specific filter, using a set of users' email as the test medium. It generally involves testing messages for 10 to 20 different users and dropping the top and bottom results from the mix. This test isn't designed to measure peak accuracy but rather average results. It is therefore in the interest of the tester to use test subjects with very diverse email behavior.

Test Criteria

It's not a good idea to use ten programmer friends for this test, but rather to find one or two different individuals each in a range of categories. Here are some sample categories to consider:

Computer programmers	Online merchants
Musicians	Corporate executives
Members of the clergy	Low-volume users
Medical practitioners	Blue-collar workers
Soccer moms	Government employees
Teenagers	Attorneys

To measure the range of accuracy for a specific filter, it will be necessary to perform several tests on different sets of high-quality corpora. Each corpus of mail should follow all of the guidelines outlined previously in this chapter:

Message continuity
The original threads for all messages must be intact. The ordering of all messages must be preserved in each corpus to ensure accurate results.

Archive window
Each corpus should be based over a period of three to six months, regardless of the quantity of messages. If a separate test corpus will be used, the test corpus should be an extension of the original training corpus, representing the seventh month. Several tests may be run on each user, using a different training period for each test.

Purge simulation

Stale data should be purged to ensure accurate results.

Interleave

The original interleave of the messages (legitimate mail versus spam) should be used. If the interleave is not available, a best estimation may be used, or multiple tests should be run for each test simulation, with the three best and worst results averaged.

Corrective training delay

The best estimation for each user should be used.

Finally, the number of training messages and the time period required for the optimal performance of the filter being tested should be determined. The software's documentation will sometimes recommend values, but it may be best to consult the filter author as well. Occasionally the documented values are too conservative or are unreasonable and require tweaking. If it is uncertain where a good training count lies, it may be necessary to perform a few different tests to identify the optimal range.

Performing the Test

The accuracy range test consists of the following events:

Training period

The period during which an initial corpus of messages is trained into the filter.

Classification period

The period during which messages are presented for classification, rather than training.

Corrective period

The period during which misclassified messages are presented for retraining.

Purge period

The periods during which purging of stale data is simulated.

Listing 10-1 outlines the entire process.

```
while messageCount < minCount or timePeriod < minPeriod
  do
    present next message for training
    if timeElapsed > nextPurgeInterval
    then
      perform purge simulation

while more messages in corpus
  do
    present next message for classification
    if classification is wrong
```

```
then
   determine nextInsertionPoint for correction
   increment incorrect classification counter
else
   increment correct classification counter

if timeElapsed > nextInsertionPoint
then
   submit erroneous message for retraining
```

Listing 10-1: Process flow of an accuracy range test

The process begins with a training cycle. During this training cycle, the recommended set of test messages is seeded into the filter, using whatever mechanism the filter provides for corpus training. The number of messages and the time period that the messages should cover is determined based on the recommended values in the documentation or from the author. The time stamps used to record the data should be stored based on the time stamp in the message's headers. If the filter does not provide a mechanism to apply this modification, it may be necessary to make minor coding changes. This simulation of a time stamp is done in order to support the purge simulation.

The decision as to whether to perform a purge simulation is made every time a message is processed, based on the time stamp of the current and/or next message. A purge simulation should be run at the intervals recommended in the filter's documentation or by its author. This is generally on a nightly or weekly basis, and therefore it will be necessary to calculate this delta from the time stamps in the message headers. When the purge simulation runs, all other processing should pause until it completes. Once the simulation is complete, the training loop may continue.

When the training corpus has been correctly trained into the filter, the next step is to present the test corpus. The test corpus should be a set of *different* messages from the training corpus, and should represent the next period of messages occurring in time right after the training corpus. The test corpus is used for two purposes. It provides the data that is actually tested, and it is used to schedule whatever corrections are necessary. As each message is presented for testing, the result of the classification should be compared with the actual classification of the message. If the result was incorrect, the message should be resubmitted for error correction at whatever correction delay checkpoint is determined by the tester. This may be based either on the number of messages processed or on the time in the time stamps. It's up to the tester to determine the most reasonable delay period for retraining.

When the message is retrained, it's important to use whatever mechanism the filter supports to correct errors. Many testers make the mistake of feeding the message back in with the inverse classification, but this doesn't necessarily correct the errors. In most cases, feeding the message through the corpus a second time will increment the relevant tokens' correct classification counts but will not decrement the incorrect counts. Be sure to use whatever error correction arguments are necessary.

Once the process has completed, the tester will be left with a number of correct and incorrect classifications. The accuracy of the filter can be calculated using the following formula:

```
100 - (100 (totalErrors / totalTestMessages))
```

If three errors were made in 1,000 test messages, the formula would evaluate the following:

```
100 - (100 (3 / 1000)) = 99.7 = 99.7% Accuracy
```

Each test will undoubtedly yield a different number of errors. An average accuracy can easily be calculated by averaging the results of the tests together. Omitting one or two results on each end of the range may provide a more reliable average, while the top and bottom results may provide a useful best- and worst-case scenario.

Measuring Adaptation in Chaotic Environments

The test to measure adaptation speed in a chaotic environment is useful for measuring the ability of the filter to adapt to an environment where new, unlearned data is presented. This test is very different from the accuracy range test and is designed to measure learning speed rather than accuracy. Because of this, the classification results are used only to determine the learning speed and not to provide results.

Test Criteria

The test criteria for a chaotic test are somewhat relaxed between corpora. Since we are measuring adaptation speed, this test requires a chaotic change in message context to occur between training and testing. Most of the same criteria as in the accuracy range test are used, but we rely upon the chaotic breakdown of these criteria between the training and all test corpora.

Message continuity
 The original threads for all messages must be completely different between the training corpus and each test corpus. Each corpus should preserve the original threads and message ordering *for that corpus only*, and the context between corpora should be very different. It is generally a good idea to use a different test subject for each corpus.

Archive window
 The archive window is generally short for this test, to be determined by the tester. The window should at the very least cover the estimated learning speed of the filter.

Purge simulation

A purge simulation should be used, but with more relaxed purge thresholds that allow for stale data to remain in the dataset for prolonged periods. If purging takes place too quickly, the test will not measure relearning speed, but only learning speed.

Interleave

The original interleave of the messages (legitimate mail versus spam) should be used. If the interleave is not available, a best estimation may be used, or multiple tests can be run for each test simulation, with the three best and worst results averaged.

Corrective training delay

This delay will depend on the tester and on the specific purpose of the test. If the test is designed to measure only the filter's ability to relearn, an immediate correction should take place. If the test is interested in real-world chaotic adaptation, use a reasonable value simulating one or more test subjects.

Performing the Test

The chaotic adaptation test consists of the following events:

Training period

The period during which the initial corpus of messages is trained into the filter.

Adaptation period

The period during which an entire set of unknown messages is presented for classification and the speed at which accurate results are learned is measured.

Corrective period

The period during which misclassified messages are presented for retraining.

Purge period

The periods during which purging of stale data is simulated.

Listing 10-2 outlines the entire process.

```
while messageCount < minCount or timePeriod < minPeriod
  do
    present next message for training
    if timeElapsed > nextPurgeInterval
    then
      perform purge simulation

while test corpora remaining
  let messageCount = 0
  let timeStart = timestamp of first message in corpus
  foreach corpus
```

```
do
  while more messages in corpus
  do
    present next message for classification
    increment messageCount
    if classification is wrong
    then
      determine nextInsertionPoint for correction
    else
      determine accuracy for previous N results
      if accuracy > minThreshold
      then
        report messageCount
        report timestamp - timeStart

if timeElapsed > nextInsertionPoint
then
  submit erroneous message for retraining
```

Listing 10-2: Process flow of a chaotic adaptation test

This test begins in the same way as the accuracy range test. An initial training corpus of messages is trained into the filter. Each test corpus is then tested sequentially. As the messages in the corpus are presented for classification, the accuracy for the previous N results (where N is a window size determined by the tester) is calculated. As the filter learns from its mistakes, the accuracy will gradually increase. When the accuracy of the window has met or exceeded the minimum threshold set by the tester, this signals that the corpus has been sufficiently learned and adapted to by the filter.

Once a corpus has been sufficiently adapted, the chaotic adaptation test will then begin training the next corpus, which should be contextually different from the previous one. The same measurements are taken and reported.

When the test has completed, a message count and time delta (based on the time stamps in the headers of the test messages) are reported for each chaotic transition. Either of the results, depending on which one the tester is most interested in, can then be averaged with those of the other corpora to determine the average message count or time period required for chaotic learning to take place.

Testing the Effectiveness of Multiple Filters

Testing to compare the effectiveness of multiple filters is a complicated task. Not only does the data need to simulate the closest possible real-world behavior, but the amount of data and how the data is trained, classified, and corrected will change with every filter. The goal of the filter comparison test is to simulate each filter's real-world levels of accuracy based on the preferences for each filter as prescribed in the documentation or recommended by the filter author. It's generally a good idea to ask the user community or even the author of a particular filter for an opinion about training thresholds, as the recommended values in the documentation are sometimes tailored to be more conservative or liberal to make users happy.

Test Criteria

The test criteria are similar to those of the accuracy range test, in that the data should be consistent and well preserved. The same data must be used to measure each filter; otherwise, the results will be meaningless. It is not uncommon to perform several different tests for each filter, using a different corpus of mail for each test.

There are two ways to determine how much data should be trained into the filter, depending on the results the tester is looking for. To achieve the fairest results, it may be appropriate to use a static amount of training data among all filters. Additional training usually only helps statistical filters, and therefore using the threshold of the filter that requires the most training and applying this threshold to all filters will prevent the test from being affected by the recommended values in the documentation. Stricter tests, which seek to measure each filter's performance based not only on the data but also on these recommended values should use the training level recommended in the documentation or provided by the filter author, possibly resulting in a different training level for each filter. In either case, it's important to take into consideration not only the number of messages being trained, but also the time period that the messages cover. A minimum of three months of training data should be considered for this test; six months is better.

Another thing to consider between filters is the training mode. Most filters support a default training mode, and so two individual tests may need to be run, one using the default training mode for each filter and one using the same training mode among filters. The first type of test is generally a more accurate representation of how filters perform together, but it may be discovered that simply altering the training mode for a particular filter could improve its performance. This should be reflected in the test results.

As with the accuracy range test, it is not a good idea to use 10 or 20 test subjects with the same background, but rather to find one or two different individuals in each of a diverse set of backgrounds.

To measure the range of accuracy for each filter, it will be necessary to perform multiple tests on different sets of high-quality corpora. Each corpus of mail should follow all of the same guidelines outlined in the accuracy range test.

Message continuity

The original threads for all messages must be intact. The ordering of all messages must be preserved in each corpus, to ensure accurate results.

Archive window

Each corpus should cover a period of three to six months, regardless of the quantity of messages. If a separate test corpus will be used, it should be an extension of the original training corpus, representing the seventh month.

Purge simulation

Stale data should be purged to ensure accurate results.

Interleave

The original interleave of the messages (legitimate mail versus spam) should be used. If the interleave is not available, a best estimation may be used, or multiple tests should be run for each test simulation, and the three best and worst results should be averaged.

Corrective training delay

The best estimation for each user should be used. This may be different from filter to filter if some filters perform their filtering at different times or are integrated into different parts of the mail system.

Performing the Test

The filter comparison test consists of the following events during each run of each filter.

Training period

The period during which an initial corpus of messages is trained into the filter.

Classification period

The period during which messages are presented for classification, rather than training.

Corrective period

The period during which misclassified messages are presented for retraining.

Purge period

The periods during which purging of stale data is simulated.

Listing 10-3 outlines the entire process.

```
foreach filter
  foreach corpus
    reset all counters
    while messageCount < minCount or timePeriod < minPeriod
    do
      present next message for training
      if timeElapsed > nextPurgeInterval
      then
      perform purge simulation

    while more messages in corpus
    do
      present next message for classification
      if classification is wrong
      then
        determine nextInsertionPoint for correction
```

```
        increment incorrect classification counter
    else
        increment correct classification counter

    if timeElapsed > nextInsertionPoint
    then
        submit erroneous message for retraining

    calculate test accuracy A_N = 100 - (100(T_E/T_M))
    optionally drop best and worst accuracy
    calculate average accuracy for filter

compare accuracy levels for each filter
```

Listing 10-3: Process flow of a comparison test

Each filter test begins with a training cycle for each test corpus. During this training cycle, the predetermined set of test messages is seeded into the filter, using whatever mechanism the filter provides. Depending on whether this threshold is static or dynamic, the number of messages and the time period to cover them may be different from filter to filter. As in the accuracy range test, the time stamps used to record the data should be stored based on the time stamp in the message headers. If the filters do not provide a mechanism to apply this modification, it may be necessary to make minor coding changes to each filter. This simulation of time stamping is necessary in order to support a purge simulation for each filter.

The purge simulation recommended for each filter should be used, and the purge intervals for each filter should be respected. Because filters manage data very differently, using a common purge value is not recommended, as it may skew the data. Unlike the training window, the purge process is very different between filters, based on many factors such as training mode.

The decision as to whether to perform a purge simulation is evaluated every time a message is processed, based on the time stamp of the current and/or next message. A purge simulation should be run at the intervals recommended in the filter's documentation or by its author. This is generally on a nightly or weekly basis, and therefore it will be necessary to calculate this delta from the time stamps in the message headers. When the purge simulation runs, all other processing should pause until it completes. When the simulation does complete, the training loop may continue.

Once the training corpus has been correctly trained into the filter being tested, the next step is to present the test corpus. The test corpus should be a set of *different* messages from the training corpus, and should represent the next period of messages occurring in time right after the training corpus. As each message is presented for testing, the result of the classification should be compared with the actual classification of the message. If the result was incorrect, the message should be resubmitted for error correction at the correction delay checkpoint determined by the tester. This may be based on the number of messages processed, or it could be based on time. It's up to the tester to determine the most reasonable delay period for retraining.

For every corpus that is processed, the accuracy of the test will be calculated. When every corpus for a filter has completed, enough data is present to determine the peak, floor, and average levels of accuracy for that filter.

Comparing Features in a Single Filter

Comparing features in a single filter can require an entirely different approach to testing, depending on the features being measured. The feature comparison test is designed to measure different levels of effectiveness among features that are autonomous to the filter's core learning algorithms. That is to say, this test is useful for testing features that do not directly affect real-world machine learning, but that play a role in accuracy. This test is frequently performed to measure the different error levels between tokenizers or tokenizer philosophy. It can be used for some learning features, but the results it provides may not be as accurate as those of an accuracy range test. To perform a real-world comparison between two features, it is recommended that the tester perform an accuracy range test.

The idea behind the feature comparison test is to create an environment that does *not* reflect real-world behavior, but rather discontinuous or diverse behavior. This allows the features to be measured on many different types of messages. An ideal corpus to use for this type of test is the SpamAssassin public corpus, available at http://www.spamassassin.org/publiccorpus. While the environment should be diverse, it should not be overly chaotic. Some contextual similarities are necessary to training, but complete message continuity should be avoided.

Test Criteria

The test criteria for the feature comparison test require a more heuristic-like approach to testing. What's being measured isn't the actual levels of accuracy, but rather the distance between the two different levels of accuracy with different features enabled (or disabled) in the filter. This test will, in most cases, yield very poor results for measuring accuracy, because it relies on sparse, discontinuous training data. The goal is to initially train the filter with a set of training text from a corpus, and then shuffle the remaining set of text messages several times, using the data to establish the peak, floor, and average delta in accuracy or error rate.

The training set used is very different from that used for the other tests, in that a somewhat chaotic environment is created to measure the effectiveness of each feature. The entire training and test corpus combined may share the same context of messages if the tester's goal is to compare the features in a diverse environment, or it may use an entirely different set of messages if the goal is to measure the filter's ability to detect unpredictable and unlearned types of messages.

Message continuity

The messages should not be continuous but should be diverse in nature. There is no need for entire threads to be preserved, although a few messages in a thread may be present in the corpus. The ordering of all messages should be mixed; several messages randomly shuffled in the test corpus will be useful for testing, although some messages may be kept in order.

Archive window
Since no long-term learning is being measured, the archive window can be any length. It is acceptable to use a static number of training and test messages.

Purge simulation
In this chaotic environment, in which there is no long-term learning, a purge simulation is generally not necessary.

Interleave
A sparse interleave of the messages should be used. The original interleave should not be preserved, but rather messages should be somewhat randomized. The test corpus should be completely randomized.

Corrective training delay
Since real-world behavior is not being simulated, corrective training may be performed immediately on error.

Performing the Test

The feature comparison test consists of the following events during each run of each filter.

Training period
The period during which an initial corpus of messages is trained into the filter. This may be a percentage of a single corpus, or it may be an entirely different corpus if the tester is measuring behavior in an unpredictable environment.

Classification period
The period during which messages are presented for classification rather than training. In this case, the messages will also be randomized.

Corrective training period
The period during which erroneously classified messages are presented for retraining.

Listing 10-4 outlines the entire process.

```
foreach feature
  while messageCount < minCount
    do
      present next message for training

  foreach test shuffle
    do
      randomize message order in test corpus
      while more messages in corpus
```

```
do
    present next message for classification
    if classification is wrong
    then
    perform corrective training
      increment incorrect classification counter
    else
      increment correct classification counter

combine results for all test shuffles
compare results between features
```

Listing 10-4: Process flow in a feature comparison test

The test process involves an initial training cycle similar to that of all other tests. Once the initial training cycle has been completed, the remaining messages to be used for testing are shuffled into N decks. The number of decks is determined by the tester, depending on how thorough the testing should be. This number is usually between 5 and 10.

Each shuffled deck is trained and classified. The floor and peak results are generally truncated, and the results from each deck are averaged. When the test process has been performed with each of the features enabled at their given time, the results of the tests are then compared to determine which features experienced the best overall performance (lowest error rate) and which experienced the worse overall performance (highest error rate).

Testing Caveats

Even the most well-planned testing can turn to mush if the testing process isn't conducted properly. In this section we'll discuss some caveats regarding the testing of statistical filters. In general, if you are experiencing very poor levels of accuracy compared to the advertised values, there is most likely a problem in the implementation of the test. These problems can be very simple oversights that, when fixed, will show a noticeable improvement.

Corrective Training

The corrective training process is unique to each filter. Two common mistakes are made in corrective training that can lead to poor accuracy.

The filter will in most cases have a special argument specifically for corrective training. This argument will be different from standard training arguments because corrective training not only involves learning the message as the correct classification but *unlearning* the message from the old classification. Tools like DSPAM use a *source* argument—for example, -class=spam -source=corpus for initial training or -class=spam -source=error for retraining. Be sure to use the specific arguments that the filter requires for corrective training, and not the same arguments that were used for corpus training.

The second error made in corrective training is in not using the original message or the output message, depending on the filter, for retraining.

Some filters store a serial number or other identifier in the message itself for managing error correction. If the original message is used to retrain, this serial number will not be present, and the message may not actually get retrained. Check the filter's documentation to identify the correct approach to retraining. If the filter implements any type of serial number or identifier, it may be necessary to use the outputted message for retraining.

Purge Simulations

Many tests fail to create a true purge simulation, which can ultimately affect the accuracy of the test. During testing, it is crucial to use the time stamps from the message headers to bind the data to a particular age. The purge cycle should then perform its functions based on the virtual age assigned to the data. Many testers make the mistake of performing a single purge at the end of the training cycle. This doesn't adequately simulate a true purge cycle.

An example of this problem can be illustrated by assigning a time period of one month to every 250 messages in a corpus. The first 250 messages in a training corpus may leave a token with 10 spam hits and 0 innocent hits. If this token is not referenced in the next 250 messages, it will have become stale, in most cases. In a real-world environment, a token that has been stale for more than a month would be purged from the system. If, in the third month, the same token was referenced with 0 spam hits and 10 innocent hits, real-world purging would leave the token with these results, as the former results would have been purged. In an automated testing environment, if the purge isn't simulated correctly, the result may be a neutral token with 10 spam hits and 10 innocent hits. This not only potentially affects the outcome of many classifications, but also increases the likelihood of classification errors in the third month.

Using an approach to purging that effectively purges stale data based on the date that the messages were actually received will prevent this condition from occurring and will help ensure the reliability of the test.

Test Messages

In tests measuring the accuracy of the filter, many testers make the mistake of using the same set of messages for both training and testing. Others make the mistake of using a completely different set of messages. In both cases, the accuracy of the filter is misrepresented because it doesn't reflect a real-world scenario.

Using the same set of messages for testing and training will cause the filter to appear more accurate than it really is, because it has already learned the messages that are being presented. Using an entirely different set of messages will cause the filter to appear less accurate because the messages being presented have no continuity with the existing messages that have been learned.

The goal of testing a filter's accuracy is to measure its ability to adapt to permutations of the present training set. Real-world users experience diverse email behavior, but with a continuity of content and message senders. When this continuity is broken, the purpose for which the filter was designed is interrupted. To effectively measure the accuracy, the test corpus should be continuous with the training corpus and should represent the next period of time for which messages were received.

Presuppositions

Probably the biggest reason that tests fail is that the tester never tries out the filters in a real-world environment to compare results. Automated, scientific testing is important, but it is all too often performed by individuals who have never run a statistical filter on their own for several months. As a result, the tester brings many presuppositions into what is supposed to be an unbiased testing process, which can lead to unreliable results. Testing a statistical filter is much the same as test-driving a vehicle. Having a focus group of 10 or 20 individuals drive the vehicle and report back provides useful information, but no sensible person would buy a car without first getting behind the wheel and taking it for a spin. The lack of *feeling* for how statistical filters function in a real-world environment can often lead to this bias simply due to lack of experience.

Before testing any statistical filters, it's important for the tester to install and run one on their own email for several months. This will have the benefit of building the tester's experience with the filter, identifying caveats, and giving credibility to the test results when published.

Final Thoughts

We've discussed four of the more common tests used to measure statistical filters. The different types of tests call for certain types of data and operating parameters. Because the state of the filter changes with every trained message, the training used to measure heuristic filters or other types of filters does not effectively measure the accuracy of statistical filters. A controlled environment must be used in order to ensure the most reliable results. There are many different caveats to consider in testing. In most cases, whenever a filter experiences terrible performance, one or more testing errors have occurred, and the environment should be examined and corrected.

It's easy to prove whatever it is you're trying to prove with testing. Be wary of tests in which the individuals performing the testing appear to have a bias for or against statistical filtering. Published results that include personal opinion or use hostile words such as "terrible" or "worthless" are most likely unreliable. Unbiased testing by a reputable group of individuals who have real-world experience in running a few filters will provide the best results.

The majority of the remaining chapters in this book deal specifically with specialized algorithms and features. These algorithms have been tested using the principles outlined in this chapter, and they should be tested in the same way when being implemented in a filter. Feature comparison tests should be used prior to each release of the filtering software, to ensure that no minor changes have had a negative effect on accuracy.

11

CONCEPT IDENTIFICATION: ADVANCED TOKENIZATION

Statistical filters perform their language classification functions based on the available data. As we've seen, all of the widely used present-day algorithms are inherently sound and accurate, but any algorithm's accuracy is directly related to the data it's provided—the "garbage in, garbage out" rule.

In Chapter 6, we discussed basic tokenization theory. Primitive tokenization allows us to identify messages based on the individual characteristics of each word, number, or other small component of a message. Content is more than just individual words like "free"; it is also a collection of concepts, like "free call" or "free software." Statistical filters that perform the advanced tokenization discussed in this chapter are capable of identifying not only raw content but also individual concepts, the true goal of concept learning. Instead of identifying a spam as a message that contains the word "free," implementing some of the concepts in this chapter allows us to identify spam content based on the concept of a "new exciting offer" or "playing lotto." This approach to tokenization flows through to the rest of the filter and allows Bayesian content filters to act more like Bayesian concept filters—filters that eliminate spam based not just on content, but on the concept of the message. Concepts don't necessarily have to be ones that are humanly understandable; they can be lexical concepts, such as grammatical pretense, word construction, and HTML generation.

Let's go back to the notion of concept learning for a moment. Suppose that we have some children sitting at a table with someone who is showing them pictures of sports cars and sedans. They're not only learning the concepts of what a sports car and a sedan are; they're learning the individual concepts that make up the larger concepts. A Bayesian content filter using primitive tokenization learns only specific characteristics, such as "four round objects" and "rectangle extending out of top subsection," whereas true concept learning would identify concepts such as "fat tires" and "engine coming out of hood." Identifying concepts is truly where content filtering approaches a new level of AI, and that is what this chapter is all about.

Chained Tokens

Chained tokens are also known as multiword tokens, word pairs, phrases, and biGrams. The concept involves a simple data processing algorithm designed to provide more specific (and much better) data for the existing statistical algorithms.

As the name implies, this algorithm is based on the concept of chaining adjacent tokens together to make new tokens. This approach creates somewhere in the vicinity of $2^n - 2$ additional data points to work with, where n is the number of tokens generated by normal single-word tokenization, providing a total of approximately $3^n - 2$ tokens, depending on any special optimizations for headers and such.

Chained tokens are tokens that are combined with their adjacent partners to form two new tokens, which eventually leads to the identification of specific concepts in a message. Chained tokens aren't a replacement for individual tokens but a complement to be used in tandem for better analysis. If the filter finds that certain concepts stick out more than some of the individual tokens in the message, these concepts will be given a slot in the decision matrix. This process involves merging different sets of tokens, some of which describe concepts. For example, if we are analyzing an email with the following phrase,

---

CALL NOW, IT'S FREE!

---

four tokens will be created using standard primitive tokenization:

- CALL
- NOW
- IT'S
- FREE!

With chained tokens, we also create the following additional tokens:

- CALL NOW
- NOW IT'S
- IT'S FREE!

Thus, the familiar concepts of "call now" and "it's free!" are created. However, just because the phrase "now it's" doesn't make sense to us as a concept doesn't mean it isn't one. The filter will eventually tell us. A few basic tokenizing rules apply to the implementation of chained tokens:

- No chains are created between the message header and the message body; individual message headers from other parts of the message are treated as separate components from their message part bodies.
- When processing the message header, no chains are created between individual headers. This means that $2^n - 2$ additional tokens will be created for each header.
- Any kind of token can be combined with any other kind of token, so long as the two tokens are adjacent to one another. For example, words can be combined with nonwords such as dollar amounts.

Chained tokens are very easy to implement and provide many different types of intelligence to statistical filtering, as we'll discuss later. The biggest advantage is that we now have more descriptive data with which to identify concepts in messages. The data generated by chained tokens isn't too specific, however, and so we'll be able to identify these concepts among many different messages, even ones written by different spammers.

Case Study Analysis

Now that we have an understanding of chained tokens, let's explore their purpose in statistical filtering. The philosophy behind chained tokens is this: given two tokens, A and B, chained tokens enable a filter to calculate not only the interest of A and B individually, but also the interest of AB, which may or may not be greater than the individual tokens.

If the two tokens combined are indeed more interesting, we may have created a concept that can be identified in other messages and that may have a context-specific probability that can help the filter better identify both spams and legitimate emails. This eventually leads to better spam identification and fewer false positives.

In most spams, any identifying language patterns or concepts can be ascertained with only two adjacent tokens. For example,

```
Play Lotto
Hot Girls
Cheap Viagra
Remove From
```

It takes only two tokens together to get a very specific idea of the concept related to the email. If someone was reading your email out loud using one or two interesting pairs of adjacent words, it would be easy to ascertain whether or not the message was spam. Therefore, a statistical filter should be able to perform this function with 15 pairs of words. Also, since spams are frequently different, it makes sense to keep the data in chunks that are as small as possible while being descriptive enough for an accurate comparison. Otherwise, you run the risk of having such specific data that you miss variations. With all these things considered, chained tokens strike a very good balance between analysis and verboseness in the building of concepts.

Pattern Identification

Let's take a look at some examples of chained tokens used in a real-life environment. Below are some individual tokens and their chained counterpart, together with their associated probabilities.

all	0.5513
the	0.5699
all+the	0.2541

This example shows that the words "all" and "the" are fairly uninteresting, in that their probability is not far from a neutral 0.5. Since they appear in a significant number of messages, both spam and innocent, the filter doesn't see much value in them, and they are likely to be omitted from any decision matrix, even if it were starved for data. While these words alone may not be interesting enough to play a role in the analysis of a message, we see that together the phrase "all the" is a much more interesting piece of data when it shows up. This chained token has a much greater likelihood of showing up in the decision matrix of a message, improving its chances of identifying an innocent message. We'll explain why shortly. Now let's look at a set of tokens with the opposite effect on a mail corpus.

color	0.3282
#000000	0.5794
color+#000000	0.9684

The word "color" is fairly innocent in this user's dictionary, as it can be used to describe a number of things—the color of a font or the color of a shirt. We really have no idea what's being described here, which is part of the problem—there are words, but no accompanying concept. The hexadecimal code for black (#000000), on the other hand, is a very neutral token for different reasons; obviously, it is used in some innocent HTML-based emails the user receives as well as spam. If these two individual tokens were used in analyzing a message, you would end up with a rather mediocre result. To make matters a bit more agonizing, the word "color" is a little more likely to show up in a Bayesian calculation and the hexadecimal code is not, since the hex code is less interesting, which could skew the result toward identifying the message as a legitimate email. However, the combination of the two individual tokens creates a concept—the idea that we're talking about the color of an HTML component (a font or background color). We thus end up with a very guilty chained token that would dramatically change the result of the calculation.

Why wasn't the chained token also neutral? After all, a font color can be part of innocent email as well as a spam. The answer is that the HTML generators used to author spams are slightly different from those used for legitimate messages. Outlook, Eudora, and Thunderbird word their HTML code differently (and in a different case) than bulk mail senders do, which will result in slightly different tokens being created. For example, a legitimate email client may use the following:

```
COLOR+#000000
COLOR+BLACK
Color+#000000
Color+Black
```

Also keep in mind that the chained token is going to appear most often when setting the font color. Black is a very popular color for big, bold text in spams. Since the hexadecimal code for black was by itself neutral, we can draw the conclusion that both legitimate messages and spams have used the color in a background setting or in some other part of their HTML code that did *not* use the color tag. For example,

bgColor	0.5076
bgcolor	0.4758

As shown here, the background color is set several times in both legitimate messages and spams, so the bgcolor tag by itself means nothing. A lot of people aren't very strong users of HTML-based email, and so differentiating HTML code from actual conversation may not need to be as granular. What we want to avoid is turning our spam filter into a mere HTML recognizer—the presence of HTML tags alone don't necessarily make a message spam (even for a user who doesn't use HTML), so we want to be very careful about which HTML tags we parse to avoid filling up the decision matrix with HTML tokens.

Differentiation

We've learned so far that chained tokens can be used to improve the accurate identification of both legitimate messages and spams, and can play a significant role in the identification of what we're calling concepts. Let's take a look at another use for chained tokens.

Content-Type*mixed	0.4334
Content-Type*multipart	0.5222
Content-Type*multipart+mixed	0.0100

The content-type headers define the presentation of data in an email. A content type of multipart/mixed is used by many legitimate email clients, and so it's generally considered a legitimate content header. Most bulk-mail senders prefer to use multipart/alternative, and so, because "multipart" is used in both forms of email, the word "multipart" becomes a very neutral token. If we were using single words only, without any concept-based implementation, we would have discarded all of this useful information. With chaining, however, we're able to catch the multipart/mixed and multipart/alternative tokens, so that our filter becomes capable of identifying the concept of multipart/mixed email—a concept that it would otherwise be ignoring. Another good example of this is found in mailing lists:

unsubscribe	0.5510
unsubscribe+from	0.0833

Spams and mailing list emails alike use the word "unsubscribe"; however, only the mailing lists this user subscribes to use the phrase "unsubscribe from." All this time, spammers have been trying to obfuscate their bogus unsubscribe algorithm to hide it from spam filters. They were so successful that it's become very unlikely that you'll find a spam with this phrase—at least until the spammers get a little brighter. When this happens, other unique concepts will simply take over. That's one of the great things about using a Bayesian window—it allows a certain amount of buffering for new types of spammer tricks. When spammers start using "unsubscribe from," the decision matrix will buffer an immediately erroneous decision and take a look at the mention of "free porn" also.

Eventually, we'll get to the point in filter development that multiple concepts can be correlated with one another. The presence of an "unsubscribe from" token in the absence of other mailing-list-like properties could be used to eliminate the token as noise, or even to invert the probability of the token in future AI logic. We'll look at the possibilities of doing this later in this chapter, when we discuss Karnaugh mapping.

HTML Classification

We've already looked at how chained tokens can be used to identify HTML tags as opposed to text used in conversation. Yet another use for chained tokens is in the example that follows, which exhibits how well chained tokens can function to identify the different patterns of HTML code used by both spammers and legitimate users.

FONT	0.4573
face	0.5506
FONT+face	0.2084

The "FONT face" token was found to have a much more innocent disposition than the two neutral tokens alone. This is due in part to the many other font tags used in spams (such as font size) that separate these two tokens. As we've discussed, many spam generators use their own type of formatting. Generators that spammers use might prefer "FONT COLOR" first, then "FACE" after, while Microsoft Outlook prefers "FONT face." The case used can also be very different between generators. "Font," "FONT," and "font" are all different data to most tokenizers. If you're looking at individual tokens, you're going to miss all this, because just about every HTML message uses the FONT, FACE, and COLOR tags. What primitive tokenizers haven't seemed to figure out is that many clients have a unique method of ordering, which chaining can capitalize on.

Contextual Analysis

Now we'll move on to one of my favorite uses for chained tokens—contextual analysis. Yes, Virginia, chained tokens can be used to identify language patterns! As normal everyday people, we frequently engage in many different types of discussions. Some are informal, some are hot and heavy, and if you're a hacker, some will most likely involve a lot of flaming.

Spammers also use their own unique style of conversation, including canned messages, raunchy and perverse advertising, and obnoxious, used-car-salesman-type pitches. Chained tokens do a great job of performing natural language analysis of these individual types of contexts. You can't tell the context of a message simply by looking at the word "that," but when it is combined with other words, you can tell that the discussion is informal. The phrase "that sent" is informal and has a poor grammatical pretense. This is a great indicator of legitimate mail to many users, and our filter will now be able to identify such types of concepts:

that	0.4233
sent	0.4042
that+sent	0.0100

Here are some more examples, selected at random. Some are innocent; others are very guilty. It's easy to figure out which ones come from what type of text just by looking at them.

always+very	0.0100
all+the	0.2541
all+you	0.6072

brought+you	0.7541
email+because	0.9901
that's+have	0.0100
that+sent	0.0100
that+the	0.0099
that+wouldn't	0.0100
that+you	0.8362
Click+Here	0.9901

Spammers have tried sending emails with "everyday common" text, and filters don't seem to have any trouble identifying the difference between their text and legitimate text. Even when a spammer succeeds in crafting a message with enough "common text," there is almost always an overabundance of guilty text to offset it. Further enhancements we'll discuss later, such as Bayesian noise reduction, can make "common-text" spams completely ineffective.

Other Uses

What else are chained tokens good for? They enable the filter to more accurately identify legitimate email addresses in the From: and To: headers. This helps to create a better "whitelist" for innocent messages. For example, our primitive approach to tokenizing would give us only these tokens:

```
From*president
From*whitehouse
From*gov
```

all of which could easily be used by many other senders than the president, including the forged headers sent with spams. Implementing chained tokens allows us to create more sender-specific tokens from these headers:

```
From*president+whitehouse
From*whitehouse+gov
```

These are arguably concepts as well: the concept of a specific email address in the header. Attempts are frequently made by spammers to "fool" primitive tokenizers into thinking that their spam is a legitimate email from McAfee, Microsoft, or some other well-known domain. They frequently fail to fool even the most basic implementations of primitive filters, but they especially don't fool multiword-capable filters. Manual whitelisting is cumbersome, but statistical whitelisting can be extremely powerful (and cool!).

The same approach can also be used to identify the x-mailer more accurately (for example, Microsoft Outlook was considered a more legitimate mailer in my dataset than Microsoft Outlook Express), and the chained token allows us to realize this with one token instead of two. This brings us to our next useful function for chained tokens, and that is de-duplication.

Traditional Bayesian combination will incorporate only the 15 most interesting tokens into a decision window. If you eliminate the somewhat interesting words by replacing them with very interesting words, you have a more accurate window that ends up playing a significant role in that very small percentage of emails (such as list digests with embedded advertisements) for which limiting a calculation to 15 tokens results in a decision based only on the randomness of the decision matrix.

Administrative Concerns

The only administrative concern that can arise when using chained tokens is the amount of extra disk space consumed by the additional token records in each user's database.

The average user's dictionary, without using chained tokens, seems to average around 500 KB to 1 MB in size. This means that an ISP with 30,000 customers will require 15 to 30 GB of additional disk space to accommodate an implementation without chained tokens (a very acceptable requirement). The average size of a dictionary using chained tokens, however, was originally around 10 to 20 MB, which would require several additional disks for a very large-scale implementation. This is still acceptable, but with a little less enthusiasm. The increased disk space requirement has inspired some alternative solutions to help manage the space concern.

Additional purge tools can be implemented to purge ineffective chained tokens from the dictionary that have been stale for a given period of time or that don't yield a particularly interesting value. DSPAM purges any tokens that fall within certain bands of probability—for example, between 0.30 and 0.70—and have remained stale for more than a week or two. It's also advantageous to remove any tokens that have remained stale for a long period of time regardless of their probability—say around 60 days. This will usually remove about half to two-thirds of all chained tokens, leaving a very tight core of useful learned concepts. In one case study, a dictionary containing a total of 70,000 tokens was purged to 34,000 tokens, 20,000 of which were effective chained tokens. The additional 20,000 chained tokens played a significant role in accuracy.

Another way to control the amount of disk space used by chained tokens is to convert the tokens into numeric values. Numeric values can generally be represented with fewer bytes and can also provide a faster implementation of indexing. Many filters convert tokens into a 64-bit checksum (an "unsigned long long" integer value). This changes the key length of each token in the database from variable length to only 8 bytes. A majority of chained tokens are well over 8 bytes, and in light of the some 100,000 to 500,000 records in a single user's dataset, this could save several megabytes of space.

A final approach to implementing chained tokens while controlling disk space is by using a merged group, as we discussed in the previous chapter. By creating a "parent" group containing systemwide data and merging it with individual users' "diffs," we're able to shrink each user's dataset down to only what is necessary to customize the global dataset.

Given that disk space is dirt cheap, and that an email system capable of supporting 30,000 users is already significant in cost, the additional disk space required for a chained token implementation is still well within the acceptable range for a serious Internet service provider that wants to provide accurate filtering services. A majority of filter users aren't huge ISPs but small- to medium-sized companies that are looking to filter spam for their thousand or so employees. It should be very comforting for these administrators to know that they will need only a few gigabytes of disk space to accommodate a chained token implementation for the whole company.

Finally, much optimization is possible in the type of back-end storage used. Stateless, random-access file implementations such as Berkeley DB and GDBM are very cumbersome in comparison to a SQL-based back end such as MySQL or PostgreSQL. SQL-based solutions seem to have a much better system for recovering unused space, which is important when purging data. Overall, it's possible to decrease the size of a typical chained dataset to between 5 and 10 MB or even as small as 1 MB using a merged group and a train-on-error (TOE) approach.

Supporting Data

Statistical filters are already very good at identifying predictable email, so it makes no sense to run the standard accuracy test to prove the worthiness of chained tokens. Instead, one test that was run against chained tokens used a feature-comparison test in which a large sample of email from the SpamAssassin corpus—email that had never been seen before by the test users—was sent through the filter. The results were very good, as shown in Table 11-1.

Table 11-1: Comparison of Primitive Tokenization versus Chained Tokens

User	Corpus	Chained?	Correct	Incorrect
USER 1	SA Spam Corpus	NO	353	147
USER 1	SA Spam Corpus	YES	431	69
USER 1	SA Ham Corpus	NO	2,274	226
USER 1	SA Ham Corpus	YES	2,433	67
USER 2	SA Spam Corpus	NO	393	107
USER 2	SA Spam Corpus	YES	390	110
USER 2	SA Ham Corpus	NO	1,820	680
USER 2	SA Ham Corpus	YES	2,007	493

The database was, of course, cleared between all tests and then retrained with or without chained tokens. As the table illustrates, the chained token approach was overall twice as accurate at identifying never-before-seen email than primitive tokenization alone. In one case, chained tokens actually hurt accuracy with one user by three messages, but they more than made up for it by correctly classifying innocent messages that otherwise would have become false positives.

Summary

In summary, chained tokens have proven their worth, both in the test lab and in actual production implementations.

One of the primary reasons to use chained tokens is the added buffering they provide, making it much more difficult for spammers to evade statistical filters with a bunch of junk text. As we'll see in Chapter 13, chained tokens also make it much more difficult to poison algorithms such as Bayesian noise reduction; by attempting to eliminate single-token noise, spammers are actually creating chained-token noise, and vice versa.

The key features of chained tokens provide more accurate classification by

- Establishing concepts of messages, rather than individual components
- Maintaining the importance of certain words together
- Providing more usable data to work with
- Classifying HTML based on its use rather than its presence
- Classifying message headers more accurately
- Identifying differences in language patterns between spams and legitimate mail

Chained tokens have been implemented in the DSPAM project and in SpamProbe, and they are presently being worked into Dr. John Graham-Cumming's POPFile filter. They have dramatically improved accuracy over other filters that don't have such an implementation, and you can be confident that any project using chained tokens is likely to be a successful one.

Sparse Binary Polynomial Hashing

We discussed sparse binary polynomial hashing, or SBPH, briefly in Chapter 6. Now we'll take a closer look at the tokenizing approach implemented as part of SBPH to see what has made it a very successful approach for full-featured language classifiers. Its most basic definition, as outlined at the MIT Spam Conference in 2003, is as follows:

> Sparse Binary Polynomial Hashing (SBPH) is a way to create a lot of distinctive features from an incoming text. The goal is to create a LOT of features, many of which will be invariant over a large body of spam (or nonspam).

SBPH is similar to chained tokens in that it identifies different concepts within the text, but it also goes beyond the capabilities of chained tokens to identify sparse phrases and lexical data. The general concept of SBPH, according to its author, Bill Yerazunis, is to "break the incoming text into short phrases from one to five words each." As further explained in the SBPH white paper,

> A phrase can have words in the middle of the phrase skipped (e.g. "BUY <skip_word> ONLINE NOW!!!" is always a bad sign.), and more than one phrase can use the same word. You can't change the order of the words, but you _can_ bridge across newlines, punctuation, etc. Make all the phrases you can make.

For example, the phrase

```
An uncommon offer for an
```

would be tokenized by SBPH into the following set of tokens:

```
An
An uncommon
An <skip> offer
An uncommon offer
An <skip> <skip> for
An uncommon <skip> for
An uncommon offer for
An <skip> <skip> <skip> an
An uncommon <skip> <skip> an
An <skip> offer <skip> an
An uncommon offer <skip> an
An <skip> <skip> for an
An uncommon <skip> for an
An <skip> offer for an
An uncommon offer for an
```

These phrases, once tokenized, are inserted into the dataset in a fashion similar to that used in standard Bayesian analysis. The total number of times each phrase has appeared in each corpus is calculated, and the most interesting phrases are used in the final calculation. CRM114 uses 64-bit hashes to convert plain-text tokens into a numeric hash. The complete process can be summed up into three steps:

1. Slide a window N words long over the incoming text.

2. For each window position, generate a set of order-preserving subphrases containing combinations of the windowed words.

3. Calculate 32-bit hashes of these order-preserved subphrases.

Each word in a text affects $2^n - 1$ features, where n is the window size (5 in our case). Needless to say, SBPH generates a whole lot more tokens than primitive tokenization! The present-day implementation of SBPH does have areas where some improvements could be made:

- The current implementation uses 8-byte characters instead of wide characters. To better improve support for multiple languages, the wide-character datatype should be used instead.

- SBPH currently preserves ordering, but it may be interesting to see what happens when ordering is not preserved.

CRM114 originally totaled up the number of spammy phrases and the number of innocent phrases and then compared the two to see which one had the most tokens in its category. In November 2002, CRM114 was reworked around Graham's Bayesian approach, and now a similar decision matrix is formed using what is called the *Bayesian chain rule*, or *BCR*. The BCR part of what is now known as SBPH/BCR is not an actual tokenizer approach but more of a decision matrix and processing approach. Yerazunis has also made some performance optimizations to make SBPH/BCR work within an acceptable range of speed. Files are mapped directly into virtual memory for less overhead. As described by Yerazunis,

> Each of the css files is mapped into virtual memory. The default size of a css file is one megabyte plus one byte, and each byte of a css file is used as a single 8-bit unsigned integer. Using the length of the css file as a modulus, each superhash value maps into a particular byte of the css file. Each css file also has a "score," initialized to zero.

Another approach used to increase performance and decrease disk space is the implementation of TOE-mode training. Tokens are trained only when an error has occurred, and so instead of having to learn an entire corpus of phrases (which would use up an inordinate amount of disk space), the filter learns only what is necessary for proper classification.

Supporting Data

Yerazunis performed some of his own testing with SBPH and presented his results to the MIT Spam Conference in 2004. His results compared standard SBPH with other tokenizing approaches, measured in errors per 5,000. We'll revisit these totals in Chapter 12 when we discuss Markovian discrimination.

Evaluator	Errors per 5,000
Pure Bayesian matching	92
Peak window value	80
Token sequence sensitive	78
Token grab bag	71
Sparse binary polynomal hash	69

One of the things Yerazunis noticed in these results is that the token grab bag approach, in which token ordering isn't preserved, scored a lower error rate than standard token sequencing. Combining a token grab bag approach with SBPH may further improve accuracy and is in fact part of the approach used in Karnaugh mapping, discussed next.

The SBPH approach showed a significant increase in accuracy, by 11 errors per 5,000, when compared with Graham's approach, referenced as the "peak window value" in the table.

Summary

SBPH is extremely effective at identifying both concepts and advanced lexical patterns. Its overhead, while greater than chained tokens, is still very manageable and ideal for small- to medium-sized classification projects. SBPH is overall a highly effective tokenization approach that will likely find its way into many language classifiers in the future.

Karnaugh Mapping

Karnaugh maps are primarily an electrical engineering and/or low-level computer science concept originally used to minimize boolean logic. A Karnaugh map provides a graphical approach to grouping together expressions with common factors and eliminating unwanted variables. It can be used in reverse to create a verbose set of tokens similar to those created by SBPH, except that ordering and even adjacency are ignored. The logic minimization features of a Karnaugh map come into play in that it can actually measure the absence of a specific token in a phrase as a meaningful piece of data. Until now, all of the tokenization approaches introduced have dealt only with data that is present, or they make exceptions for wildcard data that isn't present—but what about the concept of evaluating the presence of the word "free" next to another word that is *not* "software"? This too could be considered an important piece of the answer to the question of what content is.

Karnaugh maps can be used to illustrate logic for a range of different numbers of inputs. The ideal Karnaugh map in the setting of language classification would have a window size of 4 inputs. A 4-input Karnaugh mapping tokenizer would take input four tokens at a time:

```
CALL NOW, IT'S FREE!
```

and generate a mapping of all the different possible combinations of the tokens, including tokens both absent and present from each expression, producing a total of 2^N combinations. Literals are assigned to the individual components of a Karnaugh map, and logic is then produced for the literals.

CALL	NOW	IT'S	FREE!
A	B	C	D
A'B'C'D'	A'B'C'D	A'B'CD'	A'B'CD
A'BC'D'	A'BC'D	A'BCD'	A'BCD
AB'C'D'	AB'C'D	AB'CD'	AB'CD
ABC'D'	ABC'D	ABCD'	ABCD

Tokens in the expression that are not present are expressed in their complemented form; for example, A' is pronounced "not A."

As shown in Figure 11-1, there are 16 different combinations of logic in a 4-variable Karnaugh map. For example, A'B and C'D can be stored as two separate tokens. At the same time, A'BC', BC'D, and A'BC'D can also be stored as tokens. Finally, even the individual single tokens can be stored: A, B, C, and D. The literal representations of the tokens aren't stored, just the individual tokens that make up the expressions. In order to create a storage solution in which token phrases can be recalled in any order, two things need to be stored: a token key, using the alphabetic ordering of the tokens included in the expression, and the ordering of the expression. For example,

```
CALL+FREE!+NOW     (Alphabetically ordered key)
ADB                (Literal ordering)
```

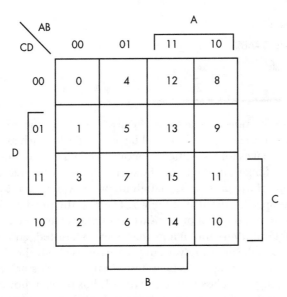

Figure 11-1: A 4-variable Karnaugh map

The literal ordering is important because even though we're not preserving order, we want to give a higher weight to tokens that are in the original order, as well as to more complex combinations. This brings us to the subject of weighting. Among the mass quantities of data generated by Karnaugh mapping, how do we know which tokens are more important than others? To address this, we can apply a 2^N weighting scheme, similar to the way Markovian-based filters do it, as we'll discuss in the next chapter. First, we give preference to more complex phrases—that is, tokens that have more phrases in them. Second, we give preference to phrases that are in their original order. Finally, we weigh the tokens by complexity and out of order.

Before we can assign weights to individual tokens, each Karnaugh map must first be evaluated. For example, if we have the phrase

---

CALL NOW, IT'S COOL!

---

the Karnaugh map against our original set of tokens will evaluate to ABCD', as D is not present. Once the Karnaugh map is resolved, we can load all relevant maps and perform our weighting:

Literal/Order	Weight
any one literal	2
any two literals	4
AB+BC+CD	8
any three literals	16
ABC+BCD+ACD+ABD	32
any four literals	64
ABCD	128

All that's left now is to factor in the absence of specific tokens. For every combination in the corpus, there will be a record with each absence in the dataset. This makes for a significant amount of data (again, this approach isn't for the faint of heart, or the faint of wallet), and so we will recall all different combinations of the present Karnaugh mapping with absent tokens and measure the specific absence of the word FREE!, the word NOW, and so forth.

Theoretically, once all of the Karnaugh maps have been evaluated and every possible combination of logic has been exhausted, enough data should be present to make amazingly accurate decisions about the data. Since this approach is theoretical, it has been tested on only very small corpora, and for generic language classification at that. It has proven, however, to provide an extremely accurate analysis of the samples being presented. Technology like this is more useful in applications where spam of other kinds is being explored, such as massive search engines trying to filter out page-ranking spam from pages on the Internet. Generally, the amount of resources needed for this type of language classification make it useful only when there is a good reason to spend a significant amount of money on hardware. This approach could potentially even be used to discover trends in DNA sequencing and other types of knowledge discovery. As Karnaugh mapping continues to be tinkered with, spam fighters will inevitably find ways to implement the approach using fewer resources. Training modes and purging could make Karnaugh mapping an extremely accurate approach to tokenization for single-user implementations.

Final Thoughts

In this chapter, we've taken a look at three very different approaches to advanced tokenization. All three approaches attempt to identify lexical patterns and specific characteristics we know as concepts. These approaches all add a different amount of data to the dataset and require differing amounts of resources. Depending on the complexity of the filter and other algorithms used to perform language classification, one type of tokenization may be more appropriate than another.

All filters should consider implementing at least one form of concept identification. Primitive tokenizers have been shown to be very effective and resource friendly, but as new types of messages are being crafted specifically for the purpose of evading filters, it is becoming more and more necessary to identify not only the components of a message but also the concepts within a message. The advanced features that this type of tokenization provides (such as HTML classification, grammatical analysis, and so on) bring an entirely new level of accuracy to modern-day filters, without necessarily requiring a significant increase in resources.

Concept learning is the foundation of true machine learning; the philosophical question, "What is content?" requires that concept identification be an important part of the answer.

12

FIFTH-ORDER MARKOVIAN DISCRIMINATION

Until now, we've been discussing the most popular approaches to language classification involving Bayesian analysis. Markovian discrimination is a new implementation used in some of the more advanced language classification projects, specifically the CRM114 discriminator.

Bill Yerazunis invested a considerable amount of research into Markovian discrimination and presented his findings at the MIT Spam Conference in 2004. This chapter was coauthored by Bill and incorporates much of his research into Markovian discrimination to provide an accurate and full understanding of how the Markov principles apply to machine learning.

Just as Bayesian learning starts out with Reverend Thomas Bayes in 1764, Markovian analysis was kicked off by Andrei Markov, a professor at St. Petersburg University, in 1886. Markov's early research included number theory and analysis, approximation theory, and convergence of series. Markov is best known for his work on random processes that have memory; these are now known as *Markov chains*. Markov chains are a basic building block for most advanced statistical theory; they are particularly useful for spam filtering.

The central idea of Markov's work was that some things in nature are more complex than Bayes' independent event statistics can describe. Markov came up with a very simple yet powerful description of nonindependent, related events that accurately models many natural processes and natural languages.

Markov's Great Advance

The critical issue Markov addressed was the concept of *state*—that is, a persistence of information from one visible event to the next. To understand this, let's look first at a system that has no state—a flipped coin.

If you flip a coin and it comes up heads, and you flip the coin again, the chance of it coming up heads again is *exactly* the same as before. There's no memory to the coin; each flip is independent (which is exactly what Bayes' Theorem requires).

Similarly, rolling a pair of dice has exactly 6 chances out of 36 to come up with a "natural 7" (as any craps player can tell you), and the next roll has *exactly* the same chance. Again, this is because the dice themselves have no memory of what has already happened.

Now consider something only a little more complex—rolling dice in a game of craps (see Figure 12-1). In craps, there is *state*; it's called "making the point." The player rolls the dice one or more times. Depending on what the player rolls, they win, lose, or have to roll again.

If the player rolls 7 or 11 on the first roll, they win. If they roll 2, 3, or 12 on the first roll, they lose. Any other number they roll is called the "point," and they have to roll that "point" number again to win. If they roll a 7 first, they lose. (There are other rules, but they aren't important here.)

What is important is that the game of craps has memory, and so the pure Bayesian statistics don't quite apply. Instead, each probability chains into the next situation; this is why it's called a Markov chain. For some systems (like craps), we can figure out the exact shape of the Markov chain. The chain is a series of states (the circles) and transitions (the arrows). We start at "Start" and follow the instructions at each state, which tells us which transition to take next.

Now let's watch a game of craps. We'll write down the history of each player—that is, what sequence of values the players rolled:

- We see someone roll 7 right at the start. That's a win.
- We see someone roll 5, then 7. That's a loss.
- We even see someone roll 6, 5, 5, 5, 5, 5 . . . maybe thirty or forty 5 rolls, then a 6 again, and it's a win. It's unlikely, but it is a win.

But no matter how long we watch, we'll never see someone roll 11, 4, 11 because the game would have stopped after the first 11. We'll also never see someone roll 3, 2, 7, 4, 3 because the game would have stopped at the first 7.

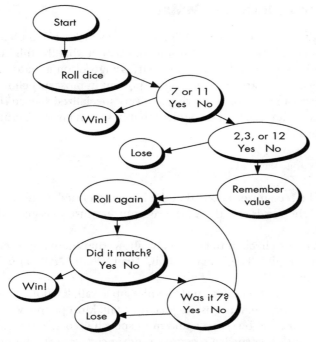

Figure 12-1: Illustration of a Markov Chain in craps

This is the whole point of a Markov chain—there are some sequences that the Markov chain model can produce and some that it cannot produce. Whenever we observe a history sequence, we know that if the Markov chain can't produce it, it wasn't from that Markov chain. This is an important point, and you should make an effort to remember it: If the sequence can't be produced by the chain, it represents some other chain.

Another great strength of the Markovian model is that it allows us to know the exact probability of any possible history sequence. We start at the "start" state of the chain and walk through each node, accumulating the chance that we'll exit the node at a particular transition. For instance, a craps game producing the rolls 5, 10, 5 could be evaluated as follows:

1. Rolling 5—that's 4 chances out of 36
2. Then rolling 10—that's 3 chances out of 36
3. Then rolling 5 again—that's another 4 chances out of 36

. . . for a grand total of 4 * 3 * 4 / 36 * 36 * 36 = .00102, or about one chance in a thousand of 5, 10, 5 being rolled in a craps game.

Notice in the game of craps that we know exactly what state we're in as well as exactly what states and transitions connect where. Unfortunately, this isn't always the way the world works. Sometimes we don't know exactly what state we're in or what the states and transitions are. That's what hidden Markov models are about.

Hidden Markov Models (HMMs)

A *hidden Markov model (HMM)* is a system in which we don't have exact knowledge of what state we're in (or sometimes even what the full list of states and transitions is). HMMs happen embarrassingly often in natural language processing and are an essential component in most speech recognizers (and we can view spam filtering as a very specialized speech recognizer).

Consider a speech recognizer that has been given a slightly mumbled sentence:

```
I picked up the ..all
```

The recognizer knows that the last word ended in "all"; it also knows the rest of the words exactly. All the recognizer must do is guess the mumbled letter.

A quick check in the dictionary shows that there are several words ending in "all." "Fall," "mall," "ball," "gall," "hall," "tall," and "wall" are all possibilities.

But how often does someone pick up a wall, let alone an entire mall? It doesn't even make sense to pick up a tall. Most people would guess "ball" as most likely to be correct, and most speech recognizers would do this as well—that's how speech recognizers advanced from 80-plus percent accuracy to 95-plus percent accuracy. It's not because the signal processing is better; it's because the recognizer knows what words are more likely to appear in a sentence as other words are recognized.

HMMs are a perfect fit for this kind of problem. The model can specify the relative chances given missing data for any word; it can also decide that a word was misunderstood and indicate what the word most likely was. The signal processing system can then back-match onto what sounds were captured and pick the best option. This kind of guessing game is how modern speech recognizers actually work.

Here's another example of an HMM. Which set of words is actually from a human?

> she hit the ball for a home run
>
> hit ball the run a she the home

Both sets contain exactly the same words. Only the order has changed. But one makes sense and the other doesn't.

Here's where we get back to spam filtering. A Bayesian filter using a primitive, single-word tokenizer deals only with single words; it doesn't see any difference between "she hit the ball for a home run" and "hit ball the run a she the home." The individual word tokens are the same, so a primitive tokenizer (like those found in many Bayesian classifiers) will not distinguish between the two sets of words. A *Markovian classifier* takes the word order into account as well; word order is actually more important to a Markovian classifier than the particular words that are used. That's the core of Markov-based text classification: *Word order is more important than what words are used.*

The rest of this chapter provides a more detailed explanation of the theory and practical implementation of Markovian text classification.

Using Markov Models to Model Text

Let's go back to looking at the average Bayesian spam classifier. We'll view it as a pipeline of processing after noise removal, HTML busting, BASE64-decoding, and so forth.

Classic Bayesian Spam Filter

A typical Bayesian spam filter will process a message like this:

1. Tokenize, breaking the text at word (or wordlike) boundaries.
2. Look up tokens in a database to find the individual appearance rates of each token in spam and nonspam.
3. From the spam and nonspam appearance rates, calculate a local probability of spam versus nonspam (usually using Paul Graham's described approach).
4. Use Bayes' Theorem to combine the individual local probabilities into an overall probability of the text being spam.

If we were to construct a Markovian model along the same lines, we'd immediately run into an insurmountable problem—we simply do not know what the actual Markovian models of spam and nonspam are. The closest models that exist are the Markovian models of spoken languages, and those are highly proprietary to the sellers of voice recognition software.

Since accurate Markovian models of spam and nonspam are not available, we use the next best thing—our own human-classified example files of spam and nonspam. The simplest way to do this is to perform a *correlation* between the unknown text and our known texts, and count matching strings. In this sense, the Markov model is the actual unadulterated text, and we assume that the text is long enough and varied enough to represent the hidden Markov model accurately.

Here's an example of correlation (a very short example, because correlation is a very expensive value to compute). Correlation takes time $N * M$, where N is the length of a known corpus and M is the length of the unknown corpus. Since N (the length of the known corpus) might be tens to hundreds of megabytes, this way of performing correlation is basically unusable for more than a single user at a time, but let's proceed with the example.

We'll use one sentence each for the spam and nonspam corpora:

GOOD:

The licenses for most software are designed to take away your freedom to share

SPAM:

Now you can save up to 60% on Extended Warranty Coverage for your Vehicle
---

UNKNOWN:

Save up to 40% for your Viagra prescriptions!

The correlation is done by "sliding" the unknown text across the two known test corpora and counting the number of sequential words that match between the two. Here the matches are as follows:

GOOD:

The licenses **for** most software are designed to take away **your** freedom to share
---

SPAM:

Now you can **save up to** 60% on Extended Warranty Coverage **for your** Vehicle
---

UNKNOWN:

Save up to 40% **for your** Viagra prescriptions!

We have two matches against our good corpus and two matches against our spam corpus, but the lengths of the matches in the spam corpus are much longer. The longer multiword features are much more indicative of similarity than are simple word counts.

It's interesting to note that this phrase-matching capability also gives very good immunity to spammers trying to use word salad, discussed in Chapter 7. This makes Markovian matching nearly immune to the word salad attack.

The only problem with this match is the amount of CPU time it takes to compute. With a small (1 MB) corpus of spam and an equal 1 MB corpus of nonspam, and a 10 KB message, performing the correlation will take roughly 20 billion comparisons (5 seconds on the fastest available single-processor machine at the time of this writing). Although that might be fast enough for a single user, it is far too slow for any widespread use.

We can speed this process up by sacrificing some of its generality. The correlation process finds all matching text strings, which is not really necessary. First, we can cut off the matching length at some reasonable cutoff (five is a good value to start with). So just like chained tokens (which have a cutoff of two words), we use a cutoff of five words. Second, instead of comparing character by character, we can lump entire words and phrases together. Third, we don't need to preserve knowledge of the relative order of our matching pieces, so instead of matching at one position and sliding, we can convert the known corpora into large tables and do lookups on each lumped word and phrase as we encounter them.

We still need to keep track of the number and lengths of the matches, but we can do that quite simply by reusing the code from our old Bayesian model.

Instead of counting matches of single words, we count matches of words and word phrases, up to our predetermined lengths. We look up those matched phrases, convert the relative counts of matched phrases to local probabilities, and then use a standard Bayesian algorithm to combine the local probabilities.

Another helpful issue to consider is whether slight deviations in short phrases are acceptable. For example, should "A B x D E" match "A B y D E" as two short two-word phrases or as a single four-out-of-five-word phrase? Experimentally, it's been found that accuracy increases if you give more weight to a four-out-of-five-word phrase than to a pair of two-word phrases.

How much extra weight is enough weight? Mathematical analysis and experimental values are at odds here. The current best published weights for Markovian classification of English anti-spam email are the exponential super-increasing weights published in 2004 by Yerazunis in "The Spam-Filtering Accuracy Plateau at 99.9% Accuracy and How to Get Past It." This set of values is based on the weighting series $w=2^{2n}$ and is shown, along with the phrase structures, in Table 12-1. Since the values were assigned through trial and error, it is quite possible that better values will be determined in the future.

Table 12-1: Example of Features and Weights for Markovian Matching

Phrase Structure	Weight
The	1
The quick	4
The * brown	4
The quick brown	16
The * * fox	4
The quick * fox	16
The * brown fox	16
the quick brown fox	64
The * * * jumped	4
The quick * * jumped	16
The * brown * jumped	16
The quick brown * jumped	64
The * * fox jumped	16
The quick * fox jumped	64
The * brown fox jumped	64
The quick brown fox jumped	256

Even without any special weighting, just using the multiword phrases as features in an otherwise Bayesian system gives a significant improvement in accuracy, as we discussed in Chapters 6 and 10.

Table 12-2 summarizes the relative accuracies of different weighting and phrasing strategies. The different strategies listed are as follows:

- Pure Bayesian matching is a classic Bayesian classifier.

- Peak window value uses the most-often-seen phrase found in the window as the only value of that window.

- Token sequence sensitive disregards mismatched words within the phrase, so A x x x B matches A x B exactly as well as A y y y B does.

- Token grab bag considers all words in a phrase without respect to order, so A B C D E matches B D A E C.

- Sparse binary polynomial hash uses a weight of 1 for each phrase, no matter what the length is.

- Markovian matching uses the weights from Table 12-1.

Table 12-2: Relative Error Rates for Different Phrasing Strategies

Evaluator	Errors per 5,000
Pure Bayesian matching	92
Peak window value	80
Token sequence sensitive	78
Token grab bag	71
Sparse binary polynomial hash	69
Markovian matching	56

Markovian matching clearly outperforms single-word tokenizers, possibly by as much as 40 percent. Although it's not the only way to achieve these levels of accuracy, Markovian matching provides a mathematically effective, unilateral approach to filtering, providing some of the same functionality as certain extended algorithms, only in a different way. As we'll discuss in the next few chapters, there are other ways to increase the efficiency of standard Bayesian filters, using feature enhancement algorithms such as Bayesian noise reduction, which can improve accuracy while scaling down Markovian matching for large-scale implementations.

Bayesian versus Markovian Classification

Let's do the math for the example of "viagra" XOR "pharmacy" for a Markovian filter versus a Bayesian filter, using a primitive tokenizer. We'll assume that "good" and "bad" have their own separate databases, so we can keep track of the "saw this feature in good" and "saw this feature in bad" counts separately.

For the Bayesian filter, each training of "viagra" or "pharmacy" separately adds to the respective database

- One count to "viagra" or "pharmacy" separately (weight +1)

and each training of "viagra pharmacy" adds

- One count to "viagra" (weight +1)
- One count to "pharmacy" (weight +1)

For the Markovian filter, each training of "viagra pharmacy" adds to the respective database

- One count to "viagra" (phrase length 1, weight +1)
- One count to "pharmacy" (phrase length 1, so weight +1)
- One count to "viagra pharmacy" (phrase length 2, so weight +4)

and each training of "viagra" or "pharmacy" separately adds

- One count to "viagra" or "pharmacy" separately (phrase length 1, weight +1)

For this example, we'll train on each of the test texts "viagra" (bad), "pharmacy" (bad), and "viagra pharmacy" (good). We'll also just count counts (knowing that from counts it's easy to convert to local probability and then combine local probability with the Bayesian chain rule).

Let's compare what's in the databases of our classical naive Bayesian filter and the competing Markovian filter after the first pass of learning. Table 12-3 shows the counts and weights as they stand after this pass. Note that the Markovian database has "pharmacy," "viagra," and "pharmacy viagra" all existing in the "good" database, because "viagra pharmacy" contains both "viagra" and "pharmacy" as well.

Table 12-3: After the First Pass: Learning for Single-Word Bayesian versus Markovian Learning

	Bayesian				Markovian			
	Count		Weight		Count		Weight	
Bad:								
Viagra	0	1	0	1	0	1	0	1
Pharmacy	1	0	1	0	1	0	1	0
Good:								
Viagra	0	1	0	1	0	1	0	1
Pharmacy	1	0	1	0	1	0	1	0
viagra pharmacy	0		0		1		4	
	(Unused)				(Used)			

Does this first pass of learning detect "viagra" XOR "pharmacy"? There are four test cases to run through—"pharmacy," "viagra," "pharmacy viagra," and "neither."

For both "viagra" and "pharmacy" separately, the Bayesian and Markovian paradigms both report a count of 1 and a weight of 1 in both the good and spam databases, so the answer is "can't tell." This is an error—we need to retrain.

For "viagra pharmacy," the Bayesian filter reports two counts of 1 at weight 1 in both the good and spam databases, so it's "can't tell" again, which is still an error. But the Markovian filter reports two counts with weight 1 in "bad" versus two at weight 1 and one count at weight 4 in "good," for a total of 6, so the Markovian filter gets it right.

Now we retrain the errors. The Bayesian filter got nothing right, so we train each test case again. The Markovian filter got "viagra pharmacy" correct, so we don't need to retrain it on that phrase This gives us the results shown in Table 12-4.

Table 12-4: After the Second Pass: Learning for Single-Word Bayesian versus Markovian Learning

	Bayesian				Markovian			
	Count		Weight		Count		Weight	
Bad:								
Viagra	0	2	0	1	0	2	0	1
Pharmacy	2	0	1	0	2	0	1	0
Good:								
Viagra	0	2	0	1	0	1	0	1
Pharmacy	2	0	1	0	1	0	1	0
viagra pharmacy	**0**		**0**		1		4	
	(Unused)				(Used)			

Did this change the performance of either classifier? Let's do the math.

For both "viagra" and "pharmacy" separately, the Bayesian matcher reports a count of 2 and a weight of 1 in both the good and spam databases, so the answer is "can't tell" again. This is still an error, but notice that every time we retrain "viagra pharmacy" we're also training "viagra" and "pharmacy" separately. That simply doesn't help; the system fails to learn. We're starting to see how Minsky and Papert proved that a perceptron can't do an XOR.

The Markovian matcher does much better. For "viagra" and "pharmacy" separately, the Markovian filter has 2 counts at weight 1, for a total of 2 points in the "bad" category, but it has only 1 point at weight 1 in the "good" category, so the Markovian filter scores the separate "viagra" and "pharmacy" correctly as bad.

For "viagra pharmacy" together, the bad-side Markovian database scores 2 counts at weight 1 for "viagra" and 2 counts at weight 1 for "pharmacy," for a total of 4 points. The good-side database scores one count each at weight 1 for "viagra" and "pharmacy," and one count at weight 4 for "viagra pharmacy," for a total of 6, edging out the total of 4 from the bad-side Markovian database. This is also correct.

The final score after two cycles of learning:

Bayesian filter: Zero correct

Markovian filter: 100 percent correct

This isn't to say that the Bayesian approach doesn't produce a good filter (it does!), but there are some things a Bayesian filter just can't do that a Markovian filter can.

We can also see why it's important to have increasing weights in a Markovian filter. If the weight for a phrase of length 2 was only 2, the Markovian filter would have the same problem as the Bayesian one—the longer phrases wouldn't be able to accumulate weight fast enough to edge out the shorter subphrases.

The actual Markovian filter inside CRM114 (as of this writing) is based on the super-increasing series shown earlier in Table 12-1. A research effort is currently under way to gain a theoretical understanding of what the optimal weights should be, so the numbers in the figure should be taken as observation, not gospel.

A side issue when implementing Markovian classifiers is that because a typical Markovian filter will use an SBPH front end to generate all of the subphrases, it will have a huge number of features in the feature stream. If each feature results in significant deviation in the local probability from 0.5, these deviations can quickly multiply in the Bayesian chain rule to cause underflow even in IEEE floating point. For this reason, CRM114 uses a local probability rule that is extremely conservative and generates local probabilities very close to 0.5. The current CRM114 local probability formula is as shown in the following equation, with $C_1 = 16$ and $C_2 = 1$.

$$P - \text{spam} = 0.5 + \frac{(N\text{spam} - N\text{nonspam}) \cdot \text{Weight}}{C_1 \cdot (N_{\text{spam}} + N_{\text{nonspam}} + C_2) \cdot \text{WeightMax}}$$

Storage Concerns

As I noted earlier, a Markovian classifier with a window length of 5 will generate 16 times as many features as a classical Bayesian classifier. With all of this extra data, storage becomes a concern. A fast and efficient way of storing features is necessary in order to make the filter fast enough for use in a large-scale environment. As we discussed in Chapter 8, one way to do this is to not actually store the data, but to store only hashes of the data. This means that a string, no matter how long, consumes only a fixed amount of storage and can always be referenced in near-constant time. The downside is that a hashes-only storage system cannot resolve hash conflicts, and so two different phrases that hash to the same 64-bit value become indistinguishable in the database. Fortunately, that's a rare occurrence. If it does happen and causes an error, the error can be trained out.

Purging Old Data

Another aspect of storage involves the purging of data. The question of when and what data to purge is frequently debated among filter authors. The conclusion is that some data purging is healthy, but not too much. The Markovian approach generates a significant amount of data that may never be seen a second time. Purging data from a FIFO queue has significant value in this sort of situation. As of this writing, research is pending on how much additional accuracy can be gained by accurate FIFO purging of old data versus random purging on hash collision, but the early indications are that FIFO purging is a much better alternative.

Floating-Point Renormalization and Underflow

Bayesian classifiers designed for the Graham model typically keep only the 20 to 50 most exemplary local probabilities and evaluate those through the Bayesian chain rule. This makes the math easy because 0.1 to the 50th power is 10^{-50}, which is still well within the floating-point range of IEEE's specification for floating point. However, 1.0 minus 10^{-50} is exactly equal to 1.0, even in 80-bit floating point. (For those readers with a vague familiarity with computer arithmetic, this is called *loss of precision due to floating-point normalization.*) This is bad; it means that once the Bayesian chain rule hits a Pout of 1.0, it can never recover change from that value.

For classifiers like CRM114 that don't throw away any of the features, this problem of loss of precision becomes much worse. Unless special steps are taken, the useful dynamic range of an 80-bit IEEE number can be exhausted even before the headers of an email message are fully processed.

To prevent this, CRM114 uses a unique two-range system. Both P(spam) and P(nonspam) are calculated separately, and the smaller is used to recalculate the larger. Thus, even though the larger probability may become numerically indistinguishable from 1.0, the smaller will retain full accuracy down to 10^{-300} which is quite useful for classifying large documents.

Final Thoughts

Markovian classification performs primitive, conceptual, and lexical analysis on a text sample, providing much higher levels of precision than the standard primitive tokenizers that usually accompany Bayesian filters. It is significantly more resource intensive than standard Bayesian analysis and therefore requires special attention to training mode and storage implementation. For small- to medium-sized systems, Markovian classification can provide very high levels of accuracy.

13

INTELLIGENT FEATURE SET REDUCTION

As we previously discussed, a feature set is the verbose collection of all of the tokens (or other characteristics we are looking for) in a message. In the previous chapters, we discussed ways to increase the feature set by generating more descriptive tokens, which ultimately led to the identification of certain types of "concepts" within an email. Another advantage to generating this additional information was the capture of more-complex lexical data. However, implementing a simple chained-token-capable tokenizer in a filter can easily produce several hundred thousand data points, and millions of data points can be generated when using sparse binary polynomial hashing (SBPH) or Karnaugh mapping.

In this chapter, we'll explore the philosophy behind intelligently reducing the number of data points analyzed by the filter, using a few different algorithms. Concept tokenizers provide us with thousands of records, but all are weighted equally when building a decision matrix, based on their appearance in previous corpora. We've taken a look at Markovian weighting and the value of weighting more important data differently. The algorithms in this chapter provide similar information to the filter when building a decision matrix, so that a relatively large dataset created by a conceptual or lexical tokenizer can be effectively cleansed and weighted more dynamically based on the messages' content.

Reducing the feature set also better defines what content is by excluding what it is not. As you'll learn in this chapter, content is not unreliable data, and neither is it injected noise.

Calibration Algorithms

Calibration algorithms provide additional weighting calibration to tokens in the dataset, based on a token's reliability. A token may have a probability of 0.9500 today, but that doesn't tell us much about what decisions the token has been involved in previously. For example, the token's value could have come from hundreds of accurate classifications of spam, or it could be an adjusted value from hours of retraining due to errors. If a token has been involved in several erroneous classifications in the past, not only do we want the token to be weighted differently than a reliable token, but we also want the token's presence in a message to suggest that the results we generate may have a higher likelihood of being incorrect.

Calibration algorithms have been applied to many different areas of science, ranging from photometric flux calibration using telescopes to calibrating radar detectors so that police can write more accurate tickets. It makes perfect sense that a calibration algorithm should be used in spam filtering too. In this section, we'll introduce a self-evaluation algorithm to calibrate standard statistical filters. The algorithm is designed to reduce the feature set by identifying the features that are the least effective at accurately identifying spam. This can be done in one of three ways:

- Skewing the final result of our decision matrix calculation
- Skewing the individual probabilities of each feature to take reliability into account
- Eliminating a token entirely from the decision matrix if it's too unreliable to intelligently base a decision on

In order to identify just how skewed our results may be, it's necessary to calculate a *misclassification skew*. This calculation is different from the one that determines the probability of the token, but it is based on some of the same data.

Calibration algorithms can also be used to increase the feature set while simultaneously reducing it. While we may find several unreliable tokens that can be eliminated from a decision matrix, neutral words with a very unreliable history can be accentuated in a type of reverse psychology. For example, the word "sell" may appear equally in both spam and innocent mail corpora, and have a probability of 50 percent. This token wouldn't normally appear in a decision matrix to determine the result of the message because it's so neutral. If this token, however, was noticed to be in a significant number of messages that were misclassified as spam (false positives), it could be made to affect not only the confidence of the filter, but also the actual disposition of the messages when this token is present. When a large number of tokens in a message are found to have previously appeared in messages that were erroneously classified, the filter should be made aware that it can't be as confident about the results and should take special measures to calibrate its own decision.

The first step in determining the reliability of each token in the dataset is to keep track of four extra counters for each token: the number of times the token has been present in misclassified spam and misclassified legitimate email, and the number of correct and incorrect classifications occurring when the token was present in the message. Some sample data is presented in Table 13-1.

Table 13-1: Sample Calibration Dataset

Token	M^S	M^I	C^S	C^I
sell	37	3	100	100
hot	13	22	125	91
deal	15	18	72	39
maybe	01	29	192	40
nailed	31	01	83	10

We can use this data to calculate a probability that will represent our misclassification skew. We obtain this value by first calculating the *skewing factors* for both spam and legitimate mail, as follows:

$$K^S = 0.5 + \frac{M^S/(S(C^S + M^S))}{2}$$

$$K^I = 0.5 + \frac{M^I/(S(C^I + M^I))}{2}$$

The variables K^S and K^I are calculated as the skewing factor, a measurement of how far in one direction each token could possibly skew in the event of a misclassification. The M^S and M^I variables represent the total number of misclassifications in spam and legitimate mail, C^S and C^I represent the total number of correct classifications in each corpus when the token was present in the message, and S represents a scaling factor between 0.5 and 2.0. We can then use Bayes' Theorem to create a combined probability, in which the resulting value is an accurate representation of how far in one particular direction a token is likely to skew:

$$K = \frac{K^S \cdot K^I}{(K^S \cdot K^I) + (1 - K^S)(1 - K^I)}$$

Since 0.5000 represents a neutral value, this neutral probability shows no risk of skew. A value below 0.5000 represents a skew in legitimate messages, and a value above 0.5000 represents a skew in spams. With a scaling factor of 1.0, the resulting data evaluates, as shown in Table 13-2.

Table 13-2: Misclassification Skew Results with a Scaling Factor of 1

Token	M^S	M^I	C^S	C^I	K
sell	37	3	100	100	0.6214
hot	13	22	125	91	0.4488
deal	15	18	72	39	0.4241
maybe	01	29	192	40	0.2919
nailed	31	01	83	10	0.5928

The scaling factor ultimately depends on how well spread the programmer wants the individual probabilities to be; a scaling factor of 0.5, for example, would cause the resulting skew values to be much more sensitive to misclassifications, as you can see in Table 13-3.

Table 13-3: Misclassification Skew Results with a Scaling Factor of 0.5

Token	M^S	M^I	C^S	C^I	K
sell	37	3	100	100	0.7487
hot	13	22	125	91	0.3915
deal	15	18	72	39	0.3167
maybe	01	29	192	40	0.0812
nailed	31	01	83	10	0.7008

We can use a neutral probability of 0.5000 to represent new tokens for which we don't yet have enough information. It's important to choose a scaling factor that won't result in values outside of the 0.0000 to 1.0000 range; 0.5 is usually the lowest value that can provide sensitivity without producing invalid results.

Once we have a misclassification skew for each token, we can do one of three things with it:

- If our goal is to weaken the effect of highly suspect tokens, we can combine the inverse of our result $(1 - K)$ with the probability of the token; be sure that K is *between* 0.0000 and 1.0000 and does not have one of these values. This is very useful for watering down or eliminating any tokens that have a high likelihood of playing a role in misclassifying the message.

- If our goal is to calculate the overall skew of the message, we can combine a subset of (or all of) the misclassification skews to create a message skew probability that can be applied to the final result of the message.

This will allow us to calculate the likelihood that this message will be misclassified based on the number of errors we've had in the past with these tokens.

- If we simply want to eliminate any unreliable tokens, we can base our elimination on a certain range of misclassification skews. This will allow us to get rid of anything that has been known to be present during misclassifications in the past.

To water down features, we can use a Bayesian combination or some proprietary formula to combine $1 - K$ with the probability of our token. Depending on how far we are willing to skew a single token, we may first want to eliminate very skewed tokens from the feature set altogether.

To produce a single skew value for the entire message, we could calculate the combined probability of the total skew for all tokens in the message and factor it into our spam decision. If there are 20 tokens with very spammy skew values and 20 others with very innocent skew values, there's little overall concern about skewing the results of the message as a whole. All tokens could be used in this case, or the N most interesting tokens, based either on the misclassification skew or the total number of misclassifications over time. Regardless of the number of tokens we use in our average, the final result will give us a number between 0.0000 and 1.0000. The closer this result is to a neutral 0.5000, the less calibration needs to be performed on our final result. As this result begins to drift farther away from a neutral value, we're able to skew the results of our decision matrix based on this skew measurement. This calibration can be performed in many different ways. The inverse of the message skew $(1 - K)$ can be added to the decision matrix as a single, static entry. It can also be factored as an entirely independent variable, in which the threshold between confidence and skew is set by the filter.

If we are using these skew measurements as thresholds for removing features from the decision matrix, all that's left to do is set a threshold—somewhere around 0.65 on the high end and 0.35 on the low end is an acceptable range for Table 13-2, although much of this depends on the scaling factor. Any tokens that don't fall within our range of acceptable skew can be eliminated from the feature set.

Regardless of how we perform our calibration, the ultimate goal is to avoid future misclassifications by calibrating the filter based on the mistakes it has made in the past. This causes our filter to adjust itself in such a way that the less reliable data points aren't given the same weight as the more reliable ones. Calibration algorithms such as this are designed specifically to improve the performance of the filter so that the data can be better interpreted based on previous mistakes.

Bayesian Noise Reduction (BNR)

Present-day filters lack true lexical intelligence. When we think of spam filtering, most of us think about the word "Viagra" mixed in with a bunch of junk text, or perhaps just a single image followed by a story.

Today's generation of statistical filters simply scans through an email and looks for the most interesting buzzwords to weigh its disposition by. Spam filters are faced, however, with a unique problem: a malicious villain is behind the scenes trying to misfeed filters with bogus data. While spammers aren't the brightest collection of minds, they seem to have a general idea of how typical content-based filters work. At the very least, they know enough to hide the "bad" words and try to add some "good" words.

With some time and a little trial and error, spammers have recently come to the point of injecting anything from non-sensible text to a target group's web page in an email, knowing that, at the end of the day, our filters are really just dumb token recognizers. Most of the time, however, this doesn't work, because a user's data is far too specialized to crack on words from obscure books or website lingo we've never used. Once in a while, however, spammers get lucky. They include just the right text in the right quantity to pass their message into our inbox. A bigger concern is that spammers may find ways to mine even more specific data from users through the use of Internet worms, web bugs, or similar means. If a spammer can find the perfect set of words to inject, they can get their spam past our filter.

Bayesian noise reduction (BNR for short) is one of the technologies I've designed in an attempt to give the filter a "lexical brain," or rather an intelligence that allows the filter to look at language in a way similar to human understanding. In order to form concepts, we must have something spam filters don't presently have: a context. Think of Bayesian noise reduction as a way to identify "out-of-context" words. If we're having a face-to-face conversation and I say something out of context, it could assume a completely different meaning and easily lead to a misunderstanding. This problem flows into language classification, in that a token can resolve to one disposition when in context (say, the word "righteous" in the phrase "righteous code") but have a completely opposite disposition when presented out of context (such as in a list of non-sensible text injected by a spammer). Filters today have no real way to deal with out-of-context words or phrases, because they don't know what a context is.

BNR identifies out-of-context data by making its own contexts. It creates a series of machine-generated contexts around a sample of text (namely, the message body) and then identifies data that contradicts itself within the context it has created. The process is illustrated in the sections that follow, using three basic steps that any statistical filter should be able to implement.

Instantiation Phase

Let's take a look at some text your filter might happen across while reading your email:

```
Mom Would Be Proud Try Viagra Now!
```

When your filter reads "Mom Would Be Proud Try Viagra Now!" it's going to assign a series of probabilities to each word because, well, that's what statistical filters do.

Text	Mom	Would	Be	Proud	Try	Viagra	Now!
Assigned Values	0.60	0.34	0.71	0.20	0.91	0.99	0.99

The first step in the noise reduction process involves instantiating a series of artificial contexts, or patterns, around this text. To create an artificial context, we first pigeonhole each of the values assigned by the filter into a band, rounded to the nearest 0.05. This helps to limit the total number of patterns we're likely to come up with, as you'll see shortly.

Text	Mom	Would	Be	Proud	Try	Viagra	Now!
Assigned Values	0.60	0.34	0.71	0.20	0.91	0.99	0.99
Assigned Bands	0.60	0.35	0.70	0.20	0.90	1.00	1.00

Next, we simply chain the bands together three by three to create patterns:

```
0.60_0.35_0.70   0.35_0.70_0.20   0.70_0.20_0.90   0.20_0.90_1.00   0.90_1.00_1.00
```

Each pattern represents the bands for three adjacent tokens in our sample text. We instantiate patterns for the entire body of our message, which leaves us with a series of what we call *artificial contexts.*

If you have a multiword-capable filter (for example, SpamProbe, DSPAM, or CRM114), you will want to instantiate a separate set of patterns for each layer of depth. For example, use the prefixes "S" and "M" to distinguish between single-word token patterns and multiword token patterns, or use 1, 2, 3, 4, and 5 to distinguish the different depths of SBPH.

Training Phase

Once we have instantiated a series of artificial contexts for an email, we take some time learning them, in a fashion very similar to the way we learn the rest of the tokens in our database. Each token is given a spam counter and a nonspam counter, and we calculate a probability for each pattern. For example, I use Paul Graham's approach to assigning token values:

```
P = (spamHits / totalSpam) / (spamHits / totalSpam + innocentHits / totalInnocent)
```

Unlike Paul Graham's standard calculation, however, no bias is used when calculating these pattern values, as we're not interested in whether the value is guilty or innocent—only whether it's consistent with the context around it. After a handful of email is processed in this fashion, our contexts are going to take on a disposition just like any other token, as illustrated in Table 13-4.

Table 13-4: Learned Pattern Contexts

Guilty		Innocent	
1.00_0.00_0.45	[0.91990]	0.95_0.25_0.65	[0.02000]
1.00_0.40_1.00	[0.81868]	0.00_0.25_0.90	[0.00900]
0.25_1.00_1.00	[0.99990]	0.65_0.20_0.00	[0.00900]
0.35_1.00_1.00	[0.99990]	1.00_0.60_0.15	[0.21000]
1.00_1.00_0.20	[0.99990]	0.00_0.80_0.55	[0.00900]
1.00_1.00_0.25	[0.99990]	0.15_0.05_1.00	[0.00900]
0.55_1.00_1.00	[0.99990]	0.60_0.85_0.25	[0.12900]
1.00_1.00_0.35	[0.99990]	0.00_0.60_0.90	[0.02000]
0.25_1.00_1.00	[0.99990]	0.70_0.05_1.00	[0.17000]
1.00_1.00_0.15	[0.99990]	0.85_0.95_0.10	[0.00900]
0.15_1.00_1.00	[0.99990]	0.75_0.90_0.50	[0.00600]
0.10_1.00_1.00	[0.99990]	0.65_0.65_0.75	[0.00600]
0.20_1.00_1.00	[0.99990]	0.40_0.95_0.10	[0.16699]

Some contexts will resolve to a very innocent or very guilty disposition, and others will be less interesting. We want to identify contexts that are both very extreme in their value and self-contradictory. A pattern context must meet two basic criteria to be interesting enough for us to use:

- The pattern's value must exceed an exclusionary radius of 0.25 from neutral, or rather the distance from a neutral 0.5 (ABS(0.5 − P)). For a typical Bayesian filter, this means that the pattern's value must resolve to 0.00 to 0.25 or 0.75 to 1.00.

- The pattern must contain at least one data point with a value at least 0.30 away from the pattern's value, or ABS(PP − PW), where PP is the value of the pattern and PW is the value of the word, or token. For example, if the pattern's value is 0.90, it must have at least one data point with a value below 0.60.

For example, in the examples in Table 13-4, we see that the pattern 1.00_0.00_0.45 has an extremely guilty value (a 91 percent likelihood of being spam). Not only is this very interesting, but the fact that the pattern includes an extremely innocent token (0.00) is a good sign that this is a token we want to look at.

Dubbing Phase

Now let's take a logical look at what we've accomplished. Given the pattern 1.00_0.00_0.45 (the first item in Table 13-4), which our filter trained to a value of 91 percent, our filter has discovered that the presence of an extremely guilty token (1.00) next to an extremely innocent token (0.00), next to a token we've not seen before (0.45 is the neutral value used by many filters), is collectively guilty. That is, this pattern of token values (regardless of the actual words used) is specifically guilty. And if this pattern is guilty, we must come to the logical conclusion that the token that the filter previously learned as 0.00 is completely contradictory in its present context—so it must be *out of its normal context!*

The dubbing phase, quite simply, involves omitting these anomalies. Given the following:

```
bnr.s.0.35.0.05.0.80  [0.99990]
bnr.s.0.05.0.80.1.00  [0.99990]

Your  Terminal  TRY  VIAGRA!
0.34  0.04    0.81  0.99    (Token Values)
0.35  0.05    0.80  1.00    (Corresponding Band)
```

we dub out the inconsistencies—any token in the pattern whose value is farther than 0.30 from the pattern's value. So instead of seeing "Your Terminal TRY VIAGRA!" we now see

```
Blah  Blah  TRY  VIAGRA!
-.--  -.--  0.81  0.99
```

Or we could get even more creative and change the out-of-context tokens' polarity to match that of the context, which provides a bit of moral satisfaction (and possibly a more accurate result):

```
Your  Terminal  TRY  VIAGRA!
0.99  0.99    0.81  0.99
```

Listing 13-1 summarizes the entire process.

```
let windowSize = 3
let windowRadius = 0.25
let tokenRadius = 0.33

program start
begin loop[cursor] (each token in text sample)
  instantiate context[context] (from windowSize tokens at cursor)
  load probability windowValue for context
  let interestingWindow = (ABS(0.5-windowValue)>windowRadius)
  if (interestingWindow)
    begin loop[token] (each token in context)
      load probability tokenValue at token
      let inconsistentToken = (ABS(windowValue-tokenValue)>tokenRadius)
      if (inconsistentToken)
        eliminate token occurrence from classification
    end loop
```

```
end loop
program end
```

Listing 13-1: The Bayesian noise reduction process

Examples

Now let's take a look at some samples of actual mail before and after the noise reduction process. It's important to note that the BNR algorithm performs the processing shown without any knowledge of the sample's disposition.

Bayesian Noise Reduction and Spam Classification

We see in the example in Listing 13-2 that much of the message is simply irrelevant text. While some of the text is useful for identifying spam against the test user, there is also an abundance of innocent and neutral text. These types of spam often provide only a minute amount of useful information to work with, flooding the message with conversational text in an attempt to fool spam filters.

```
<!DOCTYPE HTML PUBLIC "-//W3C//DTD HTML 4.0 Transitional//EN">
<HTML><HEAD><TITLE>Message</TITLE>
<META content="MSHTML 6.00.2800.1276" name=GENERATOR></HEAD>
<BODY> <DIV> </DIV> <DIV></DIV>
<DIV class=OutlookMessageHeader lang=en-us dir=ltr align=left><FONT
face=Tahoma
size=2>-----Original Message-----<BR><B>From:</B> cierra myers
[mailto:sangglenna@techemail.com] <BR><B>Sent:</B> Tuesday, February 03, 2004
10:09 AM<BR><B>To:</B> Penny Kelly<BR><B>Subject:</B> >>Attract your
mate<BR><BR></FONT></DIV><FONT face="Courier New" size=1>My Saturdays nights
are no longer spent by the fire "reading a good book". four seconds until
picture isdownloaded <BR><A href="http://www.largeinfo.com/argo.com" wjyf.com
mnhoavekpkjnimoixmomhioecwshvvl="http://
emjwxbholwirhkwwaoufvtcfamrydfnqx"><IMG src="http://www.netstarsite.com/
argo.net" fnqusjjsqenrqgwn.com
rqmjrqpkoccxavkbfhfrilkctbameurvfuepwjd="http://joydnxvnslffgngrejhustv"
NOSEND="1"> </A><BR><BR>No? drawled the dragonette; it seems to me very
babyish
<BR>How old is your mother? asked the girl <BR>Oh! I really think, continued
the
boy, nodding sagely, that it wouldn't be well to have these Records scattered
around <BR>Mother's about two thousand years old; but she carelessly lost
track
of her age a few centuries ago and skipped several hundreds Their use would
givesome folks unfair advantage over others, you know
```

Listing 13-2: A real-world microspam with embedded word list attack

Using the Bayesian noise reduction algorithm against a real-world subject with a sufficiently trained database, the filter eliminates the following text (and underlying values) from the sample:

```
HTML PUBLIC HTML HTML TITLE TITLE OutlookMessageHeader us dir ltr left Tahoma
cierra myers sangglenna techemail February To Attract Courier Saturdays nights
spent good book four seconds isdownloaded href wjyf fnqusjjsqenrqgwn NOSEND No
drawled dragonette babyish Oh! nodding sagely well these Records Mother's
about two but she carelessly lost track her age few centuries skipped several
Their use givesome folks advantage know HTML
```

```
0.16 1.00 0.16 0.16 0.43 0.43 0.40 0.27 0.31 0.40 0.44 0.24 0.40 0.40 0.40
0.40 1.00 0.23 0.40 0.32 0.40 0.30 0.22 0.09 0.25 0.39 0.09 0.40 1.00 0.40
0.40 0.40 0.28 0.40 0.40 0.40 0.40 0.40 0.40 0.17 0.26 0.40 0.40 0.24 0.22
0.49 0.61 0.40 0.43 0.16 0.76 1.00 0.41 0.40 0.16 0.39 0.24 0.19 0.40 0.11
0.61 0.38 0.16
```

This leaves the following text and values for the classifier:

```
W3C DTD Transitional EN HEAD Message META content MSHTML name GENERATOR HEAD
BODY DIV DIV DIV DIV DIV class lang en align FONT face size Original Message
BR From mailto com BR Sent Tuesday AM BR Penny Kelly BR Subject your mate BR
BR FONT DIV FONT face New size My are no longer by the fire reading until
picture BR com IMG src com BR BR the it seems to me very BR How old is your
mother asked the girl BR really think continued the boy that it wouldn't be to
have scattered around BR thousand years old of ago and hundreds would unfair
over others you FONT BODY
```

```
1.00 1.00 1.00 1.00 1.00 0.02 1.00 1.00 1.00 1.00 1.00 1.00 0.79 0.16 0.16
0.16 0.16 0.16 1.00 1.00 1.00 1.00 1.00 1.00 1.00 0.02 0.02 0.76 0.17 0.08
1.00 0.76 0.00 0.02 0.01 0.76 1.00 0.03 0.76 0.03 0.91 1.00 0.76 0.76 1.00
0.16 1.00 1.00 1.00 1.00 0.77 0.90 1.00 1.00 0.87 0.87 0.47 0.06 1.00 1.00
0.76 1.00 1.00 1.00 1.00 0.76 0.76 0.87 0.85 0.02 0.89 1.00 0.22 0.76 0.12
0.10 0.89 0.91 1.00 1.00 0.87 1.00 0.76 0.07 0.10 1.00 0.87 1.00 0.89 0.85
0.05 0.88 0.89 0.73 1.00 0.57 0.76 1.00 1.00 0.10 0.94 1.00 0.92 1.00 0.11
1.00 1.00 0.11 0.86 1.00 0.79
```

At first glance, it may appear that much would-be junk text is remaining. However, a closer look at the tokens' underlying values shows that they are very useful to the filter for evaluating the message. What's left is a much cleaner, more consistent set of data for processing.

Bayesian Noise Reduction and Legitimate Message Classification

To illustrate how statistically unbiased the noise reduction algorithm is, Listing 13-3 shows the same function performed on a sample of legitimate conversation. This particular message includes noise from the mailing list's embedded advertisements and the informal conversation itself.

```
<html><body>
<tt><BR>
-hey sassy canadian..I'll do it for ya..just email me.<BR>
```

```
I'm at mom's. We got caught in a snowstorm coming home from <BR>
Susanville..I'm exhausted! lol<BR>
-- In clovergirls@yahoogroups.com, &quot;Chris &amp; Heather Nish&quot; <BR>
&lt;hcnish@t...&gt; wrote:<BR>
&gt; Hey guys, <BR>
&gt; I need one of you to email someone for me...<BR>
&gt; My emails aren't getting to a potential customer and<BR>
&gt; now she's starting to get pissy with me...lol<BR>
&gt; any volunteers?<BR>
<BR><BR><BR></tt>

<!-- |**|begin egp html banner|**| -->

<br><tt><hr width="500">
<b>Yahoo! Groups Links</b><br>
<ul><li>To visit your group on the web, go to:<br><a href="http://
groups.yahoo.com/group/clovergirls/">http://groups.yahoo.com/group/
clovergirls/</a><br> 
<li>To unsubscribe from this group, send an email to:<br><a
href="mailto:clovergirls-
unsubscribe@yahoogroups.com?subject=Unsubscribe">clovergirls-
unsubscribe@yahoogroups.com</a><br> 
<li>Your use of Yahoo! Groups is subject to the <a href="http://
docs.yahoo.com/info/terms/">Yahoo! Terms of Service</a>.
</ul> </tt> </br>

<!-- |**|end egp html banner|**| -->

</body></html>
```

Listing 13-3: Legitimate email with common noise and embedded noise from list advertisements

As you can see in the following results, this time the noise reduction algorithm perceived inconsistencies to be primarily patterns with guilty features—which may have otherwise led to a misclassification of the message.

Unlike the first example illustrated, in which innocent tokens were eliminated, the patterns found in this legitimate message lend themselves to preventing false positives.

Eliminations:

```
I'm In com amp gt gt gt need one email for gt emails getting gt now get with
gt any your on the from this send an email mailto com subject com nbsp Your
use is subject the

0.82 1.00 1.00 1.00 0.94 0.84 0.35 1.00 1.00 0.58 1.00 0.64 0.54 1.00 0.35
0.98 0.95 0.43 0.63 0.63 0.63 0.56 1.00 0.84 1.00 0.63 0.64 0.54 0.63 0.98
0.84 1.00 0.63 1.00 1.00 1.00 1.00 1.00 1.00 0.73 0.55 0.84 0.70 0.95 0.69
0.95 0.94 0.69 0.59 1.00 0.69 1.00
```

Remaining text:

hey sassy I'll ya me mom's caught coming Susanville exhausted! lol clovergirls
yahoogroups quot Chris Heather Nish quot lt hcnish wrote Hey guys of you to
someone me My aren't to potential customer and she's starting to pissy me lol
volunteers Yahoo! Groups Links To visit group web go to href To unsubscribe
group to href clovergirls unsubscribe yahoogroups Unsubscribe clovergirls
unsubscribe yahoogroups of Yahoo! Groups to href Yahoo! Terms of Service

```
0.07 0.00 0.10 0.04 0.90 0.00 0.10 0.17 0.00 0.00 0.00 0.00 0.01 0.28 0.07
0.00 0.00 0.28 0.17 0.00 0.07 0.17 0.10 1.00 1.00 1.00 0.20 0.90 0.36 0.13
1.00 1.00 0.93 1.00 0.04 0.17 1.00 0.00 0.90 0.00 0.00 0.01 0.01 0.02 0.97
0.31 0.01 0.04 0.29 1.00 1.00 0.97 0.83 0.01 1.00 1.00 0.00 0.83 0.01 0.06
0.00 0.83 0.01 1.00 0.01 0.01 1.00 1.00 0.01 0.07 1.00 0.08
```

End Result

The results provided by this algorithm are quite impressive. In legitimate
messages, the number of guilty identifiers that could lead to a false positive
are substantially reduced. In spam messages, there is a significant reduction
in innocent identifiers that could lead to a spam misclassification. And this
all takes place without the noise reduction algorithm having any knowledge
of what the true disposition of the message is. After performing tests on random system users, I've found that the BNR algorithm appears to improve
confidence by an average of 20 percent and, in a few isolated cases (which
could be considered false positives), reduced confidence by only about 5 percent. Table 13-5 shows two such users on my system and their results.

Table 13-5: Bayesian Noise Reduction, Illustrating Improved Confidence in
Most Samples

Total Samples Analyzed	3,948	2,280
Total Improved Confidence*	2,523	1,522
Total Decreased Confidence*	26	16
Total N/C in Confidence*	1,399	742
Average Increase in Confidence*	21.51%	20.80%
Average Decrease in Confidence*	5.26%	4.00%

* Confidence calculated using Robinson's Geometric Mean Test Inverted.

Efficacy

I've found that BNR's ultimate effectiveness (and long-term efficacy) depend
on how its pattern contexts are trained by the user's filters. At present, I am
training the contexts on every message processed (and retraining on errors),
but I've found that training only on hard-to-classify messages makes BNR a
little more sensitive to different types of noise. I believe there's also a threshold for purging that should be developed through trial and error. Perhaps

dividing all of the counter totals by 2 at certain milestones could help keep the pattern contexts dynamic enough to adapt to new types of context. Training philosophy will most definitely affect BNR's performance, and so it's a good idea to find a happy medium through a little testing.

Since BNR behaves based on the context values it has learned for a specific user, your actual mileage may vary. I'm confident, however, that this approach will come in handy as spammers continue to grow their word-mining databases. At some point, spammers will be able to generate enough accurate junk to increase their success rate against typical content-based statistical filters. The great thing about this algorithm is that its function is abstracted from the actual words. So in order to circumvent this type of approach, a spammer not only needs to mine words likely to be innocent, but also needs to mine both guilty and neutral words to the nearest 0.05. The spammers also need to somehow mine the learned patterns and values from a user's filter (which may not even be possible) and then put it all together to create a series of artificially "in-context" junk text. This is, at the very least, computationally infeasible today.

The BNR algorithm appears to be very useful at identifying out-of-context data within any type of message (good or spam), and it does its job remarkably well, considering that it has no suppositions or knowledge about the true disposition of the message. I tested this algorithm against my own corpus of mail and was very surprised to see my accuracy jump from 99.96 percent to an astonishing 99.985 percent (from 1 error in 2,500 to 1 error in 7,500).

This implementation of Bayesian noise reduction has been included in DSPAM versions 3.4 and later (older versions sported a more heuristic approach) and is also available in a GPL library for other filter authors at http://bnr.nuclearelephant.com.

Final Thoughts

In this chapter, we've taken a look at some unique algorithms designed to remove unimportant features from a decision matrix. Although the scope of this chapter has been related directly to language classification, these types of algorithms can be incorporated into several unrelated fields. Various types of analysis in economics immediately come to mind, using the BNR algorithm to identify the more important data points of interest on noisy revenue or stock charts and perhaps even as a means of steganography detection. An implementation in general data mining could also apply to network event filtering or log mining.

In the next chapter, we'll take a look at collaborative algorithms, which can be used to network different groups of users together to make collaborative filtering decisions.

14

COLLABORATIVE ALGORITHMS

Statistical filtering has a reputation for taking place in isolation, since filtering is better when it's more personalized. The problem with this isolation, however, is that there's a lot of value in sharing information too. Collaborative algorithms can help improve the accuracy of a filter by providing information about important new email so that the recipient's filter doesn't have to learn it from a misclassification. Several different collaborative algorithms are used today by popular filters, and all attempt to serve the same purpose, which is to make two heads better than one. Collaborative algorithms help us to further define content. Content is not only my content; it's also the other guy's content or, more specifically, the content we might have in common.

Collaborative algorithms can be used correctly and incorrectly. The correct way to use them is as supporting algorithms to present information about other users in a network and their results. We'll discuss some of the more popular collaborative algorithms in this chapter.

Message Inoculation

Message inoculation is a concept originally invented by Bill Yerazunis of CRM114. It is best explained by Yerazunis himself:

> Part of the problem is that spam isn't stationary, it evolves. That pesky .1 percent error rate is in some part due to the base mutation rate of spam itself. Maybe the answer is "vaccination." Vaccination is allowing _one_ person's misery to be used to generate some protective agent that protects the rest of the population; only the first person to get the spam actually has to read it.

> My expectation is this: Say you have ten friends, and you all agree to share your training errors. Each of you will (statistically) expect to be the first to see a new mutation of spam about 9 percent of the time; the other ten friends in this group will have their Bayesian filter trained preemptively to prevent this. Net result: you get a tenfold decrease in error rate—down to 99.99 percent accuracy. With a hundred such (trusted) friends, you may be down to 99.999 percent accuracy.

A message inoculation is an antigen that is introduced into each participating member's filter. The antigen inoculates the user not only from receiving the original spam, but also from receiving any other spam that is contextually similar. The antigen trains the right amount of lexical data in the user's dataset to seed it against any permutations or similar messages that happen to share some contextual similarities.

Inoculation takes place only when a training error has occurred. This is important for two reasons. As accurate as language classifiers are today, they are still capable of making errors, and we don't want to accidentally inoculate users with misclassified mail (this will cause a snowball of errors to occur). Also, one of the goals in fighting spam on a large scale is to reduce the number of resources that spam is allowed to use. If we were to fire off an inoculation every time a spam was caught, we would be doubling the amount of bandwidth spam uses already. As erroneous classifications are made, inoculations get sent out as the user attempts to correct the error. We end up sending only information that is most likely to be missed by someone else's filter.

It's also important to note that inoculation groups comprise trusted users; that is, every member in the group has chosen to trust inoculations from every other member. This is very important, since message inoculation is protected with an authentication mechanism to prevent malicious injection. A list of shared secrets and/or public keys is exchanged between users in a group, so that they can authenticate one another's inoculations. Presently supported mechanisms include an MD5 checksum with shared secret and public key signatures.

Message inoculation was drafted into a message format outlined in the Internet-Draft available on the Internet Engineering Task Force (IETF) website at http://www.ietf.org/internet-drafts/draft-yerazunis-spamfilt-inoculation-04.txt. The Internet-Draft describes a specific MIME encoding for sending message inoculations through email. The benefit of using this encoding is that inoculation groups may consist of different users on different systems, even using different spam filters. The message inoculation is generally sent by the user's spam-filtering application, which could be run on the server side or embedded in the mail client itself.

According to the Internet-Draft, the message inoculation encoding consists of six different components:

> 1. The inoculation subtype, which identifies that the message being received is an inoculation and should be treated accordingly.

The inoculation subtype is explained further as a subtype used in conjunction with a standard content-type header. Three primary media types are currently supported: message, text, and multipart. The inoculation subtype is used to define an inoculation either in the top-level headers or in one or more parts of a multipart message.

```
Content-Type: message/inoculation
```

A multipart inoculation is capable of delivering multiple inoculations in a single message. Each part of the message contains its own additional inoculation headers, such as authentication information.

> 2. An Inoculation-Sender field, which identifies the sender of the inoculation and provides an identity the recipient can query locally for authentication information (such as a shared secret, public key, et cetera).

The sender of the inoculation must be in the recipient's trusted group in order for the inoculation to be accepted. Since an authentication mechanism is used, the inoculation sender's identity is looked up in a table where it will exist in conjunction with either a shared secret or a key. The inoculation-sender field is also a header field.

```
Inoculation-Sender: bill_yerazunis
```

The sender's identity may be a username or an email address but should be specific enough so that it doesn't risk confusion with any other users in the group. Since it's possible for some users to have many different email addresses, using the naming convention firstname_lastname is usually less ambiguous.

> 3. An Inoculation-Type field, which specifies the type of inoculation payload being sent (spam or nonspam), to instruct the filter how to proceed with importing the inoculation payload.

There are essentially two different types of inoculations a user can send. The most common type is a spam inoculation, to protect all other members of the group. Depending on the group's makeup, it may also be appropriate to send a message inoculation for a particular nonspam to the members of the group. If the group consists of employees at a company, for example, a nonspam inoculation could be used to retrain a company message the user received as a false positive.

4. An Inoculation-Authentication field which specifies the method of authentication provided (if any) to verify that the inoculation is from a trusted user.

Depending on the type of authentication being used, the inoculation-authentication field will contain the authentication method and any additional data necessary to the correct authentication of the message. For example, if the authentication mechanism being used is an MD5 checksum with a shared secret, this field will include the checksum sent by the other user.

```
Inoculation-Authentication: md5; checksum="c3a47b29744062288cbd5c305897eaa9"
```

The Internet-Draft does make provision for an authentication type of "none," but it strongly recommends against implementing this authentication type, as it would be relatively easy for a spammer to send bogus inoculations to a large group of users if no concept of authentication is being used.

5. Extended authentication message components, such as a public key signature, may be present depending on the authentication mechanism used.

If the authentication mechanism being used involves a public key, the signature for the inoculation payload will be present in a different part of the message, identified by a "signed" subtype.

6. The inoculation payload, which is the actual information provided to seed the filter tool.

There are a few different types of inoculation payloads, depending on the actual inoculation type. For example, a message inoculation will contain an Internet message in RFC 822 format, complete with headers and a message body. If the inoculation is a standard text inoculation, unformatted text will be sent as an inoculation payload. Unformatted text is generally processed differently than an Internet message, as the tokenizer will generally process message headers differently from the message body.

Once the inoculation has been received, it is up to the filter to determine whether or not the user requires the inoculation, and it will apply the inoculation using whatever training the filter sees fit. A complete example of the process of receiving and processing an inoculation using MD5 with a shared secret authentication mechanism follows.

1. The recipient's inoculation-aware spam tool notes that this is an inoculation-type message.
2. The recipient's spam tool parses the headers to find that the claimed sender is a trusted user and the claimed inoculation type is spam.
3. The recipient's spam tool checks the local set of authorized inoculators and finds that the identified user is permitted to inoculate spam.

4. The recipient's spam tool looks up the identified user in its configuration and finds that the corresponding authentication shared secret is a particular string of text.

5. The recipient's spam tool tests to confirm that this is not a multipart inoculation and that the payload is the entire data text area.

6. The recipient's spam tool forms the authentication text by concatenating the authentication shared secret, a newline, and the full data text area (omitting the obligatory newline-newline after the last header line) and continuing to end-of-file on the email text or the length of the content, specified in the content-length field, if present.

7. The recipient's spam tool calculates the MD5 checksum of this authentication text.

8. The recipient's spam tool compares the calculated checksum (from step 7) with the claimed checksum found in the message header. If the checksum does not match, no automatic inoculation is done, and the mail server may either notify the user of the failure of an attempted inoculation or may simply drop the message and exit with nonerror status. It is recommended that this behavior be user configurable.

9. Having validated the authenticity of the sender/checksum/payload, the spam tool forwards the payload (and only the payload) to the learning interface of the proper user-configured spam-filtering program, including the type of payload presented.

10. The filter then determines whether the inoculation is useful (for example, it won't inoculate if you already have the "disease") and applies the inoculation if appropriate.

An example of a message inoculation is provided in Listing 14-1.

```
To: Everyone on my list <spamsucks@myhouse.com>
From: Jonathan A. Zdziarski <mymailbox@mydomain.com>
Subject: This is a test inoculation
Inoculation-Authentication: md5;
    checksum="dcdac94fab6ded79f33b0134d665d02f"
Inoculation-Type: spam
Inoculation-Sender: jonathan_zdziarski
Content-Type: message/inoculation
Content-Length: 169

From: Bob Denver <bob@dead.com>
Subject: This is a spam
To: You <you@youremail.com>

This is a test innoculation. The checksum is correct, however.

    -Bill Yerazunis
```

Listing 14-1: Example of a message inoculation

Supporting Data

As a trial test of message inoculation's ability to adequately protect a group of users, ten live users were selected and grouped together in a single message inoculation group. The users' mailboxes were mirrored, so that an uninoculated mailbox and an inoculated mailbox were created. The users then continued along with their daily lives for 30 days. At the end of the 30-day period, each user's inoculated mailbox had an average of 20 fewer spams than the uninoculated mailbox. Each user experienced a total of about 3,000 spams during this period; the accuracy level dramatically improved from an average of around 99.3 percent to 99.96 percent. If this were implemented at a medium-sized Internet provider of 10,000 accounts, it would decrease the total amount of spam received by approximately 2.4 million messages annually.

This test proved that message inoculation works, at least for the test group. Larger groups of mature users should be able to count on even higher levels of accuracy from a larger base of inoculation.

External Inoculation

Real accounts don't necessarily have to be the only source of inoculation. External inoculations involve the use of *honey pots* (mailboxes set up specifically to receive only spam) and have become quite popular recently to capture spam in the wild.

The theory behind external inoculation is this: why put *anyone* through the misery of being the first to receive a new spam when you can have the spammers themselves send it directly to you? On top of this, you can combine external and internal inoculation by taking spam you receive externally and inoculating your friends with it internally. This is all accomplished by establishing one or more honey pots.

The email address of a honey pot is frequently circulated in invisible text and other types of places where harvest bots are likely to pick it up. The satisfying thing about using honey pots to perform message inoculation is that the spammers themselves are really inoculating you from their new distributions of spam without even knowing it!

Message inoculation has two primary uses. First, it provides a way for users to collaborate with other trusted users and learn important lexical data for new types of spams before they arrive. Second, message inoculations provide a way for users to collaborate directly with the spammers and to inoculate themselves and other members of their group from new types of spam.

Classification Groups

Classification groups are another type of collaborative filtering algorithm that is generally found exclusively on server-side spam filters. The concept behind classification groups is to seek assistance from a group of other trusted users when a user's filter is uncertain as to whether a given email is spam. Clearly, we don't want to ask the users themselves for input, which is why this is performed on the server side. Classification groups are a small-scale version of neural mesh networking, which we'll discuss later in this chapter. Classification groups don't require the additional overhead of parallel processing or even the need to process every node in the group. Instead, a groupwide spam hunt is started and iteration stops whenever enough qualifying results come back from the query.

A series of nodes is defined, with one node representing one user on the system. When a node in the classification network receives a message, the node's filter instance determines its own confidence level in the result. If the confidence level is determined to be "uncertain," the user's filter instance then queries several other nodes in the network sequentially. In a classification network, the first positive, majority decision, or a percentage of decisions play a role in final classification, depending on the size of the network. For example, in a network of ten nodes, a user's filter instance may seek two confirmations that the message is spam in order to classify the message as such. All nodes are considered equally accurate, and therefore once a minimum threshold has been met, iteration can stop. Other implementations iterate through the entire classification group and then tabulate which classification fell to a majority of the nodes. This results in smaller queries and faster execution time than a large-scale neural networking algorithm and can yield results that are just as good on smaller systems or in smaller groups where the users have specifically opted into membership.

Classification groups can also be used to establish a global-type training user to provide out-of-the-box filtering to new users on the system. A global dataset can be generated, either as a composite of several users' training data on the system or, more likely, trained directly by the systems administrator to provide mediocre, generalized filtering for new users during their initial training period. This global group can provide an acceptable level of filtering for new users until they are able to build their own set of training data. If a new user on the system has fewer than X legitimate messages and Y spams in their corpus, the filter may then assume that the user isn't ready to perform their own classification, at which point the global user's dataset will be queried. During the time that the global dataset is being used, the user's filter instance can be training based on the results provided by the global decisions. When the user's dataset has come into maturity, the global dataset will be disengaged and consulted only when the user's filter instance is uncertain about the particular classification of a message.

Classification groups work very well in well-maintained environments but can cause problems among users with different email behavior. Since one person's spam is another person's legitimate email, it's possible that classification groups could generate some false positives at first about messages that require additional classification. Classification groups are also designed for users with mature datasets. New users should never be placed in a classification group until they have built up enough data to be able to filter spam accurately. One of the nice safeguards of classification groups is that errors will be retrained, making the user's dataset more confident in the particular types of messages received, so that the classification group may not even need to be consulted the next time.

Collaborative Neural Meshes

The term *neural network* is rather generic. The Wikipedia (http://www.wikipedia.org) definition of a neural network is "a mathematical model for information processing based on a connectionist approach to computation." The original inspiration for the technique was from examination of bioelectrical networks in the brain formed by neurons and their synapses. In a neural network model, simple *nodes* (or *neurons*, or *units*) are connected together to form a network of nodes—hence the term "neural network."

The type of network discussed here is closer to a neural mesh. It is similar to a classification network in that it deals with discovering collaborative results, but the neural mesh approach is implemented with a different architecture.

Contrary to a classification group, which requires only as many nodes as are necessary to make a positive identification, in a *neural mesh* all nodes within a certain proximity to the input "neuron" are queried. Individual nodes are interconnected with other nodes to form a mesh of synaptic circuitry. The interconnections between nodes are best built using specific logic to identify nodes that are more contextually similar to each other. Once the results from all relevant nodes have been returned, the results from the most reliable nodes are then used to make a final decision.

Reliable nodes are determined based on how accurate they have been in the past. Reliability is generally calculated by keeping track of the number of correct and incorrect classifications each node has made against the mail of each of the other users. This series of neural decisions is stored in the system as temporary data. Each decision contains a list of all the users (or nodes) involved in the decision and what the decision was. If the user determines that the message was erroneously classified, the retraining process will trigger a lookup of the neural decision. Decisions that were incorrect will then be subtracted from the affected nodes' "correct" totals and added to their "incorrect" totals, which could result in the "rewiring" of certain interconnections. At execution time, these interconnections will identify reliable nodes as closest. These will also be nodes that are more contextually similar to the user. Figure 14-1 shows an example of nodes interconnected in this way. Nodes can be interconnected in a variety of different practical implementations. In the neural mesh paradigm, the interconnected roots are shifted based on reliability and will provide a structure in which the most reliable nodes are the most closely interconnected.

A practical implementation of this approach can use varying "strengths" and distances. The reliability (and results) are then combined to form a probability based on the results.

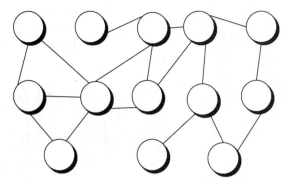

Figure 14-1: Neural mesh interconnections

The advantage of using a neural network rather than a classification group is that the filter is capable of "learning" which users have datasets closer to their own mail behavior, therefore providing better results. Apart from being very cool to watch, this also is what makes collaborative algorithms such as these successful, since there is such a diverse set of users on most systems.

Another application for a neural mesh is to create dynamic dataset groups to better scale system resources. For example, if our neural mesh includes 100 users, and it finds that 25 of those users appear to have an extremely high reliability rate with one another, those 25 users could potentially be clustered together using a single dataset with only minimal train-on-error data in each user's own database, which could be merged at run time. Merged groups are sometimes also created by systems administrators to provide a global set of data for all users, allowing individual users to store necessary training data and merge it with the global information at run time. This approach allows users to quickly ramp up their filtering by using a global group without the need to wait for their own corpus to become mature before their training data is applied to the decision. The same approach can be used to merge groups of contextually similar users together, using only minimal training data to "tweak" the parent group.

Neural Declustering

An inverted approach to neural networking, called *neural declustering*, can be used to break up a series of global groups into smaller, more contextually similar groups. Let's say you started out with three servers and 20,000 users on each server. Each of the three servers could be split in half, to form six nodes of 10,000 users each, and linked into a neural network group. The neural network would then be able to determine which of the six nodes were closest to one another. The nodes could then be split up based on their contextual similarities into 12 different parent datasets. These datasets would use the neural network to find the ones that they were the most contextually similar to, merge them again, and split up into 24 different datasets, and so on. Figure 14-2 illustrates the process of declustering three large systems into several smaller ones based on similarities.

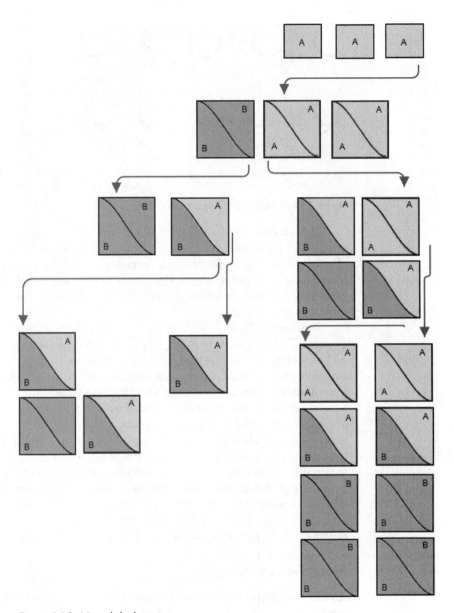

Figure 14-2: Neural declustering

Machine-Automated Blacklists

Machine-automated blacklists are a new spin on an old concept. In their previous form, blacklists were maintained by humans, which frequently resulted in long delays, inaccuracy, and a lot of maintenance problems. (See Chapter 2 for more information about the historical blunders of blacklists.)

Machine-automated blacklists are blacklists that are powered by the statistical filters themselves. Statistical filters, for the most part, are more accurate than the average human at identifying spam, so why not also put them in charge of blacklisting networks? Statistical blacklisting has recently become quite popular in light of the many problems with manual blacklists. It is generally far more accurate and has a much shorter propagation time than traditional blacklists in providing up-to-the-minute real-time spam phenomenon tracking. It is a great first-level defense against spam, and also a good way to seed your filters with spam from known senders.

The general idea behind statistical blacklists is to allow filters to report spam caught for particular source addresses and to share this information with other networks using spam filters. Unlike traditional blacklisting, no manual adding/removing of host information is necessary—when the spammer starts spamming, they get blacklisted. When they stop, they will eventually become allowed again, automatically.

Streamlined Blackhole List

The Streamlined Blackhole List (SBL) project is one such type of blacklist and can be found at http://www.nuclearelephant.com/projects/sbl. The SBL is a network-based client/server tool designed to provide the same basic functionality as an RBL (real-time blackhole list) or DNSBL (DNS blacklist), but it is retrofitted to work exclusively with statistical filters.

- All submissions are machine-automated, providing up-to-the-minute intelligence and high accuracy.
- Blacklisting is determined based on the infectious spread of the offending network addresses and not on the number of complaints received.
- Blacklisting has a rolling 24-hour dark period, so old data is immediately purged from the system.

On top of its unique mode of operation, the SBL has been designed with a proprietary TCP-based protocol using very little bandwidth (sometimes 5 or 6 bytes per query) and enabling a single stateful connection to process many queries per second. The SBL has shown great promise and has illustrated the power of collaboration by blacklisting large numbers of IP addresses, even with only a few different participating mail servers. Because of its weighting based on infectious spread, it hasn't experienced a single false positive to date. Statistical blacklists provide not only a great way to conserve resources but an even better way to tie spam directly into corpus feeding of statistical filters. In addition to standard public collaborative filtering, the SBL server can be downloaded and used internally to track just about anything, from a cluster of mail servers to intrusion detection data or addresses originating denial of service attacks.

Weighted Private Block List

Another statistical blacklist is called the *Weighted Private Block List*, or *WPBL*. The WPBL is similar to the SBL, except that actual weights and measures are used to calculate the percentage of spam coming from a host in contrast to the amount of legitimate mail. The following description is from its website (http://wpbl.pc9.org):

> WPBL is a fully automated real-time blocklist that uses distributed mail sightings from many users to list IP addresses that are relaying spam. Our goal is to list individual IP addresses that are actual spam sources as judged by highly accurate statistical (mostly Bayesian) filters running on real email accounts. All IP blocks are temporary and disappear when spam stops. Our IP sighting system also takes into account non-spam sent from IPs, to avoid listing legitimate hosts.

Distributed Attacks

One of the concerns with statistical blacklisting involves dealing with viruses and other types of distributed attacks. As it turns out, this hasn't been a problem yet, as virus emails are frequently sent directly from an individual user's machine and not through a provider's relay. If we block receiving SMTP from a user's machine, the user still has the ability to send mail, since any legitimate mail would be relayed from their ISP's mail server. Unfortunately, many new CPU time-sharing projects have emerged on the Internet that earn money by sending spam. In the near future, it will be necessary to block individual hosts sending mass quantities of spam, even from residential networks. Tools like the SBL and WPBL will make this task much easier.

Filters That Fight Back

FFBs, or *filters that fight back*, have become quite controversial, as they have the ability to generate a significant amount of traffic and perform denial of service attacks. On the other hand, they are one of the biggest collaborative tools for fighting spam. An FFB will scan for URLs in all inbound emails that are received. The filter will then perform an HTTP GET of the URL(s) in the email. If the email being sent is legitimate and is going to only one or a group of people, then a few HTTP GETs of the data won't bother anybody and will consume minimal bandwidth. If, however, the message is originating from a spammer and is being sent to millions of users, widespread use of FFBs will generate millions of HTTP GETs to the spammer's website, effectively knocking it out for a little while and hopefully costing the spammer money in bandwidth and computing resources.

FFBs can also perform statistical analysis on the actual web page(s) at the other end of the URLs in messages. If the filter instance isn't certain whether the message is spam or not, the HTTP GET can return more information to help the filter decide.

One of the biggest concerns with FFBs is the possibility that a massive, widespread denial of service attack could be launched against legitimate corporations simply by spamming. Anyone who wanted to take out eBay could easily send a massive spam with the URL to eBay's website on it. This can be countered in two ways: first by manually creating a list of exceptions to the FFB GET rule, and second by performing statistical analysis on the URLs themselves to determine whether their makeup truly consists of spammy components.

Fingerprinting

Many new types of fingerprinting technologies, a majority of which are based on collaboration, are emerging for detecting spams. *Collaborative-based finger-printing* involves multiple networks submitting their spam into a central analysis engine. This analysis engine compares trends in the spam with trends from thousands of other spams reported by other service providers. The goal is to fingerprint the spams, the senders, and even the general style.

Many collaborative efforts, such as Vipul's Razor, use a form of spam signature identification. Fingerprinting provides a great way to identify well-known spams and eventually leads to what Terry Sullivan calls SpammerPrinting, in which a message's characteristics can help identify the actual sender of a spam.

Probing

Probing is an approach used by some filters to perform a check directly back to the sender to determine whether it is acting as an open relay. Probing isn't really a collaborative algorithm as we know it (it doesn't involve collaborating with other recipients of spam), but it does collaborate with the sender to determine whether it has the characteristics of a spammer.

Many different tests can be performed, such as checking whether port 25 is open on the sending host, seeing whether it acts as an open relay, and even determining whether some basic SMTP commands are supported. Probing is one of the easier ways to identify spam, but it does create a slight delay in every message received, as the filter has to probe the sender before it can accept the message.

Automatic Whitelisting

Automatic whitelisting isn't considered a typical collaborative algorithm. What makes it collaborative is the direct relationship the approach has with the spam filter user. One challenge to developing artificial intelligence that can perform statistical filtering is that humans don't always base judgments on the email content; sometimes they base them on the sender of the message.

Many humans still judge an email by its cover and believe an email to be legitimate based solely on the sender of the message. The primary reason most language classifiers do not implement whitelisting is the burden of work that must be performed by the end user and the lack of any mathematical or statistical significance to whitelisting. Spam filtering should be as effortless as possible for the end user, and maintaining a whitelist of known senders is considered too much work.

As a result of manual whitelisting, many advertised accuracy rates have been bloated. On the other hand, whitelisting is a powerful yet simple tool, but the knowledge exchange it requires is a deal breaker. Users perform whitelisting by preferring to read emails from individuals they know and believe are relevant based on the From address of a message. In spite of what a message may contain, it is deemed relevant by the reader if it is from a specific individual. In Chapter 2, we discussed the fact that this approach is fallible because the recipient address can be forged.

Automatic whitelisting attempts to provide a whitelisting service that is

Effortless
The user does not need to maintain a list of trusted senders.

Resistant to forgery
It is not compromised by a simple, automated forgery.

Fault tolerant
In the event of forgeries or other circumvention, it utilizes a fallback to statistical analysis.

Automatic whitelisting creates a useful solution to the problems presented by manual whitelisting and takes advantage of this human approach to classification without requiring any effort by the human user. For every message classified for a user, the entire From header (not just the email address, but the whole header) is tokenized into one large token, which is stored. The number of messages from a sender that have appeared as spam and as legitimate mail is tracked. If N messages from the sender have been delivered with zero spams, the sender is considered tentatively trusted.

If the From header for an incoming message is from a tentatively trusted source, automatic whitelisting will perform the same human-type classification as the recipient would and will automatically pass the message through as a legitimate message. The filter author has the option of implementing an analysis-free pass-through, or of analyzing and learning the message as a legitimate message to assist in filtering.

Tentatively trusted sender status is revoked immediately when a spam is reported from a trusted sender. The "trusted sender" status for that sender is dropped, and the sender will continue to be classified by the same statistical analysis as all messages from untrusted senders. Depending on how automatic whitelisting is implemented, the filter may then invoke the trusted status again for the sender only in the event of a false positive or if the sender information becomes old and is purged from the system.

The advantage to automatic whitelisting is that a statistical (albeit very simple) algorithm is used to determine whether a particular sender is trusted or not, without any work on the recipient's part. Automatic whitelisting also has the benefit of being very low risk. A single malicious message will result in automatic whitelisting being disabled for that particular sender, and as a result automatic whitelisting can be used only once per spammer's sender address to the recipient. This would require a spammer to send $N+1$ messages in order to pass one through to the user, where N is the whitelisting threshold. Sending these messages would consume a significant amount of bandwidth. On top of this, the first N messages would need to be legitimate enough to pass through statistical analysis without being tagged as spam. Special restrictions can easily be added to automatic whitelisting, such as counting only a single sender address per time period to prevent these types of floods. In general, N is set to a relatively high number, but not so high that legitimate senders will not be granted tentative trusted status within a reasonable amount of time. N is usually set to around 10 or 20.

The present state of email doesn't exhibit the behavior of a spammer flooding all of their recipients with legitimate messages, but if this took place in the future, setting maximum thresholds per time period would be a relatively easy remedy to ensure the efficacy of automatic whitelisting.

URL Blacklisting

URL blacklisting is another supporting algorithm for statistical filters, designed to block an entire network's ability to access a particular web address if it is deemed to belong to a spammer. America Online has recently adopted this practice and is blacklisting the websites of known spammers. This approach makes perfect sense if you consider the spammer's agenda. The spammer's only means of contact (in most spams) is the web address provided in the email. Even if the message is delivered to its intended recipients, it doesn't do the spammer any good unless someone clicks on the link. When a spam recipient clicks the spammer's method of contact, the spammer gets paid and spam continues to flow.

The idea behind URL blacklisting is to extract the web addresses sent in emails and to blackhole, across the network, those that are used in spam. This prevents anyone on the network from clicking the link if the spammer's message should make it past the filter. Now consider an automated blacklisting approach to this, where multiple networks could share this information. Whenever a new spam distribution is sent out, the spammer's website would become automatically blacklisted within the first few spams received. Even if the spammer succeeds in getting their messages through to unprotected individuals or past filters, the recipients will not be able to respond to the message by visiting the website.

There are many free speech concerns about this type of blacklisting because it dictates the web addresses a user can and can't reach. It also opens the door to potential attacks on legitimate web addresses, but this can easily be avoided in a large-scale networking environment. The biggest argument against this type of blacklisting is the belief that users deserve the right to censor themselves and that it is unconstitutional to censor them without their consent. Some smaller networks have responded to this concern by providing users with an override link after warning them about the site they are about to visit. This, at the very least, helps to educate users about spam and can even be used as a way to identify those on the network who respond to spam advertisements. Supporters of URL blacklisting simply believe that users should get another ISP if they don't support their current provider's policy.

Minefields

Email-based minefields are similar in concept to message inoculation and were originally devised by Bill Yerazunis and me. They consist of a series of mailboxes (referred to as *land mines*) on the Internet for which there is no human recipient, and the mailboxes themselves are likely to receive only spam—similar to honey pots. The email addresses of these land mines are quietly advertised in places on the Internet where only harvest bots are likely to acquire them. If a spammer sends mail to one of these land mines, the address will immediately become blacklisted. The concept of minefields can easily ride on top of the framework of a statistical blacklist such as the SBL.

When a message hits one of these land mines, the explosion occurs. The IP address of the mail server sending the message is reported to a minefield network and is then distributed to any spam filters that are subscribed. An entire distribution of ten million spams can be thwarted by a single land mine. This information can then be used in a number of ways. The spam filters can use it to block all inbound email from the reported IP addresses for a period of time, routers can use it to block all traffic from the reported IP addresses for a period of time, and most importantly, it can be used to alert the administrator of the network being abused that a spammer is sending a distribution.

One of the positive side effects of email minefields is that they have the ability to render email harvest bots obsolete. If using a harvest bot only results in the spammer becoming blocked every time they send a spam distribution, the spammer will be less likely to use a harvest bot in the future. The email address of a land mine can be made available in many of the same ways that a normal email address is made available on the Internet, and if done correctly, no harvest bot would be able to tell the difference.

Final Thoughts

In this chapter, we've discussed many different collaborative algorithms that can support existing statistical filters and bring user intelligence together. Statistical filters themselves perform very well on their own, and implementing these additional layers of intelligence can only improve them. As public collaborative services become more widely used, several different statistical filters will benefit by linking into them.

It's easy for our filters to learn from their mistakes, but it's even better if they don't have to make mistakes in the first place. By sharing intelligence, many filters have been able to increase their accuracy tenfold.

SHINING EXAMPLES OF FILTERING

Throughout this book, we've described statistical filtering as the next-generation framework for spam filters. In this section, you'll get to see just how successful they are. Several best-of-breed filters will receive their due credit in this chapter.

Every one of the tools outlined in this chapter is available as open source software; they won't cost you a dime to download and use. They also happen to be some of the finest tools available for the task of spam filtering.

POPFile: The POP3 Proxy

Author: Dr. John Graham-Cumming
URL: http://popfile.sourceforge.net

About POPFile

According to Graham-Cumming, POPFile didn't originally start out as a spam filter, but was intended to perform generic email filtering using a Bayesian engine:

> . . . in fact, over 63% of users use it with more than 2 categories. There's even someone who is of doing automatic sorting of 48 separate categories (one is spam, of course).

POPFile performs as a POP3 proxy, meaning that it doesn't have to be integrated with any particular mail server software. It can perform well both in server-side and client-side installations. When installed on the client side, the user points their mail client at their own IP address. POPFile will then make a connection to the user's SMTP server and filter mail in transit. When running on the server side, an ISP can direct its users to connect to the proxy machine (running POPFile), which in turn will establish a connection their mail server. Both implementations provide an advantage over other filter applications in that they filter mail at MUA time instead of MTA time. *MTA time* refers to the time period when the mail server is receiving the incoming message. *MUA time* refers to the time period when the user is downloading and reading their mail. The advantage to filtering at MUA time is that more information about spam (or ham) may be available when the user reads their mail. In a collaborative filtering environment, in which one user can vaccinate another from a particular spam, this could mean catching a new spam that wasn't identified when it was delivered.

Another advantage to using POPFile is that it can function as a filter for SMTP (outgoing) traffic as well as NNTP (news) traffic. POPFile is easily portable to many other operating systems and is known to function under Unix, Windows, Mac OS, and even NextStep.

POPFile also supports i18n and l10n internationalizations. This means it is capable of supporting 28 languages, including Arabic, Hebrew, and many Asian languages, including Chinese, Japanese, and Korean.

POPFile is best suited for individual users or small workgroups, although the author is familiar with at least a few large companies that are using his software. Graham-Cumming is working on officially providing large-scale support in newer versions of the software.

One of the things that sets POPFile apart from other filters is that it's a straight Bayesian filter, rather than being based on Paul Graham's approach to filtering. The author refers to it as "straight up naïve Bayesian on word counts." Graham-Cumming has put a lot of work into the tokenizer, which has been written with many intelligent properties designed to address spammers' trickery. These are documented on a web page entitled "The Spammers' Compendium" (http://www.jgc.org/tsc).

The latest additions to the tokenizer include logic to specifically address tricks using cascading style sheets.

Accuracy

The author provides a very well-kept statistics page, which tracks the peak and average accuracy users are reporting. A total of 300,000 reports have been made in his tracking system from June 2003 to April 2004. According to the author,

> The summary is divided into two parts: the first is based on the complete set of statistics processed, the second counts statistics reported by users who have passed more than 500 messages through POPFile. The first set of statistics includes the initial period where POPFile is making frequent mistakes; the second set shows POPFile's accuracy after initial training and during normal use.

The recorded statistics at the time of this writing are:

Average bucket count	4
Percentage of users with more than two buckets	62.77%
Average accuracy	95.3%
Percentage of users with accuracy greater than or equal to 95 percent	76.97%

The table below shows the different levels of accuracy reported into the statistics recorder by users of the software. The majority of reports (29.19 percent) show levels of accuracy between 99 percent and 100 percent.

Accuracy	Reports	Percent
100	6,561	2.1
99	91,208	29.19
98	64,238	20.56
97	37,550	12.02
96	24,386	7.8
95	16,499	5.28

Accuracy	Reports	Percent
94	11,856	3.79
93	9,071	2.9
92	6,982	2.23
91	5,505	1.76
90	4,543	1.45
below 90	33,973	10.87

Below are similar results reported after the first 500 messages have been trained. Again, the majority (33.98 percent) rules with a level of accuracy between 99 percent and 100 percent.

Accuracy	Reports	Percent
100	1,215	0.46
99	88,189	33.98
98	60,388	23.26
97	34,198	13.17
96	21,637	8.33
95	13,909	5.25
94	9,492	3.65
93	6,779	2.61
92	4,811	1.85
91	3,587	1.38
90	2,656	1.02
below 90	12,651	4.87

Interview with the Author

Q: Have you noticed spammers trying to bypass your filter? What are some of the results of their attempts?

A: Yes, I've seen various things with invalid HTML tags (e.g., <<font> or <font>>), which at one time confused the parser. Naturally, there's all the stuff in "The Spammers' Compendium." Their attempts are futile.

Q: How do you think statistical filtering plays a role in today's fight against spam, and where do you see it tomorrow?

A: [I] think it's working well. Tokenizers will continue to be updated with recent trickery. I hope to see adaptive filters everywhere!

Q: What originally got you interested in a spam-filtering project? How does spam make you feel?

A: I wasn't interested in spam filtering at all; I was interested in sorting all the real mail I receive every day. Spam was one category that was just a nuisance that I wanted out of the way. It turned out that POPFile did a good job of spam, and when I started looking at spams that got through I realized that spammers were up to all sorts of spam filter avoidance tricks. That's when I got more interested.

Spam annoys me; spam helps pay my bills.

Q: What are some of the urban legends you hear about spam filtering that you think may hurt the credibility of projects like yours?

A: I have heard that "word salad" is defeating Bayesian filters. That's not true in my experience or through my experiments. I'm not very interested in fighting that battle, I'm more interested in making a great implementation.

Q: What are your plans for the future, in relation to your project?

A: Basically: fully skinnable user interface, SSL and SOCKS support, ship XML-RPC API, and add support for massive numbers of simultaneous named users.

Q: If a spammer offered you a million dollars to close up shop and sell the rights to your code, what would your reaction be?

A: The answer is no on two grounds: firstly I don't want to take money from a spammer and help them in any way, and secondly my code is released under the GPL. I believe in software freedom.

SpamProbe: A Modified Approach

Author: Brian Burton
URL: http://spamprobe.sourceforge.net

About SpamProbe

SpamProbe is a statistical spam filter written by Brian Burton of Burton Computer Corporation. It is based on Paul Graham's research, but some variations to enhance Graham's original algorithms have been made to the software, with excellent results.

SpamProbe uses the author's alternative Bayesian approach. This approach implements a decision matrix with a window size of 27 elements and allows for repeating terms in the matrix (presently up to two repetitions). The top 27 terms are populated into the decision matrix based on their interest. The calculations are rounded to five decimal places so that minute differences in the data have less impact. Ties in term calculations are resolved by allowing innocent terms to have precedence over guilty ones, and the frequency of each term's appearance in the message is used to resolve any remaining ties. SpamProbe uses a modified form of Graham's Bayesian algorithm to compute a spam probability for the message.

SpamProbe also incorporates an alternative set of tokenizer rules and implements a concept-based tokenizer, using *multiword pairs* (also known as *chained tokens* and *nGrams*), discussed in Chapter 11.

SpamProbe trains on nonobvious emails and uses a "train when hard to classify" algorithm in conjunction with a "train to balance message counts" algorithm for adding terms to its database. When SpamProbe classifies a new message, it adds the message's characteristics to its database only if the message was either an error correction or not obvious (for example, if the spam classified with a probability less than 99.5 percent). A majority of messages are "obvious" and are thus ignored for training purposes, leaving approximately 5 percent of the messages to be trained. SpamProbe will also train on a message if its type is underrepresented in the database.

SpamProbe is designed for use with a mail delivery agent such as maildrop or procmail. It provides an easy-to-understand command-line interface, including simple training commands and plenty of options for tweaking the scoring algorithms.

SpamProbe is intended for Unix-like systems in conjunction with these local delivery agents. The target user maintains a mail server and provides spam filtering for their users. It works best with IMAP servers, since IMAP provides a convenient system for providing feedback to the filter—server-side storage. Some users have reported using SpamProbe on high-volume mail servers with thousands of users, but SpamProbe also accommodates a small-scale implementation.

Accuracy

With all of SpamProbe's modified approaches, the tool is able to provide accuracy in the range of 99.7 to 99.9 percent in many cases. Users have reported various levels of accuracy, but the majority of those using the tool experience around 98 to 99.*x* percent accuracy. SpamProbe stresses avoiding false positives more than attaining perfect accuracy.

Accuracy depends on the flow of email for each user. Users who receive only 25 percent spam will generally experience lower accuracy—say, in the low 90 percent range—than those who receive 90 percent spam.

Interview with the Author

Q: Have you noticed spammers trying to bypass your filter? What are some of the results of their attempts?

A: Yes. I have not observed any direct attacks on SpamProbe's tokenizer, but I certainly see frequent attempts to fool filters using random word inclusion and image-only content. Almost all such attempts fail. I have plans to include Bayesian noise reduction in the near future to slam this last door in the spammers' faces.

Q: How do you think statistical filtering plays a role in today's fight against spam, and where do you see it tomorrow?

A: I believe that if statistical filtering were universally applied, spam as we know it would vanish. Unfortunately there are many impediments to its widespread adoption (most of them nontechnical). Even without universal adoption, the technique still provides the best defense for individuals and companies that want to eliminate spam.

Q: What originally got you interested in a spam-filtering project? How does spam make you feel?

A: For years before reading [Paul Graham's] article, my inbox had been heavily spammed. I have had the same email address for years and have never shied away from using it publicly. In 2001, I saw a dramatic increase in the amount of spam I received and knew that I had to do something (I was afraid to open my email at client sites for fear they would see one of the subject lines and think that I WANTED to receive that sludge). I had plans to learn about neural networks and develop a learning filter "when I had some free time."

Then, in August of 2001, I read Paul's article and saw the promise in his method. I wrote a quick prototype in Ruby (wonderful language, by the way) and started using it on my own email. The prototype filter learned quickly and became over 70 percent accurate. A week later it was over 90 percent accurate. I was hooked.

I have been a heavy user of open source technologies for my whole career and have always wanted to give something back to the community. Also I wanted to help other people to reclaim their inboxes, so I decided to publish the filter on SourceForge. Unfortunately, the Ruby filter was too slow for practical use, so I rewrote the filter in C++ and named it SpamProbe. I enjoyed writing the filter and loved some of the email I received from users thanking me for saving them from spam. I still modify SpamProbe whenever time allows.

Q: What are some of the urban legends you hear about spam filtering that you think may hurt the credibility of projects like yours?

A: I have had exchanges with zealots on the Internet criticizing Graham's idea. Generally speaking, they are spreading FUD to protect their own product or pet technology. It's sad to see companies pushing bad ideas (challenge response, blocking lists, simple word detection, etc.) and ignoring an excellent technology that would provide a genuine cure for their customers' spam problem.

Q: What are your plans for the future, in relation to your project?

A: Most of my plans for improving SpamProbe involve practical usage improvements such as wide-character support (for Asian languages), pluggable tokenizers (to support language-specific token boundaries), and improved performance. I also plan to implement Bayesian noise reduction and experiment with some new ideas for token selection.

Q: If a spammer offered you a million dollars to close up shop and sell the rights to your code, what would your reaction be?

A: I'd laugh, take his money, and dedicate myself full time to improving the most recently released version of SpamProbe. The source is out there forever, and it can't be stopped by writing a check. I hate spammers and virus writers sufficiently that I have dedicated countless hours developing a free program to stop them. I'm not going to stop just because they offer me money.

TarProxy: IANA Spam Filter

 *Author: Marty Lamb*
URL: http://www.martiansoftware.com

About TarProxy

TarProxy is unique in that it is not a filter. Rather, it uses existing filters to make decisions about SMTP transfers in progress and then acts on those decisions. Actions might include throttling the connection, rejecting the message, or *tarpitting* the remote server (that is, appearing to accept the message very slowly, but silently discarding it). Of course, it might also accept the message. At the time of this writing, TarProxy is still under development, with hopes that its use will be widely adopted in the future.

TarProxy is an amazingly satisfying tool to use on one's network. Not only does it provide the satisfaction of using up all of a spammer's resources, but it allows you to do so in a humorous, demoralizing way. As we discussed in Chapter 2, there are three distinct ways to use TarProxy to cause spammers grief by using SMTP response codes. Either reject the message outright:

```
554 I don't need any Viagra. Go Away.
```

pretend we are experiencing a hardware failure:

```
451 I'm tired of this. Spam me Later.
```

or just flat-out lie to the spammer and ask them to sit there until we're ready to receive their message.

```
451-Your spam is important to us. Please stay on the line...
```

TarProxy is designed to work for anyone running their own SMTP server for inbound mail. It performs all of its work upstream of the mail client, so the client machines don't require any knowledge at all that TarProxy is even running.

TarProxy is algorithm-independent. Fiercely so, in fact. This is because the author believes that an anti-spam genetic diversity is required in order to be effective. As a result, TarProxy has been designed to accept input from any software capable of making judgments about a message or an SMTP session.

Accuracy

Accuracy naturally depends greatly upon the filters used in conjunction with TarProxy. If the administrator is not 100 percent confident in the filter being used and is concerned about false positives, TarProxy can be configured to accept suspect messages very slowly, rather than flat-out refusing them. This has the interesting side effect of lowering the bar for filter accuracy, which should increase the genetic diversity of compatible filters.

And that's the nice thing about TarProxy. Spam filters all have their own levels of accuracy, but when the filter is wrong, the user loses a message—it gets dropped, quarantined, or tagged into a spam bin somewhere. With TarProxy, a filter can experience false positives and still allow the message through. If a spammer is sending a mass distribution of spam, it can be slowed down to a trickle without causing a loss of email.

TarProxy is also one of the few tools available today that are designed to actually conserve resources. A spam filter by itself is useful only for preventing spam's arrival; it still allows the spammer to use up the recipient's bandwidth and processing resources. But front-ending the spam filter with a tool like TarProxy will effectively stop many messages at the borders, or at least help throttle the amount of bandwidth and processing resources being used. A full-scale implementation may also include network address blacklisting to prevent certain networks from being allowed to even deliver mail.

Interview with the Author

Q: Have you noticed spammers trying to bypass your tool? What are some of the results of their attempts?

A: A test installation that ran for approximately two months did not indicate active countermeasures. This will probably change if TarProxy is widely adopted.

If spammers do modify their software to get around TarProxy, they will end up announcing their presence very loudly. Open relays and proxies would still be affected by TarProxy, as spammers do not generally have the ability to update the software on those computers.

Q: How do you think statistical filtering plays a role in today's fight against spam, and where do you see it tomorrow?

A: I'm not aware of any filtering methods BUT statistical filtering that can take into account individuals' varying personal definitions of spam. I see it only becoming more prevalent, although there will need to be a standard interface to mail client programs (such as Thunderbird, Evolution, or Outlook) that will allow users to easily train their filters. If filter usability continues to improve as it has for the last couple of years, I doubt it will be long before everyone is using some form of statistical filtering.

Q: What originally got you interested in a spam-filtering project? How does spam make you feel?

A: I had been using the same email address for several years, and spam had been getting sufficiently out of hand for me to think about ways to eliminate it. TarProxy was probably my 100th idea or so—the first 99 either had obvious flaws after more careful consideration or were already being developed by someone else. Mostly the former.

Q: What are some of the urban legends you hear about spam filtering that you think may hurt the credibility of projects like yours?

A: I haven't heard much of anything. I don't think the general public is aware of what's available—they're certainly not aware of free/open source software in this area. Earlier this week I encountered what I believe to be one of the reasons for this. I was sent an invitation to exhibit and speak at a conference on email and instant messaging. I called the conference organizer and discovered that they were simply looking to fill display booths to the tune of $6,000/booth—minimum. The opportunity to speak was purchased with the booth.

There's no way any open source projects can appear at events like these. So without awareness, there's unfortunately no credibility to be hurt.

Q: What are your plans for the future, in relation to your project?

A: First, to finish the core functionality. Second, to work with the authors of the various filters so those filters can serve as the brains behind TarProxy. I've given some thought to providing some "Professional" or "Enterprise" features as an add-on purchase to the free base installation, but I'm still on the fence with that.

Q: If a spammer offered you a million dollars to close up shop and sell the rights to your code, what would your reaction be?

A: I'd take it. TarProxy wouldn't vanish, as its source code is available under the GPL. Someone would just have to pick up where I left off at the time of the transaction.

DSPAM: A Large-Scale Filter

Author: Jonathan Zdziarski
URL: http://dspam.nuclearelephant.com

About DSPAM

DSPAM's primary focus is strong R&D and high accuracy in server-side environments. Its core engine is a shared library that can be linked to other applications for drop-in spam filtering, meaning that it can support many other projects, both on the client side and on the server side. The core engine's wrapper (known as the *DSPAM agent*) turns DSPAM into a high-performance command-line language classifier capable of being incorporated into most types of Unix mail server packages. It integrates nicely with Sendmail, Exim, Postfix, Courier, and others. It can be implemented as a gateway service capable of blocking spam before it ever gets to the mail server and can even be configured as a POP3 proxy. In its most common implementation, DSPAM masquerades as the local delivery agent and filters inbound mail prior to delivery. However, it can also perform more complicated functions, such as emulating an LMTP proxy.

DSPAM works well on smaller installations, but it is designed specifically for large corporations or Internet service providers with heavy loads. Its execution time is measured in hundredths of a second, with an average of about 0.01 to 0.03 second real classification time, or 0.03 to 0.10 second real training time on average hardware.

Another unique feature of DSPAM is its storage driver interface. This interface allows the administrator to choose among many different storage paradigms, including MySQL, PostgreSQL, Oracle, SQLite, and others. This allows for an easy installation for smaller implementations but adds the flexibility of supporting hundreds of thousands of mailboxes.

DSPAM is a hybrid of basic statistical functions and advanced research to improve on the quality of the data. Some of the techniques it uses include custom training algorithms, Bayesian noise reduction, and many different forms of collaborative models. It also uses a concept-based tokenizer implementing chained tokens, as well as many customizations to Graham's tokenizer rules.

Devoted to R&D, DSPAM has given birth to several new technologies. Bayesian noise reduction was originally created as part of the DSPAM project to improve accuracy by reducing features that appear as noise in a message. The message inoculation standard being used in other filters such as CRM114 was also codeveloped with the DSPAM project.

DSPAM was designed to function with or without a collection of mail for each user. With a corpus, DSPAM will train based on historical data and will provide immediate filtering on the first day. Without a corpus, DSPAM uses other algorithms, such as one known as *statistical sedation*, which dampens the effects of guilty data to prevent a high rate of false positives while learning a particular user's email behavior. DSPAM has been shown to learn very quickly and has even started filtering spam for some users after training as few as seven spams.

Research and development on the DSPAM project is funded primarily by some of DSPAM's larger users and business partners using DSPAM in their products. Yet it remains General Public License (GPL) and therefore open source for the world to use freely.

Accuracy

Many different tests are performed prior to every DSPAM release, which help to quantify many of the changes made to the software. In some situations, DSPAM has proven to achieve peak levels of accuracy up to 99.985 percent (approximately 1 error in 7,000 messages, including spams and legitimate mail) and in one recorded case broke four 9s accuracy. A majority of hands-off users experience between 99.5 and 99.8 percent accuracy, while users on a system tuned by a savvy systems administrator will generally experience 99.8 to 99.95 percent accuracy or better. It is very common for users to achieve 99 percent accuracy within the first week or two of training, depending on their inbound mail. Users who make a diligent effort to maintain training over a longer period of time (months) are known to easily achieve 99.95 percent accuracy (1 error in 2,000 messages).

Accuracy can also be improved by taking advantage of the many collaborative algorithms DSPAM supports. Setting up message inoculation groups and utilizing DSPAM's neural networking functions will undoubtedly improve accuracy, possibly even beyond what the filter is capable of doing on its own.

Interview with the Author

Q: Have you noticed spammers trying to bypass your filter? What are some of the results of their attempts?

A: I've seen a lot of different attacks on Bayesian filtering in general, and a majority of them don't work against today's filters. There was always that one-off perfect combination of microspam and word salad that might have made it through once or twice in the past, but those were quickly learned. Word salads don't work against a majority of Bayesian filters, and I think spammers are finally starting to get a clue about this.

What irks me more than word salad attacks is the amount of broken RFCs spammers will resort to using to try and break filters. A lot of filters, including mine, were originally written to understand email based on the various RFCs that define how email should be formatted. I was a bit too naive at the time to believe that somebody would deviate from the standards, but they did. Since spammers have started breaking RFCs, I've had to make a few tweaks to my code to help it read broken email. The spammer doesn't succeed very often, mind you. It's fortunate that you can only break email so much.

Q: How do you think statistical filtering plays a role in today's fight against spam, and where do you see it tomorrow?

A: Statistical filtering has struck a nerve with the spammers, and that's a good thing. I don't see it as a complete solution, because filtering alone doesn't conserve any networking resources—but it does play a significant role. Combining statistical filters with other solutions like TarProxy and network ACLs will end spam for the particular network using that solution.

It's going to take more than just filtering the spam to stop it. That 20 or 30 click-throughs the spammer might get makes their services well worth the money. A lot of people have thrown their hands up about spam, and don't realize there are viable solutions out there that aren't just snake oil scams to capitalize on spam. That small percentage of brain-dead marketers who thought it would be a good idea to spam people about buying their spam filter gave the industry a bad name.

I think spam will eventually come to an end, but it will probably take many more years before we start to see it. Right now what's important is the public education about tools like these, and getting more people to become interested again in fighting spam.

Q: What originally got you interested in a spam-filtering project? How does spam make you feel?

A: I was getting sick of seeing raunchy porn ads come into my email box every day. My wife was sick of it, and even with some level of primitive filtering I was unable to even be in front of my computer when my children were around for fear they'd see some new spam come in. My church has their own mail server, and so the people close to me also wanted a solution. In 1996, I started coding the first version of DSPAM, which was more or less just a simple phrase-matching program. Over the next few years, it got better and was filtering around 60 percent of my spam. I had been thinking there must surely be a better way to do this, and that's when I came across Paul Graham's article. When I read about Graham's approach to fighting spam, I had to try it. I soon ditched my old code and began coding a new prototype. From there, I got hooked and started coding all types of improvements and optimizations. The rest is history.

Q: What are some of the urban legends you hear about spam filtering that you think may hurt the credibility of projects like yours?

A: There is a small community of misinformed people who think Bayesian filtering doesn't work. Unfortunately, they also happen to be the ones writing articles about it . . . people who have clearly never used a real statistical spam filter in their life. Misinformation is probably the biggest risk that could possibly hurt Bayesian content filtering. The only way to get around a Bayesian spam filter is not to run one, and bad press is a free tool spammers benefit from. There are a lot of skeptics out there who will market their opinion as fact, and unfortunately a lot of people believe it.

I also think a lot of commercial companies have done more harm than good. The creative license for statistical filtering really belongs to hackers like Paul Graham, Gary Robinson, and Bill Yerazunis and the rest of the community that has invented many of these approaches. Some companies have claimed the technology as their own, which gives people the idea that any other solutions are nonstandard, when it's really borrowed technology. Most commercial solutions today aren't nearly as accurate as their open source counterparts, which certainly doesn't help either.

Skeptics think Bayesian content filtering isn't adaptive enough for "the spams of tomorrow" and that eventually filters will all crumble. Spammers have been attacking statistical filters for years now, and I only see the filters getting better—look at where we are today, almost achieving 99.99 percent accuracy, compared to 99.9 percent last year. That's ten times better than last year! And this is amidst the number of increased attacks on BCF by spammers.

I think education is going to be the only solution to this sheer insanity.

Q: What are your plans for the future, in relation to your project?

A: I'd love to see my research into DSPAM become fully funded one day, so that I can dedicate my career to machine learning. There are a lot of neat ideas rattling around in my head that I just haven't had time to work on.

Q: If a spammer offered you a million dollars to close up shop and sell the rights to your code, what would your reaction be?

A: Well first, I'd make him triple his offer—a million dollars is chump change compared to the amount of money the project has already saved companies in managing spam. The next logical thing would be to say that since it's GPL I'd just continue working on the last public release, but I would suspect that the spammer would probably require some kind of noncompete agreement preventing me from working on anti-spam projects for a year or two.

I'll gladly take the devil's money and dedicate my efforts at designing "generic machine learning" algorithms and publishing them. I'm sure other filter authors could benefit from some of this research, and when the non-compete agreement was fulfilled I'd go off and either contribute to someone else's spam project (probably Bill Yerazunis' CRM114) or pick up DSPAM where the last public release left off.

Three million dollars in my pocket is three million that's not in the spammer's pocket.

The CRM114 Discriminator

CRM114 · Discriminator

Author: William S. Yerazunis
URL: http://crm114.sourceforge.net

There are spam filters, and then there is the CRM114 Discriminator. The CRM114 Discriminator is in a league of its own. It originally got its name from the classic movie *Dr. Strangelove*, which had a black-box communications device that was designed not to receive at all—unless, of course, the message was properly authenticated.

About CRM114

Most spam filters you run across are single-purpose programs. They are designed with one paradigm in mind, one particular *style* of filtering. Some are heuristic; some are blacklist/whitelist, Bayesian, word pair, fingerprint, and so on. But almost all filters have one filter design paradigm at the foundation of the software, and you can't change the paradigm without rewriting the entire filter program from scratch.

CRM114 is different: it's not a filter. CRM114 is a filtering-optimized, Turing-complete programming language. This means that CRM114 is not just *a* filter, but it can be *any* filter. Unlike the single-paradigm filters, it's relatively easy to create a heuristic filter, or a blacklist/whitelist filter, or even a Bayesian filter in CRM114. You truly can do as you need—or do as you please.

If you want it to *just work*, the standard CRM114 kits include a feature-rich mail filter based on Markovian weighting (discussed in Chapter 12), all ready to use. The first-time user on a Linux machine will need to type about a dozen commands (all of which are in the HOWTO). No programming is required, nor are any other mathematical or computer skills needed other than typing and mouse clicking.

If you *are* a programmer or a power user, you'll find that CRM114 is fairly feature rich; you can create a customized filter fairly easily. The programming language is fairly straightforward and vaguely reminiscent of Latin; in fact, one of the keywords *is* Latin.

Under the Hood

Under the hood, CRM114 is implemented in multiple layers. The four layers are (from bottom to top) the special-purpose, made-to-be-fast libraries; the language (and microcompiler); a presupplied set of handy filters written in the microcompiled language; and a set of parameter files that make it easy for nonprogrammers to customize the behavior of those presupplied filter files. The parameter files control the filter language files, the filter language files tell the compiler what code to generate on the fly, and the generated code invokes the libraries.

CRM114 is several times faster than many filters that are only a tenth or a hundredth as accurate. Execution times generally range about 0.05 second real-time for classification. Part of CRM114's speed and power is due to the use of Ville Laurikari's GPLed super regex library named TRE. The TRE library provides very fast pattern matching, including approximate pattern matching. Although you *can* build CRM114 with the GNU regex library, the TRE library is smaller, faster, and far more powerful, and it is the recommended companion regular expressions library for all CRM114 installations.

The feature that makes CRM114 different from almost all other filters is the language component. The CRM114 language has high-level statements for matching, hashing, surgical alteration, and I/O. It also has higher-level statements that in a single operation do "move to the next block of input," "run the following command as a subprocess," and "perform a match by some particular means, and tell me which of the inputs this particular sample is the most 'like.'" This capability is what most people think of as a filter—it's a text classifier.

The default CRM114 classifier as of this writing is termed a Markovian classifier. It attempts to match the Markovian process that generated the input sample against two or more previously generated Markovian models, and whichever one matches better wins. Markovian discrimination is covered further in Chapter 12. Although the default CRM114 classifier is Markovian, power users can easily change it to be straight Bayesian, entropic, or something else they'd like to experiment with.

CRM114 is targeted toward running on a Linux (or Unix) server. It's designed to sit in the mail delivery pipeline and filter in real time as messages arrive. The easiest way to use CRM114 is either through the .forward mail hook that most mail delivery agents honor or via procmail. Both ways work equally well.

Accuracy

For best accuracy, it's necessary for the CRM114 user to train CRM114 to their own ideas of spam and nonspam; a fresh CRM114 installation has no idea what's good and what's not. For the first few hours, CRM114 will make many mistakes. After a few days, it will make only a few mistakes a day, and after a week, only a few mistakes a week. Many users find this extremely rapid learning to be the most astonishing part of CRM114; after a couple of weeks of use it often provides 99 percent or better accuracy.

The CRM114 author presently experiences approximately one error per week, or roughly 99.95-plus percent accuracy, with a peak of 1 error in 8,000 (or 99.987 percent) during one cycle. Interestingly, CRM114 is far more accurate than most humans. The CRM114 author once tried to manually classify the same set of over 3,000 messages twice over a period of about a week. The result was that he was only around 99.84 percent accurate—less than one-fifth as accurate as his creation. CRM114 regularly performs at 5 times human accuracy and occasionally hits 10 times human accuracy for as long as a month.

If a user absolutely needs filtering *now*, there's a set of prelearned Markovian models that can be downloaded and installed, and that will give 95 to 98 percent accuracy. However, these models are only about half as accurate as the models that users can generate for themselves with the built-in learning capability of the CRM114 mail-filtering programs.

Interview with the Author

Q: Have you noticed spammers trying to bypass your filter? What are some of the results of their attempts?

A: The only real attempts have been the "dictionary salad" and "book report" spams. The dictionary salad spams use huge blocks of random words. But since those random words don't form meaningful sentences, they don't match the Markov models of spam or nonspam; those blocks of random words just drop out of sight. This leaves the spam standing unhidden.

The "book report" spams use a chunk of innocuous text (usually someone's book report for a class that made it to a website) to provide some plausible, nonspammy text. But again the Markov model for a book report doesn't match the Markov model of either spam or nonspam, so again the spammy part of the text stands out and the Markov model detects the spam quite easily.

I suppose that if you're a high school English teacher who accepts emailed assignments, the "book report" spam might get past your personally trained copy of CRM114, but for most of us, it's just not an issue.

The bottom line is that I've never seen a successful attack that gets spam past CRM114. Two or three times a week, I'll see something that looks like an error, but when I check into it, it turns out that I was fooled and CRM114 was right.

Q: How do you think statistical filtering plays a role in today's fight against spam, and where do you see it tomorrow?

A: Statistical filtering is the only thing that is sufficiently accurate for me to use. I had a heuristic filter for two years (it's the best-known one), and it had a sufficiently high error rate that I found it was better for me to just read everything.

In the future, it will be a different game. First, *SPF (Sender Permitted From)* is a wonderful hack that sits right on top of DNS; it allows the legitimate owner of any domain to "lock out" anyone else from forging that domain as a sender. The real beauty is that SPF doesn't require a new protocol and servers; SPF comes for free as soon as you get your DNS working.

I think we'll also start to see minefields: accounts that are set up to intentionally attract spam. These are accounts that no human ever sends email to (or perhaps even that no human even knows the actual address of). When the spammer sends an email to one of these minefield accounts, the spammer's IP address is instantly forwarded and blacklisted from a large number of sites; it's as though the spammer stepped on a land mine.

Q: What originally got you interested in a spam filtering project? How does spam make you feel?

A: Well, spam bothers me on a number of levels, because it's an intrusion on my time and attention—and (true story) almost cost me a VERY large amount of money.

What had happened was that a job offer came in for . . . well, we'll say it was a *substantial* amount of money. We're talking "buy a new Ferrari . . . or maybe an airplane" kind of *substantial.*

And I had been hitting "d" for delete, wading through spam, and deleted the job offer due to brain-faded inertia.

I didn't find it till two days later when I was wondering why the HR person hadn't gotten back to me, and I went back and did a careful search. There it was. Much money. Deleted without thinking.

Now, it turns out that I didn't take the job after all (and so still don't have a Ferrari or an airplane) . . . but it would have truly been awful if the job offer had fallen by the wayside without further thought on my part.

I've related this story to others, and I've since received similar stories— job offers, house sales, that sort of multi-hundred-thousand-dollar kind of thing . . . being accidentally deleted because it was hidden in a flood of spam.

Q: What are some of the urban legends you hear about spam filtering that you think may hurt the credibility of projects like yours?

A: There are some people (not many, and none that I've actually spoken at length with) who don't understand the principles of Bayesian filtering, let alone Markovian filtering. From some of their writings, I suspect that a few have never even tried a Bayesian spam filter, let alone tried to understand it.

But that's OK. They'll either learn or they'll drown.

Q: What are you plans for the future, in relation to your project?

A: Well, one goal is to create filters so good that you never need to review your spam bucket. But filtering is far more general than that.

Consider Usenet; it would be wonderful to reclaim Usenet from the spam, or let people using LiveJournal or Yahoo not have to regularly delete all of the spam that gets posted. Or consider the problem of "sock puppets"— people who create huge numbers of pseudonymous accounts in order to provide a denial of service against someone they have a personal grudge against. Some friends of mine have used CRM114 to automatically identify and expose these sock puppets for what they are . . . and often for *who* they are. The default Markovian matcher in CRM114 is accurate enough to identify individuals with about 70 percent accuracy, just by their writing style; proving the identity is then a matter of plain old gumshoe work.

Consider the Web itself. I'm not in favor of censorship, even for kids (much preferring just to leave the computer in the living room), but some people working for the French school systems have set up web censoring software based on CRM114; they found it much more accurate and scalable than the commercial offerings.

Or even consider "filtering" of semistatic data. When you type search terms into a search engine, you're filtering, but on keywords. How much more powerful would it be to filter with a Bayesian or Markovian filter?

And that's not even touching the question of *Is a Markovian the ultimate in filtering technology?* In my opinion, it isn't even close. Look at history: the heuristic and keyword-style filters were basically defined by Aristotle and the Stoics around 350 B.C. Bayes did his work around 1750 and Markov around 1900. That leaves 100 years of very solid math that we haven't even touched yet for filtering technology, like Kalman filters, Minsky's theorems, or Hopcroft's work.

Q: If a spammer offered you a million dollars to close up shop and sell the rights to your code, what would your reaction be?

A: Sure. I'd talk.

I'll probably negotiate for a while.

Then, after the check clears, I will point out to them that since the language design and Markovian classifier have been published and in the public domain for over a year, they can't patent any of it. What they own is the code as of the day they bought it, not any of the real value (the designs and theories) nor any of the code as copyrighted under the GPL as of the day before.

In short, they've bought a pig in a poke; they're out a million dollars and I'm just laughing and smiling as I fork the code from the previous public release and add a few new cool optimizations and hacks.

The most that they will be able to do is sell binary-only copies of CRM114 to other spammers—the same code that their *customers* could have downloaded as GPL source for free in the first place.

Now, if you say that I had to *really* close up shop? No, I would probably turn them down. Why? Because it's too much fun. A Ferrari is nice, but it only lasts a dozen years at best . . . and hacker glory is forever.

In one sense, spam filtering is the next great AI challenge, the next Turing test. Now it's not just "Prove to me that you're a human." Now it's become "Prove to me that you are my friend." No more HAL 9000 computers.

And in that sense we *already* have succeeded; CRM114 is now one of several filters that can detect spam more accurately than its own creator.

It's all just a fascinating problem.

INDEX

basic delimiters in tokenization, 98–99

Bayes, Thomas, 49

Bayesian

Burton's approach, 76–78

combination algorithm, 75

Graham's approach, 75–76

noise reduction, 231–232

poisoning, 127

Bayesian filters

Bayesian chain rule, 209

Bayesian combination, 74–78

Bayesian content filtering, 49

Bayesian Noise Reduction. *See* BNR (Bayesian Noise Reduction)

in language classification, 49

in Markov models, 219–222

vs. Markovian classification, 222–225

Bayesian poisoning, 127–130

Bayes's Theorem, 49

BCF (Bayesian content filtering), 49

BCR (Bayesian chain rule), 209

Berkeley DB (BDB), 147–148

BGP (border gateway protocol) networking, 172–173

biased filters, 71

biGrams. *See* chained tokens

binary encoding, 90

binary trees, 147

blacklists, 27–28

machine-automated, 250–252

Osirusoft list, 28–29

propagation and maintenance problems, 28

URL, 255–256

BNR (Bayesian Noise Reduction), 231–232

dubbing phase in, 234–236

efficacy of, 239–240

end results of, 239

examples, 236–239

instantiation phase in, 232–233

training phase in, 233–234

body of message encodings, 89–92

Bogofilter, 49

border gateway protocol (BGP) networking, 172–173

bots, 38

braces ({}) as delimiters, 100

brackets ([]) as delimiters, 100

Brightmail filter, 29–30

buffer overflow, 162

Burton, Brian

Bayesian combination by, 76–77

PBL ISAM library solution by, 151–153

SpamProbe by, 261–264

C

C languages, 161

C/R (challenge/response), 34–35

calibration algorithms, 228–231

Cancelmoose spam, 13–14

Canter, Laurence, 10–13

Canter & Siegel spam, 10–13

case study analysis of chained tokens, 199–200

chain letters, 8–9

chained tokens, 198–199

administrative concerns, 205–206

case study analysis, 199–200

contextual analysis, 203–204

differentiation, 201–202

HTML classification, 202–203

miscellaneous uses, 204–205

pattern identification, 200–201

summary, 207

supporting data, 206–207

chains, Markov, 215–217

challenge/response (C/R), 34–35

chaotic environment adaptation measurements, 185–187

character sets in tokenization, 108–109

chi-square in statistical filtering, 79–80

Children's Protection Registries, 43

classification

in BNR, 236–239

language. *See* language classification concepts

exclamation points (!)
    as delimiters, 99–100
    for HTML comments, 116
Exploits BlackHole List (EBL), 17
external message inoculation, 246

F

fail-over estimates, 170
feature set reduction, 227–228
    Bayesian noise reduction in,
        231–232
        dubbing phase in, 234–236
        efficacy of, 239–240
        end results of, 239
        examples, 236–239
        instantiation phase in,
            232–233
        training phase in, 233–234
    calibration algorithms for,
        228–231
Federal Trade Commission, 20
feedback
    in image spams, 133
    in language classification,
        54–55
FFB (filters that fight back),
    252–253
fiber-channel controllers, 166
FIFO purging, 226
fifth-order Markovian
    discrimination, 215
    vs. Bayesian filters, 222–225
    floating-point renormalization
        and underflow in, 226
    hidden Markov models,
        218–219
    state concept in, 216–217
    storage concerns in, 225–226
    for text modeling, 219–222
filters
    accuracy measurements,
        182–185
    Bayesian. *See* Bayesian filters
    biased, 71
    collaborative. *See* collaborative
        algorithms
    comparing, 191–193

examples, 257
    DSPAM, 266–270
    language classification,
        58–60
    POPFile, 258–261
    SpamProbe, 261–264
    TarProxy, 264–266
    FFB, 252–253
    heuristic, 29–32
    statistical. *See* statistical filtering
    success of, 112–113
    testing, 187–191
    weak links in, 113
filters that fight back (FFB),
    252–253
fingerprinting, 43, 253
Fisher, Ronald, 79
Fisher-Robinson's inverse chi-
    square, 79–80
floating-point renormalization and
    underflow, 226
Floodgate spamware, 16
foreign languages in tokenization,
    108–109
forgeries in whitelisting, 33
419 spams, 20–21
free space, disk
    managing, 142
    in scaling requirements
        assessment, 159–161
    for stateless database
        implementations, 147

G

GDBM (Gnu DBM), 147
general resource planning, 168–169
geometric mean test, 78
global datasets, merged, 160–161
global ingress for disk space, 161
Gnu DBM (GDBM), 147
Graf, Peter, 151–153
Graham, Paul
    Bayesian combination by,
        75–76
    and Bayesian content filters, 49
    example filter by, 58–60
    on heuristic filters, 63

inoculation groups, 37
instantiation
in BNR, 232–233
in scaling requirements
assessment, 163–164
intellectual property, 44
interleave in testing, 181
internal layer in filter processing,
165
internationalization
in POPFile, 258
in tokenization, 108–109
Internet Death Penalty, 17
Internet-Draft, 242–245
interpreted languages, 161–162
inverse chi-square, 79–80
invisible headers, 131
ISAM library, 151–153
iterative training, 82–83

J

Jarad, Joe, 28
Java language, 162
JavaScript, 125
Jay-Jay's college fund, 7–9
Jesus spam, 9–10

K

Karnaugh maps, 210–213
key size for records, 142
Knuth, Donald, 163

L

Lamb, Marty, 35, 264–266
land mines, 256
language classification concepts,
45–46
accuracy in, 46
components of, 49–50
data storage for. *See* data
storage
feedback in, 54–55
fighting spam with, 47–49
filter instance example, 58–60

future of, 61–62
machine learning in, 46–47
primitive analysis, 26–27
statistical filtering in, 49, 60–61
training in, 48, 55–57, 60
languages, computer, 161–162
large-scale filters
CRM114 discriminator,
270–274
DSPAM, 266–270
less than signs (<) for HTML
comments, 116
Lightning Bolt product, 17
Lipsitz, "Krazy" Kevin, 15
litigation, 41–44
locking
row-level, 164
storage, 143

M

machine-automated blacklists,
250–252
machine capacity sizing, 167–170
machine learning
in language classification
concepts, 46–47
in token reassembly, 102
Mail-Abuse Prevention System
(MAPS), 27–28
mailing list attacks, 126–127
maintenance
in blacklisting, 28–29
in heuristic filtering, 31
MAPS (Mail-Abuse Prevention
System), 27–28
maps, Karnaugh, 210–213
Markov, Andrei, 215
Markovian discrimination. *See* fifth-
order Markovian
discrimination
mathematical operators as
delimiters, 100
MD5 checksums, 242, 244–245
measurements
chaotic environment
adaptation, 185–187
filter accuracy, 182–185

word pairs
    chained tokens. *See* chained
        tokens
    in tokenization, 107–108
word salad, 111, 135–137
word values for historical datasets,
    69
WPBL (Weighted Private Block
    List), 252

Y

Yerazunis, Bill
    on Canter & Siegel spam, 12–13
    and collaborative filtering, 37
    CRM114 discriminator by,
        270–274
    and Markovian discrimination,
        215
    and message inoculation, 242
    and minefields, 256
    and SBPH, 108, 155

Z

Zdziarski, Jonathan, 266–270